ADVANCE PRAISE FOR

NAMING THE WORLD

"I always thought there were no secrets to writing well, that only hard work, rare talent, and plenty of luck made a writer good. *Naming the World* proved me wrong—it opens the doors to some of the best writing classes in the country, the best teachers, and the minds of many of the best writers themselves. A fantastic resource for any writer (or writing teacher) looking for inspiration or guidance or support."

—HEIDI PITLOR, series editor of *The Best American Short Stories,* and author of *The Birthdays*

"Forget about getting an MFA! Bret Anthony Johnston has put together the equivalent of a master class in writing by some of the best writers/teachers around. Here are the nuts and here are the bolts for any writer struggling with the essentials of his craft."

—BETSY LERNER, author of *The Forest for the Trees: An Editor's Advice to Writers*

"Here's a book full of bright doorways into our writing, set out with specificity and reason. Not only is *Naming the World* a rich compendium of provocative prompts, but as a whole it serves as a timely conversation of the larger aesthetic of well-made fiction, a roomful of caring experts. Mr. Johnston, by assembling these worthy exercises, has done us all a valuable favor."

—RON CARLSON, director of the Graduate Program in Fiction at the University of California, Irvine, and author of *Five Skies*

"At last—the book about writing I have been needing for years and that I will now keep on my desk at all times. Witty, warm, intuitive, inspiring, and hopeful, the writers gathered here feel like the best possible company as we all attempt to do this impossible, vital thing called writing."

—STACEY D'ERASMO, assistant professor of writing at Columbia University, and author of *A Seahorse Year*

NAMING THE WORLD

NAMING the WORLD

And Other Exercises for the Creative Writer

EDITED BY

Bret Anthony Johnston

RANDOM HOUSE NEW YORK

Published in the United States by Random House Trade Paperbacks, an imprint of
The Random House Publishing Group, a division of Random House, Inc., New York.

RANDOM HOUSE TRADE PAPERBACKS and colophon are trademarks of
Random House, Inc.

Illustrations: Daniel Wallace (p. 27) and Rob Torres (p. 242)

LIBRARY OF CONGRESS CATALOGING-IN-PUBLICATION DATA
Naming the world: and other exercises for the creative writer/edited by Bret
Anthony Johnston.
p. cm.
"A Random House trade paperback original"—t.p. verso.
ISBN 978-0-8129-7548-2
1. Authorship. 2. Creative writing. I. Johnston, Bret Anthony
PN137.N36 2007   808'.02—dc22   2007016001

Printed in the United States of America

www.atrandom.com

9 8 7 6 5

Book design by Casey Hampton

In memory of Frank Conroy,
whose presence here is as profound as his absence

CONTENTS

CHARACTER

POINT OF VIEW AND TONE

PLOT AND NARRATIVE

DIALOGUE AND VOICE

DESCRIPTIVE LANGUAGE AND SETTING

INTRODUCTION

DON'T BELIEVE IN TALENT. NOR DO I PUT FAITH IN THE idea of inspiration, the muse, or the muse's shadowy and malicious twin, writer's block. (That is, of course, unless you're considering buying this book because you *have* writer's block; if that's the case, it's a tragic, insidious affliction, and these exercises provide immediate, lasting, and entirely affordable relief.) Truth be told, I'm not at all sure that writing can be taught. I am positive, though, that it can be learned.

What I believe in, as a writer and a teacher, is dedication. And stubbornness. And discipline. Being a writer is, in the fullest sense of the word, a vocation. It's labor, to be sure, often very lonely and stilted and compromising labor, but it's also more than that; it's a calling, an act of courage, an act of faith. I don't mean this in any New Agey, touchy-feely way; quite the opposite. Much of the writer's work must be—can only be—accomplished by doggedly venturing into territories unknown, by risking failure with every word. With this in mind, I strive in my classes—and in this book— to create an environment in which each writer feels invited and prepared to take such risks; I try to provide concrete and specific— rather than abstract or stock—lessons that might increase the student's chances at thematic, aesthetic, and technical success; and above all else, I encourage the aspiring writer to show up at her desk every day. This is what I believe in, what I trust will ultimately distinguish those who want to write and publish from those who *do* write and publish: work. I believe in rolling up your sleeves and buckling down when a sentence or story or chapter is struggling. I believe, to paraphrase Henry James, that every writer is a reader moved to emulation, and I believe that the act of writing is itself the muse. The articles of my faith are revision and perseverance and rigor and commitment and craft and what Frank Conroy, on a muggy Tuesday afternoon in Iowa, so aptly referred to as "butt-in-chair time."

On the first day of my fiction workshops at Harvard, my students and I tell a story together. This is an exercise devised, I believe, by the angelic writer Nancy Willard. There are usually twelve of us sitting around a seminar table, and we're feeling simultaneously excited and terrified and hopeful and more than a little worried that we'll be unmasked as impostors. (At least I'm feeling these things, and because I've never met a writer who wasn't constantly enduring some mishmash of this weird and potent anxiety, I assume student writers are likewise afflicted.) I tell them that I'm thinking of a character, a man named Bill. Bill, I say, wants a glass of water. Then, with the students confused and staring at me in silence and thinking maybe they should've opted for that economics class taught by the professor who eats his chalk, I turn to the person on my right and ask what happens next in the story.

And like that, they're at home. It's one of my favorite moments in teaching, seeing this particular relief deliver the students to solid ground. With the parameters of the project established—each writer contributes to the narrative, then passes it to the right—their imaginations soar and they're eager to spend the next twenty minutes telling Bill's story. (Bill's story, you should know, is almost always of the Old Testament sort: abject poverty, intestinal parasites, wolverine and black widow and IRS agent attacks, alien abduction with requisite probing, projectile vomiting resulting from nonpotable water ingested earlier in the story, pachyderm stampedes, and so on. A sadistic bunch, tomorrow's literary lions.) And soon there's this important and undeniable and infectious air of confidence filling the room; I always imagine it's what a locker room would feel and sound like after an underdog football team has won a championship. When the impromptu narrative comes full circle and ends, the students clap and laugh and debate who rained down the most creative trouble on good ole Bill. Was it the iron maiden? The quicksand? The botched sexual-reassignment surgery? Then, in my most professorial tone, I ask a serious question, the question that the whole exercise has been building toward: "Where did the story change?"

Again the room fills with voices, with the impassioned noise of bright students trying to identify and articulate the narrative's fulcrum, to find where the story pivoted from rising action to falling action. *It was when he fell face-first into the den of water moccasins! No, when his wife chased him with the flamethrower! No, it was when he realized he was wedged between the fourth and fifth dimensions, and the opposing existential gravities slowly tore him apart!* Eventually, and with increasing certainty and precision, the writers will zero in on whoever is sitting directly opposite me in the group. I never steer them in this direction, but the students' instincts always lead them to the top of the circle; this is not dissimilar from how baby sea turtles start inching toward the ocean seconds after they hatch. And of course, like the turtles, the students are exactly right.

But why? Why will the story *always* turn, *always* reach its climax at the point diametrically opposite to where it started? There's no collusion between the professor and the would-be linchpin, no literary sleight of hand or narrative shill, and none of the students could have possibly heard Bill's traumatic tale before, yet without exception, the fundamental "change" always manifests itself in precisely the same place. (Try the exercise at a party or dinner table. You need only supply a single character and a tangible desire; the story will take care of the rest. Your guests will think you're brilliant or practicing witchcraft or both.) I've used the exercise in elementary and high schools, in juvenile detention centers and MFA programs and writers' conferences around the country, and it always plays out in the same spooky and complex way. Yet the reason behind the phenomenon is as simple as it is affirming: we know how to tell stories.

Stories are how we make sense of our lives, how we attempt to impose some discernible order on the chaos of existence, and such attempts make the chaos bearable. Either by instinct or by experience, we understand the shapes and nuances, the contours and expectations and demanding subtleties of the stories we tell and hear, and through practice we've become enviably proficient at the art of giving them voice. For example, I've yet to deploy Willard's circle exercise and *not* have the students introduce conflict—which, along with empathy, is the lifeblood of fiction—and often they include more sophisticated aspects of narration as well: humor, metaphor, flashback, alternating points of view. Yet despite this proficiency, something happens when we (and I include myself) endeavor to *write,* rather than tell, a story. Somewhere, somehow, we blow it. I think of this as a breach that opens between the conception of a story and the actualization of that story, the distance between the perfect idea in your mind and the foundering jumble of words on the page. Writing exercises, I believe, serve to introduce or elucidate techniques and strategies that authors can use to bridge that void. As with Willard's circle, the goal is to draw out the writer, to cultivate her confidence, and to provide the tools and raw material to make her work the best version of itself. The exercises here aspire to do exactly that.

The book is divided into eight sections. Each of sections one through seven orbits around an element of fiction, and within each section are exercises designed to demystify the common and complex mechanisms by which that specific element operates. They aim not to constrain the imagination but to awaken it. Faced head-on, the pressures of creating art can prove too intimidating, too daunting; the infinite possibilities of language and story can paradoxically paralyze rather than liberate the writer. By focusing on one element at a time, however, the writer can make the task more manageable, and the writing itself becomes more inventive and original. The last section of the book is a compilation of more than three hundred daily writing prompts. Many of these are designed to be completed in ten minutes or less, and they aim to stoke your imagination, to heighten your attention to language, and to focus your concentration before the day's real writing begins. Think of them as literary jumping jacks or a shot of tequila, a regimen to get the blood pumping and the muscles limber so that your work is as strong as possible.

I make no claims of fairness in my choice of contributors. Quite unabashedly, I recruited my favorite writers and teachers of writing, those whose work and guidance continue to influence my own fiction and whose examples have proven invaluable to my students over the years. In many ways, every exercise is a master class with one of the country's most eminent authors, an invitation to peek behind a magician's curtain, to rifle through a carpenter's toolbox. In these pages are finalists for and winners of the Pulitzer Prize and the National Book Award; there are magazine and book editors; there are short-story writers, novelists, international bestsellers, and professors from the finest universities and graduate writing programs in the world. I gave them no specific instructions or requests, but asked only for the exercises that had been—or would be—most beneficial to apprentice fiction and nonfiction writers. The results are as varied as the authors themselves, and as illuminating and inspiring. One by one, they offer their wit and counsel, their compassion and perspective and insight, their experience and goodwill and intelligence and the profound, abiding assurance that writing fiction is a dignified and worthwhile way to spend your time.

And now we pass the story to the right, to you. And now we wait to see where you will take it, to hear what happens next.

GETTING STARTED

GERMS

ERE ARE SOME GERMS, SEEDS, VIRUSES FOR YOUR WRITING. They come in different forms. You'll think of more. Get used to starting with something small and exact, not with anything as large and as vague as an idea.

THE EXERCISES

1. Start with a line. I'll give you one. You can find them everywhere in what you read, in what you hear. Find them in poems, newspaper stories, on billboards, in the conversation of the people behind you at the supermarket checkout. Take the line as the opening of your novel. Write it out and keep going. Let it take you where it will. Write for ten minutes or until you want to stop. The line will likely be gone when you revise the piece, if you do. Maybe it will become the epigraph for your novel.

   Here's one line: "Most things will never happen; this one will." Taken (with grammatical liberties) from Philip Larkin.

Here's another: "Last night the moon seemed to say something." (From Frank O'Hara.) One thing I hope these lines do is pull you out of your world and plop you into an imagined one.

2. Start with a list. Your novel begins with a list. Who's making it? Why? What does it reveal about the list maker?

Here's the heading for one: "Things That Make One's Heart Beat Faster."

And another: "People Who Seem to Suffer."

(And read *The Pillow-Book of Sei Shonagon,* from which these lists were taken.)

3. Start with a title. Why not? What does the title suggest to you? Certain themes, perhaps. Characters. A place? Titles are always important. They can be symbolic, can suggest tone, characterize, can push you along. The title is the essence of the novel—which is why, despite our exercise, the title often comes last. Here are a few titles. Do them one at a time. Write and then think.

> *The Heart Specialist*
> *Murder Your Darlings*
> *You Belong to Me, I Believe*
> *Stirred, Not Shaken*

4. Start with a character. Many stories (most of mine) begin with a character.

Here's one from the unfortunate news of the day: your character is a parish priest who hears the confession of his colleague and fellow curate at St. Paul's Church and learns that his trusted companion has molested a child.

Here's another: a mother whose child has been abducted. A chance to deal with our greatest fears, certainly.

5. Start with a situation. The situation should be odd and perhaps a bit troubling. It should make you wonder. Here's an
   intriguing situation; make it the opening of your novel or
   perhaps the end of chapter 1: a landscape architect cries in
   a restaurant while dining alone. And: a stand-up comic
   (you'll have to write jokes!) listens to the neighbors in the
   next apartment as they fight.
6. Start with an event.

   A high school prom
   A death in the family
   The birth of triplets
   A frightening diagnosis

7. Start with an image.

   The smell of clothes drying on a line
   The sight of salt-crusted work boots tucked under a
       radiator
   The taste of Play-Doh
   The sound of fingernails being scraped along a chalkboard
   How it feels on your skin when a cloud passes before the
       sun

8. Start with a subject.

   Happy puppet syndrome (a neurological disorder)
   High school
   Mountain climbing
   A drought

9. Start with an oddity.

For instance: a neurology professor (say, at the University of Florida) takes home body parts and stores them in his freezer.

Or try this: The poet Hart Crane committed suicide by leaping from an ocean liner into the sea. His father, Clarence, invented the Life Saver candy in Cleveland. Crane's Peppermint Life Saver. Since we're speaking of Cranes, Anton Chekhov had a pet crane in Yalta, a raggedy, one-legged creature that followed Chekhov around. (Was it named Heart, do you suppose?)

Joyce Carol Oates

WRITING PROMPTS

I N MY PRINCETON FICTION WORKSHOPS I DEFINE MY ROLE, or one of my roles, as that of an ideal editor: not a rejecting editor, not a censorious or severely critical or interfering editor, but one who defines herself primarily as a friend of the text and a friend of the writer, in that order.

THE EXERCISES

Here are some prompts to start stories:

> *"An unsolved mystery is a thorn in the heart."* This is the opening line of a short prose piece you are to write, meditating upon an "unsolved mystery" in your own life. You may wish to transpose this into purely fictional terms.

> As minutely as possible, you will describe a significant place, conveying by means of language the emotion generated by this place in your imagination.

You will "interview" an older relative, asking questions, eliciting answers, and then, in presenting the speaker's voice, removing yourself entirely from the text.

A miniature narrative, consisting of a single, very supple sentence.

NOTHING BUT THE TRUTH

A T MOST READINGS I GIVE FROM MY TWO NOVELS, SOME-one—usually a man—asks, "So, how come you don't just write nonfiction?"

Let's deconstruct this question for a moment.

First, there is the intimacy suggested by the "so," as if he and I are old friends. I have just read to him from a novel set either in an Italian-American neighborhood in the 1950s or an isolated mountain village in central Italy during World War II. As a thirty-something author who (reportedly) can pass for twenty-six (on a good day), I am obviously not writing from personal experience. The novels tell stories inspired by my parents' lives, not mine. I choose to take the questioner's tone—and the question overall—as a compliment: he's telling me I've created a convincing fictional world. He believes he was *there* strongly enough to request that I confirm that *there* actually exists.

Next: "How come?" Not "why," which would be too formal, too scholarly. We are in not a university lecture hall but a community bookstore, surrounded by frothing baristas and beefcake calendars and the homeless. The mood is casual, collaborative. I'm a novelist, therefore an accessible storyteller who's assembled a group to entertain. (I don't mind this one bit, by the way; it's a great joy and honor.) What I find interesting is that most readers view the novel form (and fiction in general) as both common *and* mystical. Fiction belongs to the people, like IKEA art, and yet fiction writers still invariably inspire respectful awe from those who can't fathom shaping their riotous imaginations into a sustained plot of interconnected story lines. The questioner might have asked me, "How come you're such a genius?" Or, at least, "How'd you get so lucky to publish your stuff?"

The next and most important word: *just*. Despite the fact that nonfiction outsells fiction, and that a book gains instant credibility and increased interest when the phrase "based on a true story" is slapped across the jacket, there is an enduring (mis)perception that nonfiction writers are "just" note takers or recorders of information rather than artisans. Some readers think, "If I had time and a stack of index cards, I, too, could write nonfiction." And so when they meet someone like me, who is blessed with a rich and colorful family history spanning two continents, they ask, in so many words, "Why'd you bother inventing stories when they can basically write themselves?"

The truth is that nonfiction (a broad genre, of course, but in this case, the questioner and I really mean the memoir or personal essay) is incredibly difficult to write. Moreover, its authenticity is virtually impossible to certify. Truth, after all, is more elusive and less flexible than the imagination; the details and complexities of our experiences vanish as we live them; and, obviously but most importantly, our understanding of these experiences is purely subjective. The memoir or personal essay writer is heavily constricted by such realities, and it is within those restrictions that she shows her remarkable talent: to re-create lived experience using the techniques of fiction (dialogue, description, point of view, scene) while staying uncompromisingly true to "what really happened." It's somewhat analogous to a poet choosing to write a pantoum rather than in free verse. The best nonfiction writers are exquisite storytellers and expert craftsmen; they turn the inescapability and inevitably of reality into the most thrilling and satisfying of tales.

That's the long answer to why I don't write nonfiction. The short (and guilty) answer might be: It's incredibly hard. Your plots, settings, and "characters"—yourself included—are too limited. You can't "just" do a ton of research and hold interviews and make outlines; you must have the human insight of a great novelist with double the vigilance and discipline in your analysis.

But maybe you (like many of my students) have a great true story to tell, and you are undaunted by the challenges I've put forth. Maybe this true story is important to you because it is yours alone or your parents' or your deceased neighbor's; or maybe it is broader, the untold chapter of your city or country's history. There is a good chance that the story seems overwhelming in its complexity—with numerous potential digressions and connections popping into your head as you mentally outline it—and you're feeling defeated before you've even started. Here's a purely generative exercise to help you focus. And, because I'm a novelist at heart, I've included a few options for fiction writers as well.

THE EXERCISE

Make a list of five to ten significant "firsts" and as many significant "lasts" (or "finals") in your life. Do the same if you are writing about someone else or some*thing* else (a city or neighborhood). The significance can be subtle or dramatic. For example:

1. The first time I shoplifted
2. The first time I saw the Grateful Dead in concert

3. The first immigrant family who moved into Anytown, USA
4. The first boy who broke my heart

1. The last time I saw my father
2. The last cigarette I smoked
3. The last major sports team victory in Bigcity, USA
4. The last day of college

For Nonfiction Writers

Pick the first or last you find most compelling or about which you either remember the most or can research most thoroughly. Write a five-hundred- to one-thousand-word description of this event using as many sensory details as possible (sight, sound, touch, taste, smell). Your primary goal here is not to analyze the event or capture it in its entirety but to transport the reader to that time and place, to create a scene the way a director or cinematographer might.

Set the scene aside for a while, maybe a week or so. Then go back to it with fresh eyes and fill in what you can't see, smell, or touch vividly enough. Alternately, you can give the description to a trusted reader and ask him or her what may be missing.

You now have the raw material for an excellent essay, but you're missing a key element: the "turn." The turn—which some call, quite appropriately, the "So what?"—is that bit of insight or connection beyond the event that keeps it from being purely personal or arbitrary. It is a gesture toward your ultimate goal: relevance and resonance. I think of Steve Almond's wonderful nonfiction book *Candyfreak*, which extravagantly describes the color, taste, smell, and texture of all sorts of chocolate bars and odd regional confections and, in many cases, the first and last times the author tasted them. The descriptions are pure pleasure in themselves but would not succeed as compelling nonfiction without the many turns and "so whats" Almond includes: that is, that his desire and near fetishizing of candy is really a desire for the family acceptance he never felt as a child; and that the disappearance of regional candies is a metaphor for a loss of American character and soul.

You want your inherently significant first or last to have this sort of meaning beyond the literal, and it is now your job to examine the raw material you've created and ask yourself if it does. If it doesn't—if it is merely a pleasant or dramatic memory that is significant only to your own life, with no metaphorical or broader implications—then it is likely not fertile enough ground for an essay or memoir.

For Fiction Writers

Though "write what you know" is perfectly sound advice, I always encourage my students to live other lives in their fiction. I think one of the main reasons new writers don't finish short stories or novels is because most adhere too closely to "what really happened" and burn out during the increasingly arduous task of rehashing the scenes and emotions. Also, no matter how talented the writer, fiction can never live up to the richness and texture of actual experience. To expect it to do so is to set yourself up for major disappointment, which may lead you to unfairly question your skills as a writer.

So, after you have written your lists of firsts and lasts, pick the entry that feels most compelling to you. Take, for example, "the first time I shoplifted." Jot down all the things you remember about the experience, focusing on the sensory: sights, sounds, smells. Now write the scene *but* change something fundamental about the experience. For example:

- The gender of the main character
- The time period in which the experience occurred; for example, make it happen in the 1920s or the 2020s
- The outcome of the experience. If, in reality, you got away with it, show what happens if the main character gets caught.
- The basic situation. Instead of stealing a Milky Way from CVS, maybe you stole a condom. Or maybe a tie from Saks.
- Switch "first" with "last" in the statement and then change something else. For example: "The last time this person shoplifted a tie from Saks."
- Combine one of your firsts with one of your lasts: Maybe the last time the main character saw her father was at a Grateful Dead concert. Or the first boy who broke your heart did so the night the Red Sox won the 2004 World Series. To me, this option has the most exciting possibilities.

This exercise works because the author is confidently grounded by the actual experience but still forced to stretch his or her imagination. The more drafts you write, the further from "real life" you will get, and yet the entire piece will likely still retain a sense of authenticity.

FICTION THROUGH ARTIFACTS;
or, How to Justify a Love of Accumulating Junk

THE BLANK PAGE CAN REALLY SUCK, ESPECIALLY IF YOUR brain feels just as blank. But lucky for you, the world happens to be enormously full of STUFF that's yours for the taking. Getting at fiction through the use of "artifacts" not only allows you to short-circuit or circumnavigate your censorious internal editor, it enables you to fill (or begin to fill) that proverbial and ubiquitous blank page *without actually writing anything*. Skeptical? Please proceed.

THE EXERCISES

Postcards—Character, Voice, Situation, Maybe Even a Plot . . .

I keep a collection of blank postcards—vintage, contemporary, odd, mundane, whatever; you can find these at thrift stores, antiques stores, on eBay, or in old family albums in the attic. Choose a postcard, then try to imagine who on earth (i.e., what sort of *character*) might have selected *this particular* postcard to send to someone. Did they go to a store and pick it out? Find it in a drawer? Steal it? Get it free at a hotel? To whom are they going to send it?

The first part of your exercise is to write the postcard *as* the character who is sending it. Write it as that character would write it. Consider the audience. Consider the motive for writing. Consider occasion. Consider that it's a postcard (other people will be able to read it on its way to its destination). Consider handwriting, perhaps, if you're artistically inclined enough to do so. Consider your writing implement, should that be relevant. Consider anything else you happen to find yourself considering. Address it.

This next part of the exercise is optional, but it can be fun and helpful as well. You can do this exercise with a partner, in a group, or you can take on all the roles yourself if you are alone and/or stranded on a desert island.

After you finish your card, trade with your partner, or shuffle the group's cards and redistribute them, or simply put on another hat. Now you're the person who *received* this card. All you know is what has been implied through the card, but that's probably enough to start germinating a second character, one who might, say, write a letter in response to said card . . .

And there you have two characters, with voices, in relation to each other. Great plots have been founded on a lot less than that! If you want to get really crazy (and you happen to have discovered a warehouse full of old, weird postcards), you can even have the second character respond to the first character's postcard on a postcard of her own (randomly selected, of course), thereby making you have to contend not only with the characters outlined in postcard No. 1 but with why character No. 2 would have chosen postcard No. 2 to send to person No. 1 in response to postcard No. 1. Are you tired yet? Or do you suddenly have a great idea for a novel in postcards . . . ?!

Snapshots—Dialogue, Scene, and Beginnings

I'm always collecting cool photographs (most of which are from *DoubleTake* magazine or art books, and all of which depict two or more people in a situation). Start your own collection of such photos—they can be snapshots too, as long as you don't know the people in them—or just find one or two photos that speak to you in some way. Make sure each has two or more people in it.

1. Write a short-short story of the *scene* of that photograph. The piece must *begin* with a line of dialogue spoken by one of the people in the photo to someone else in the photo. Set yourself a time limit (thirty minutes, tops) or a page limit (two) or word count (one thousand). What I like about this exercise is that it helps you trick yourself into dramatization. The scene is there, in front of you; it's virtually impossible to keep yourself from inferring some form of narrative from it, or *con*ferring some sort of narrative *onto* it. There's your story: what's happening here. Then, if you begin writing with a line of dialogue within the scene, you'd be hard-pressed to do anything *but* write that fully dramatized scene. The time limit keeps you from taking on too much outside the scene, from extrapolating too much. Keep it short and you're forced to stay within the scene and draw the detail from within the photograph. This exercise is almost guaranteed to produce whole, autonomous, integrated, weight-bearing short-short stories.

2. Choose a new photo and begin a story about this photo in one of the following ways:

   "She/He was the kind of person who ..."
   A sentence that establishes the "where" of the story

A sentence that establishes the "when" of the story
A grand, sweeping generalization
A command to the reader

Then choose one and write that story—a short-short—the same way as above.

Cheerleader Possessed by Demons—from Title to Story

Go to the grocery store. Buy a copy of *Weekly World News* (or another tabloid, though *WWN* is the best, in my humble opinion). (Or do this once a week and amass yourself a hearty collection like mine.) *Do not read the stories.* This might sound like me telling you to buy a copy of *Playboy* and not look at the pictures, but really, it's not. The headlines are the best part of *Weekly World News.* The stories are pretty much crap, mostly because they're entirely implausible. I like to cut out the headlines and paste them onto cardboard backing for durability. (I recycle the rest of the paper, and so should you.) Choose a tabloid headline from the selection and then— *unlike* the lame *WWN* writers—write a story that attempts to take the headline seriously or, maybe, reinterprets it.

I Undo—Point of View

The Vows column appears every Sunday in the *New York Times* Sunday Styles section. I collect them, but you can also find them online at nytimes.com.

Pick a couple, any couple.

What do you know or what can you infer about these people from the story in the column?

What *don't* you know about them? Given what you know, how would you fill in things you might not know: What kind of toasts were made? In what formation did they walk down the aisle? Had the families met before? What was served at the reception? Sit-down dinner? Buffet? Drinks? How's the weather? Where's the honeymoon going to be? How did the couple leave the reception? What's the story of this wedding that people will tell for years to come? What's worrying the bride's mother? The groom's? What's on the minds of the best man, the maid of honor? Aunt Ethel? The flower girl? Get the idea?

Write:

1. In the third person, as omnisciently as possible, and beginning with a line of dialogue, write the scene of this couple's final fight before the divorce.
2. Choose one point of view (husband, wife, parent, child, friend, lover, therapist, bartender, babysitter, previous spouse, next spouse, divorce attorney . . .) and in either a close third person or first person, give us a "Portrait of a Marriage."

Dumpster Diving—Fiction Through Artifacts

Go out into the world! Bring a shopping bag with you. (Wear gloves if you are particularly concerned about filth or suffer from OCD or something.) You are looking to collect anything that might be of any use in sparking a story. Don't judge too much for now; just scavenge. You can always throw it all out again, you know. You may climb into dumpsters if you so desire, but you do not have to. There is a chance it might be illegal to do so where you live; "dive" at your own risk. But nowhere that I'm aware of is it illegal to pick crap up off the street after people have dropped it. Grocery store receipts, Post-it notes, a broken taillight, a fizzled purple balloon, a Barbie shoe, a double-exposed photo ripped in half and tossed away . . .

anything! I've done this with groups of students young and old across the country. They've found a sorority-rush ratings book; a half-incinerated, sparkly blue, fuzzy bear costume; tickets to a Red Sox game that hadn't yet been played; love letters; To Do lists; breakup notes; kindergarten drawings; religious tracts; books on contemporary nursing practices; a door . . .

Set yourself a scavenging time limit—an hour, maybe, to start (inevitably, you will soon enough devote your life to wandering the streets looking for cool stuff, but for now, just take an hour).

Return home, sort "finds." If you do it in a group, you can have show-and-tell, which is always fun.

Some things you might do with your artifacts:

1. You may well return from scavenging with ideas already bubbling in your brain. Sit yourself the hell down and start scribbling.

2. I like to sort of *catalog* my finds when I return from a dumpster dive, particularly the ones that are text-based. I copy down the notes, grocery receipts, lists, and so forth on pages of my notebook. Somehow this helps me to appropriate the material as my own. Once it's on *my* page I can futz with it as I like, adding to it, subtracting, leaping off from it. . . . Some people might even call this *writing*.

3. Select five artifacts from your collection and write a story in which all five must make an appearance.

4. Lay your artifacts out before you—or select a group to work with and spread those out on the floor or a table—and begin "collaging," which is to suggest that depending on their relative placement to one another your artifacts might take on different meanings, that these artifacts might *associatively* begin to form narratives among them-

selves. You could, you know, write a whole story just in artifacts.

And if your actual *found* artifacts start suggesting a narrative to you, you might think, "Oh, how great would it be if I had a report card to put between this D+ English paper and this grocery receipt for fourteen bottles of Jim Beam," and then you can feel free to create an "artifact" of your own devising. You could even write a whole story composed of "artifacts" you make up.

THE IMPORTANCE OF BEING ENVIOUS

A T THE ONSET, I HAVE TO STATE THAT I'M NOT CONVINCED that there's any such thing as "writer's block." I suspect that what we like to call "writer's block" is in fact a failure of nerve or a failure of imagination or both.

If you're willing to break rules, risk ridicule, and explore the unknown, and if you've somehow managed, despite social conditioning, to hold on to your imagination (more's the pity if you haven't), then you can dissolve any so-called block simply by imagining extraordinary, heretofore unthinkable solutions, and/or by playing around uninhibitedly with language. In other words, you can imagine or wordplay, conjure or sport your way out of any impasse.

Prolonged neurotic "blockages" aside, however, it would be false not to acknowledge that every working writer experiences days when the ideas and images reveal themselves more reluctantly than usual. Biorhythms could be at fault, it could be a savage hangover, external or internal distractions, or one of those ruptures that occur periodically in the pipeline from the Other. (Writing imaginative fiction is such a mysterious enterprise that often there's no way to explain its sources except to attribute them to Something Out There Somewhere.)

On those dreaded occasions when your muse shows up wearing army boots, it may be time to tap into one of the strongest and most persistent, if seldom discussed, human emotions: jealousy.

Yes, we should never underestimate the valuable role that sheer envy plays in the creative process. Whereas in a romantic relationship jealousy is stupid and destructive, as a lubricant of the verbal brain machinery it can be highly effective. It's elementary: you read a few pages (sometimes a few paragraphs or even a line or two will suffice) of work of which you are in awe, and in minutes you'll find yourself motivated—burning!—to try to compose passages of equal merit.

Well, at least envy can usually motivate me. On a pedestrian morning, grounded in a no-fly zone without a banjo on my knee, I'll read, say, a poem by Pablo Neruda or César Vallejo, turn to the early pages of Anaïs Nin's *Seduction of the Minotaur,* sample a bit of Pynchon, Nabokov, or Henry Miller, or even put Bob Dylan on the stereo, and soon I've waxed six shades of pistachio and kiwi. The green beast has awakened and is starting to chase me down the street.

Call it forced inspiration if you will, call it literary Viagra, but as a writing exercise envy works. "Could I not coin phrases that smoke and pop like those do?" I'll ask. "Is that guy's word bag really that much bigger than mine?" Or: "Do I have the guts to work as close to the bull as she does?" Feeling almost ashamed in the presence of such verve, I'll return to my idling narrative primed to redeem—and entertain—myself.

By no means is this a case of competing for fortune or fame. It isn't as if I want to elbow Norman Mailer out of line at the bank or steal Louise Erdrich's ink. What I desire is to feel for myself the rush Mailer or Erdrich must have felt when they pulled that particular rabbit out of a hat. What I covet is to have the kind of effect on language-conscious readers that Norman and Louise have just had on me.

Ultimately, it doesn't matter whether your prose actually meets the master's unintentional challenge. That degree of success is probably not in your cards. But you have to believe it might be. And in merely attempting, with every muscle in your envious psyche, to climb to that elevation—to be that inventive and amusing and tough and daring and true—you may well have mooned the drab angel of mediocrity, and if nothing else you will have let loose your juice.

THE EXERCISE

Use the green sparks of envy you sometimes throw off when you read a particularly dazzling piece of prose to jump-start your own literary motor.

Daniel Wallace

MOURNING FALLS, USA

SOMETIMES IT'S HARD FOR A WRITER TO . . . WELL . . . BEGIN. Given the alphabet, a life, and a big blank computer screen, the world and all the creative possibilities it offers can be overwhelming. Do you write about Grandpa's false teeth, love, dogs, or maybe a combination of the three? How about that time you went to Italy and got mugged?

That's why I drew this map. Look at it as a small town in the middle of Somewhere, USA. It doesn't have a name, it doesn't have a history, it doesn't even have people who live within its prescribed borders.

That's where you come in. Your job is to create this town—in other words, to become a god. What's it called? Who lives there? Where do your characters work and play? Who do they love or hate? The only rule is this: *You can't leave town.* Everything you write about has to happen here. You can go to the park with your girl, work at Wal-Mart with your mother, and swim in the river with your dog. But you can't go anywhere that's not pictured in the map, and you can't interact with anyone who's not living there.

What does this achieve? By limiting the imaginary world available for discovery, you have a sort of creative safety net that encourages you to explore; there's nothing that can't happen here—love, death, all of life's baggage—but the fact that it can *only* happen here—your own "postage stamp of native soil"—somehow makes it less frightening. The stories that arise from it in my classes are amazing. It's always surprising to see who chooses to be the town prostitute.

My last class named this town Morning Falls. Or is it Mourning Falls? There's a story there . . .

THE EXERCISE

Use the map as a blueprint for a fictional town, and use its perimeters, landmarks, and landscape as tools to generate characters and stories of your own.

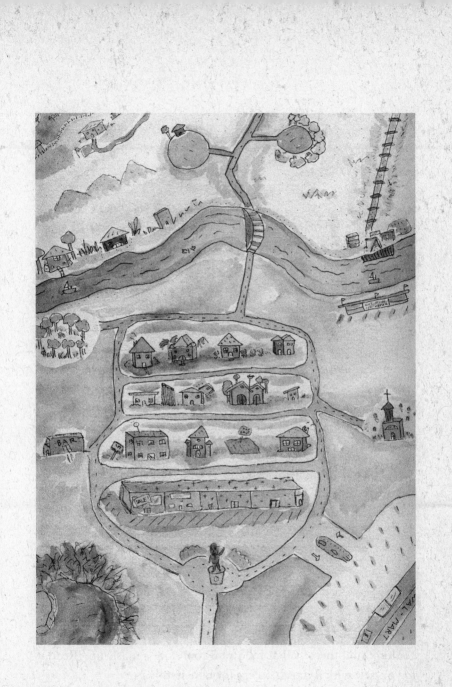

A POSTCARD FROM THE
VELVET REVOLUTION

WENT TO FILM SCHOOL IN THE EARLY 1980S. THE FACULTY was thick with Eastern Europeans, especially Czechs who had studied together in Prague and left after 1968. In screenwriting class, we worked through thirty pages of writing exercises that, it entertained me to believe, had come over with our professor—I never actually asked, but the typeface was strange and the letters had been broken up into artifacts by generations of photocopying. On the other hand, the document was written in English. It didn't make a screenwriter out of me, but it provided hours or possibly even years of fun.

After the publication of my first novel, in 2004, I discovered the problem of "show, don't tell." I didn't actually discover it; it was pointed out to me. Repeatedly. It did sound awfully familiar. "You must write only what the camera sees," my screenwriting professor liked to tell us. His was even more of an injunction, but a friendlier one, I still think. Maybe it was the accent. In any case, I went looking again for the exercises in our screenwriting samizdat, but I couldn't find them. What follows is therefore a mash-up. (Read it to yourself with a Czech accent for best results.)

THE EXERCISE

Picture a postcard with a girl alone on a road. What do I mean by a girl, how old? How can you tell at this distance? Get closer. Is she sitting or standing? Well or ill? And what do I mean by a road? Where is it? What can you see on either side? Decide who your girl is and what she's doing there. Decide where she came from and where she's going. Decide why. Now, what does she have with her? What time of day is it? What year? Describe the girl on the road. There is no one she knows nearby. Use only what can be seen, smelled, touched, heard, and possibly tasted to dramatize her situation. If she speaks, it can only be in reaction to something that occurs in her surroundings. No interior monologue, no recollections, no omniscience. In essence, you are a camera, but a camera with five senses and a decent vocabulary, and the film is free. Keep shooting until something happens.

If you get stuck, try a genre: suspense, romance, science fiction, sure—but even surrealist, postmodernist, absurdist, fairy tale. Use conventions of setting, appearance, and mood to create expectations that you can later satisfy or subvert (or both). "Suspense is the tension between hope and fear; pull the strings!" said my professor. When you think of your girl and your road, what do you hope will happen? What do you fear might happen instead? The most fun things to read, in my opinion, are the ones that allow me to entertain the possibility of more than one outcome. Do that.

———

After you've gotten to a stopping place, and after you have put this exercise away for a day or a week or ten years, reread what you wrote and ask yourself what it would mean if this piece came at the end of the story instead of at the beginning. What if your girl is not the main character at all but a bystander in someone else's story?

What if this scene is a dream or a memory and the real story is happening somewhere else or at some other time? Write about that for a while and then put the whole thing away, again.

The third time you look at this story (for this is a film school exercise and so it must have three acts), go back and break all the rules. Add the memories and interior monologues that I forbade you earlier. Decide that Prague is really Mexico and your girl is an old woman now. Introduce a character who can answer some of the questions that stumped you earlier and, then, remember that *that* character is a liar.

Lee Martin

WHAT IF IT WAS MORE THAN THAT?

Here's something I can't get out of my mind these days, which seems as good a place as any for me to begin to see what I have to tell you about writing creative nonfiction.

So much of the genre centers on exactly what the writer doesn't know. It's that curiosity and uncertainty that requires the essay, which is ideally an attempt on the writer's part to discover what he or she really thinks and feels about a particular topic. A good essay is an act of exploration, an examination of character and situation, but also an examination of the writer's own intellectual and emotional responses to something that simply won't let him or her go.

What do you have right now that you can't stop thinking about? Something from the present? The past? The future? Something you lived through or, as in what I'm about to tell you, something you heard told or something you read about in print?

I come from a rural part of southeastern Illinois, and from 1969 through 1975, I lived in the small town of Sumner, population in the neighborhood of one thousand at the time. Just prior to my birth, in 1955, the town celebrated its centennial. My parents purchased one of the books, *Trails of Yesterday,* printed to commemorate the occasion, and that book has survived these last fifty-one years, somewhere along the line coming to rest on my shelves. On the first page, there's a message addressed to the future, specifically to those who will be around to plan the second centennial celebration, in 2054. "We have faith in the future," the 1954 townspeople write, "and we anticipate a continuously steady development of our community." No hope could have ended up more unfulfilled, for what happened, boiled down to its simplest elements and directly stated, is this: the economy went sour, and folks, looking for a little extra kick, figured out how to make methamphetamine. Now the place is filthy with it, but there happens to be a police officer who's determined to do everything he can to reduce the problem. He finds the meth labs, makes the arrests, and turns the violators over for prosecution.

Then he comes home one evening—here's the hard part to say, the thing that won't let me go—and finds his bird dog in his backyard beat so near to death the only thing to do is have the vet put him down.

The report in the paper quotes the county sheriff, who says that of course it had to be retaliation for all those meth arrests. It had to have been a lowlife like that.

And maybe it was. Wicked people do wicked things all the time. We know that. But the path they travel—this path from innocence to corruption (innocence because aren't we all innocent before life gets a good hold on us and shows us exactly what we're capable of?)—is often much more complicated than the final result would indicate. It's so easy to rush to judgment when we forget that fact, when we only hold the despicable event in our hearts and minds. Hold it there, we should, of course, but to hold only that is to simplify our common lot in a way that goes against the grain of what we know about human beings. We know that all of us are made up of contradictions. The most loathsome among us can at times be charming; the most saintly can have their moments of ill-advised behavior. These contradictions are what make us noteworthy—interesting because we can't, at any given moment, be fully defined and known.

So this person who beat the police officer's dog? I don't mean to condone that action, only to point out the difference between news and story. The former relies on facts but in a superficial way. Yes, this is what happened. Yes, someone beat that dog. We read that item in the newspaper, and we get angry, sad, vengeful. We shake our heads. "What kind of a person?" we mutter, and suddenly we're in the land of story, that land that exists just beneath the facts, and this is the place where essays begin, at this point of unknowing, this point of sensing there's more to the event and the people involved than a newspaper report can hold.

When I wrote my first memoir, *From Our House,* I wanted to take a hard look at my father, who lost his hands in a farming accident when I was barely a year old and became an angry man. I knew him as a father who was quick-tempered and inclined to reach for a belt, a yardstick, or a persimmon switch with which to punish me. I knew the clench of his jaw muscles, the sign that his temper was about to boil over, and I knew the welts he often left on my skin, but those memories alone weren't enough to require the writing. You see, I also recalled perfectly pleasant moments in my father's company—listening to baseball games on the radio, replaying my basketball games when I was older, accompanying him as he did good turns for neighbors down on their luck—and the intersection of those moments of temper and those moments of pleasure made it difficult, as it had all my life, to know what I really thought about him and the life we had as father and son.

This way of looking at characters from more than one angle, thereby seeing more and more aspects of the personality, is common to the fiction writer. When I wrote my most recent novel, *The Bright Forever,* for example, I wanted to explore characters—each of them affected in some way by the central event of the book, the kidnapping of a nine-year-old girl—who weren't wholly good or evil. I had to find moments of shortcoming for the "good" characters and moments of innocence for the "bad" characters. Sometimes I see nonfiction writers who are just beginning to attempt the genre—particularly writers of memoirs that feature childhood experiences with people bent on causing harm to them—determine early on exactly who their characters are. A person who hurt them is cast as a villain in the early pages, and, because the writer can see that person only in a narrowly defined way, the character never has the chance to demonstrate any other facets of his or her nature. It's important, then, to remind the nonfiction writer that, like the fiction writer, who deals with invented characters, his or her obligation to the real people and places that make up the stuff of the nonfiction is to see them as fully and with as much generosity as possible.

Fleshing out people in a piece of nonfiction and making them multidimensional is often a matter of paying attention to research. Yes, you can find the facts attached to a specific event and the people involved, but what's the story beneath those facts? Here, like a good archaeologist, the nonfiction writer often unearths artifacts and then uses them to come to conclusions about the people who once possessed them. After my father's death, for example, I found a Farm Bureau pamphlet upon which he had written his name again and again in a beautiful, flowing script. I knew from the date of the pamphlet and the grace of the penmanship that he'd written his name there when he was still an unmarried man, past the age of thirty-five, living alone on the farm with his aged, nearly blind mother. When I looked at his name, written over and over with such insistence, it seemed to me that he was expressing a desire to escape his bachelorhood—which he soon would, marrying my mother when he was thirty-eight. When I looked at that handwriting, he became someone much different than the angry father I'd always known. Likewise, when I found a school photograph of him at the end of a line of classmates—I estimate that he was in the seventh or eighth grade at the time—I took note of the way he stood slightly apart from the next person in line and the way he just barely tipped his face up to meet the camera and the hesitant look on his face, and I imagined him as a shy, gentle boy who had no idea what life would do to him and how it would remake him into a person he didn't know he was going to become.

Artifacts such as the pamphlet and the photograph brought me closer to my father and also took me farther away from him because they made him more difficult to classify. In a sense, they made him into something new, and they took me deeper into my unknowing. How was I to respond to him? Was he the angry father I so often knew, or was he the shy boy who was hesitant in the world, or was he the hopeful bachelor desperate to escape his loneliness? He was all of those people, of course. The artifacts suggested as much as they took me deeper into his character and then, by extension, led me more completely into our relationship, which was the thing I'd come to explore. There's always more to something than meets the eye—more to people, particularly—and the good nonfiction writer uses the artifacts at hand, as the following writing activity asks, to cast off across an uncharted river of unknowing, eager to see what waits on the other side.

THE EXERCISE

1. Write down everything you think you know about a person, a place, or an event. "This is the sort of person who would . . ." "This is a place where . . ." "This event occurred because . . ." Act as if you know everything there is to know.

2. Then do some research with the challenge of finding out something you didn't know. Read newspaper reports, conduct interviews, look at photographs, poke around in the county courthouse records, visit a local or state historical society. Find something that makes you look at the person, place, or event from a different angle. Find something that opens the material up in a way you couldn't have predicted.

3. Create a passage that contains a moment of surprise, a moment where for the first time you knew something in a way you never knew it previously. If writing about a person, you might begin with the prompt "Usually my father [or whomever you're exploring] . . ." The idea here is to establish a baseline for the person by offering up what may be the prevalent aspect of his or her character as you recall it. You're looking for habitual action. "Usually my father checked the locks each night at bedtime and then tromped up the stairs, pausing at the top to tell my brother and me to pipe down and go to sleep." Then continue by veering off from that baseline with the prompt "Then one night [or day] . . ." You might say, for example, "Then one night, we didn't hear him coming up the stairs. We waited and waited, but all we heard was the ticking of the grandfather clock on the landing. Finally, we crept out of our bedroom, looked through the stairway railing, and saw our father kneeling on the floor below us, his hands clasped together in prayer." You can do the same, of course, by using not memory but something discovered in research, as I did with the Farm Bureau pamphlet and the photograph. You can also do the same for a place or an event. All you have to do is write about what you knew and then show us the information or artifact that turned your certainty on its ear.

FOR FURTHER CONSIDERATION: It's important that nonfiction writers know enough to get a piece of writing under way. They know what it was like to be a part of their family, for instance, or they know what it's like to live in a particular town, or they know the facts of a specific event. It's equally important for these writers to admit to themselves and to us that they don't know everything, that there's still much to be learned. Their research, then, as long as they're open to such learning, can take them to interesting places that will complicate what they think and feel. If indeed the essay is a conversation between the various parts of the writer's self as he or she attempts to come to some sort of meaning, then it's absolutely crucial that the writer open him- or herself to the various contradictions within that self as well as within others, and the places that they occupy. Research isn't just gathering facts; it's also a chance to discover something new and unanticipated in our responses to the world at large.

Dan Chaon

THE TITLE GAME EXERCISE

THE FOLLOWING EXERCISE IS DESIGNED TO HELP YOU think about your own creative process, and especially about the complex process by which stories are generated (or germinated, if you prefer a more organic metaphor). In her essay "The Reading and Writing of Short Stories," Eudora Welty talks about what it is like to read an analysis of her stories. "When I see them analyzed—most usually, 'reduced to elements'—sometimes I think, 'this is none of me.' . . . I could not remember starting with those elements." She goes on to talk about the actual seeds that start her mind going—birdsong, a tune on the radio, something seen from a passing car.

It's hard to tell where stories come from. We troll through the subconscious, hoping to hook a spark that might lead to a story. Yes, most of the time it is deeply personal, but I don't think much of it is autobiographical. Most of us don't lead especially interesting lives, or if we do, we write our memoirs. In fiction, the spark we're searching for isn't reality so much as a conglomeration of words, memories, and imagination. We seek out not what we know but what stirs our hearts, a little minnow-flash of unshakable emotion—an image, a character, a situation, a voice. It is the person we might have been, the things we might have done, if we'd been braver or more dramatic or more reckless; it's the secret that flashed by in the newspaper or on the TV news, the moment that whispered by when you were on the bus; it's the story you would tell if someone was there to put a cocked gun to your temple. You know you've got it when you feel a little tingle in your chest, a flip-flop of your stomach.

THE EXERCISE

In this exercise I am going to offer you a little bait for your hook: a title. For this exercise, you will need:

- One weird word that you like (it has to be a real word)
- One word (verb or gerund) that evokes a complex, troublesome memory for you
- One song or album title
- One adjective-and-noun combo
- One question
- One word or phrase evocative of your childhood—something your mother or father would say, a piece of a joke you liked, or a game you used to play, for instance

Take six separate pieces of paper; write the weird word at the top of the first sheet, the verb on the next, then the song, the adjective and noun, the question, and the evocative phrase.

Each of these is the title of a story you are going to write.

Don't second-guess yourself too much on these; go with your first instinct—trust the dreaming part of your brain. I am asking you to free-associate, to drift your line through dark, unexplainable waters. Meditate on the titles until you feel a tug. Think about the images, or characters, or situations, or setting that a particular title evokes for you. See what a title feels like at the top of your page. Then begin to write. Make sure that you complete at least one full page for each title, but don't write too much beyond one or two pages. In fact, try to make yourself stop in the middle of a scene, *before* you run out of steam; try to leave each piece at the edge of a cliff. If you're lucky, you may now have the beginnings of six new stories; if you're lucky, one of these may actually stick compellingly in your head, may lead you into a real story of your own. In any case, you've created half a dozen possibilities for yourself.

Norma E. Cantú

LIVING TO TELL, TELLING TO LIVE: THREE LITERARY EXERCISES

BECAUSE WE ARE ALL UNIQUE BEINGS, WE ALL HAVE STORIES that are particular to our own experience. The following exercises will lead you to produce three pieces of writing based on these experiences. Each takes about an hour, although you can shorten or lengthen them as you wish. Each exercise can be repeated with a different focus so that you may generate numerous pieces of writing. You can use these exercises for fiction and nonfiction writing. You may want to read through an exercise first so that you know what it entails and then return to do it, allowing plenty of time for reflection and for writing. You may want to have an alarm clock handy—or use the alarm setting on your cell phone or PDA while turning off the ring tone.

THE EXERCISES

Exercise No. 1: My Name

Names are power; so is knowledge. Names are important in fiction, for the character's identity is often directly linked to her or his name. On a personal level, the more we know about our names, the more we know about ourselves. Just as we assume various roles during our lives (daughter, sister, aunt, mother, teacher, friend, etc.), each one of us bears various names throughout our lifetime: the formal given name our parents or caretakers chose for us when we came into this world, the childhood nickname, the family pet name, the "school" name teachers use, your married name (if you are a woman and marry and choose to change your name; in the United States, that is, because women in some countries do not change their surname to their husband's name), the name that appears on formal papers—Social Security card, driver's license—and the name that identifies you to yourself! The same holds true for characters. Although the following exercise asks that you focus on your own name, you may want to try it using a character's name instead and with that character's history and life in mind.

Focus on your name—what it means to you and how you feel about it. If you don't know how it was chosen for you, you may want to ask someone who may know why you were named as you were. But also feel free to imagine or to create a reason for your name. If you are a parent and you have not told your children how you chose their names, you may want to do so at some point.

As you read the following questions, you may jot down notes or just relax and let your mind wander as you answer them in your mind. Take your time; read each question and give yourself a minute or so to reflect. Let your imagination fly and you will be surprised to see what comes to you.

1. If your name were a flower, what kind of flower would it be? A rose? A hibiscus? A dandelion? The blossom of the prickly pear cactus or of the gigantic magnolia? What flower would signify your childhood? What about now?
2. If your name were a color, what color would it be? The yellow of the sunflower? The pastel blue of the evening sky?

The deep purple of the eggplant? Close your eyes and focus on your name. See it in your mind's eye. What color is it written in and on what color background?

3. If your name were a musical instrument, what instrument would it be? A blaring trumpet? A soft violin? A piccolo? A recorder? A tuba? A drum? Close your eyes and say your name aloud. What instrument does your name remind you of? Does it sound like the soft ding of the triangle? The deep notes of the saxophone?

4. If your name were an ice-cream flavor, what flavor would it be? Pistachio? Plain vanilla? Mango? Close your eyes and imagine your name in your mouth. What was your favorite ice-cream flavor in childhood? What is it now?

5. If your name were a fabric, what would it be? Denim? Silk? Nylon? Rayon? Duct tape? Moiré? Taffeta? Take a mental inventory of the clothes you own. Are they mostly cotton? Or synthetics? Do you prefer the feel of wool or of silk? Cloth is very sensual, and your name is what clothes your identity. What fabric is your name?

6. If your name were a city anywhere in the world, what city would it be? Paris? San Antonio? London? Chicago? Hong Kong? Laredo, Texas? Would it be the city or town of your birth? The place where you had your first kiss? What city are you attracted to? You may never have visited Madrid or Helsinki or Boca Raton, Florida, yet it may have a strange attraction for you. Are there any cities that hold that fascination for you?

7. If your name were a street or a highway in your town or city, what street would it be? Pick a highway or a street that you enjoy driving on. When I was a child my father would take us for Sunday drives, just to enjoy his favorite streets, to see other parts of town. So when I travel these streets, I

am flooded with memories of those Sunday afternoons in the car with my family, the wind blowing my hair every which way. Is the one you chose a quiet secluded road or a busy, much-traveled street? Is it rural or urban? The paths that we take often reflect the roads we prefer to travel on. I rarely take the interstate if I can get to where I am going on city streets. But when I am in a hurry, it is that same highway I usually avoid that becomes my favorite.

8. If your name were a food, what would it be? Italian? Chinese? Mexican? Midwestern? Be specific. Is it pasta? Or is it moo goo gai pan? Is it enchiladas? Or is it roast beef? What dessert is your favorite? What dessert would say your name? After all, we are what we eat!

If you have been answering the questions, taking your time with each one and not rushing through to the next without reflecting on your answers or jotting down something, you may want to go back and revisit the questions. For now we are ready to write about your name.

Freewrite for about fifteen to twenty minutes, just letting go and using the answers you jotted down as a springboard for the writing. (Freewriting sounds like what it means: write anything that comes into your mind. The goal is to get down as much language as possible, so try not to lift your pen from the page or your fingers from the keys.) Don't stop to edit, and don't worry about putting commas in the right place or finding the exact word at this point. Just get your thoughts on the page or the screen. This first draft will yield the kernels that will become the finished piece. Now expand on the piece, taking time to develop and enlarge the ideas, allowing the images to come alive for you.

After you write your piece, read it aloud. Doing so will allow you to catch things that you may want to change. Whenever you

find yourself tripping up on a word or phrase, note it and go back later and revise it so it feels more like your voice. It will flow more naturally. I recommend that you use colored pens or pencils to mark areas that need more work. Remember to use adjectives that reflect the senses—touch, smell, sound, sight, and taste.

Exercise No. 2: Lost

At one time or another we have all been lost, either literally or metaphorically. Also, we have all lost something or someone. Loss is part of our life experience and can teach us many lessons. This two-part exercise will ask you to recall and write about such losses.

a. As a five-year-old child, I was lost in a huge marketplace. My parents were frantic until they found me. In my view, I was not lost; they were! This exercise asks that you recall a time when you felt lost, or perhaps were truly lost. As you read the following questions, reflect on the feelings and the images that come to you and then write down some key words that you can then expand on in your piece.

Think of a time when you got lost, and answer these questions:

1. What is the occasion?
2. Where are you?
3. What time of day is it?
4. Are you driving? Walking? With someone else?
5. If it applies, think of whether you had a map. Was the map misleading? Were you ignoring directions or the map?
6. How did you find your way? Did someone else "find" you? Were you afraid? Were you tenacious?

Were you talking to yourself? What were you
saying?

7. What consequences did you encounter? Were you
late? Never arrived? Were you embarrassed? Teased?
Are stories still around of that time you were lost?

b. Items tend to get lost. Notice that I didn't say "I lose things"
but that *they* get lost. Actually, in most cases, they turn out
to be right where I left them when I finally find them, and
at the most unlikely place I think to look, that is where I
find them! Now think of a time when you lost an item, an
ideal, or a person. You might recall when you lost your
faith in someone or something, or when you lost a significant artifact, such as a graduation or wedding ring. Perhaps you lost a loved one or a friendship. The following
questions are designed to help you focus on your loss.

1. What is the significance of the item, ideal, or person?
2. What would have happened if you had never lost the
item, ideal, or person?
3. Did you ever find the item, ideal, or friendship or did
you reconcile yourself to the loss? If so, how? What
helped you come to terms with the loss?

Exercise No. 3: The Photo

Photographs are frozen memories. We can use photos, real or imagined, to trigger memories that can become the basis for wonderful
writing. For this exercise, think of a photograph or snapshot—
whatever comes to mind—of you at any age between five and
twelve. It is preferable that it be a photo where you appear alone,
but it will be fine if you recall a photo of yourself with others.

As you reflect on the following questions, you may want to jot down key words or thoughts that you will use later as you write your piece. It works better if you do not have the photo in front of you as you answer the questions and write, although you may want to look at the photo afterward and see how your memory of the photo compares with the actual photo.

1. What is the occasion? A birthday? A school photo? A holiday? Nothing special?
2. What are you wearing? Describe the color, fabric, and design and how you feel about what you are wearing. Even if you can't see your feet in the photo, describe what shoes, if any, you are wearing. Sandals? Loafers? Boots?
3. What does your hair look like? Who combed it? Do you like it?
4. Who is taking the photo?
5. What sounds are around you? Is it indoors? Outdoors? Are there voices? Whose?
6. What are you standing on? Wooden floor? Cement? Grassy lawn?
7. What do you feel, looking back at that photo?
8. If you, the adult, could talk to the child in the photo, what would you say?
9. If the child could talk to you, what would she or he say to the adult?

Now write for fifteen minutes. Just let the story flow from the photo. You may begin by describing it and using the key words you jotted down when answering the questions, but allow your voice to tell the story behind the photo. Explore how you feel and how the child that you were is still with you.

You may want to repeat this exercise, thinking of a different photo each time. Or you may want to make it a different exercise by recalling a photo where you appear in a group; then ask the questions as you ponder who else is in the photo and what has happened to them since the photo was taken.

You may want to allow the writing to "rest" for a while and then return to it a few days later and add to it, revising and editing the piece.

Alan Cheuse

MY FAVORITE FICTION-WRITING EXERCISE

PASTICHE WRITING, OR MAKING IMITATIONS OF THE WORKS of fine writers, has helped my students at nearly every turn in their early writing careers. I've always looked to painters for examples. They send their students to the museums, where they copy portions of the canvases, or sometimes even entire paintings, of the masters. In this way they learn, among other techniques, how to use their wrists in brushstrokes of genius.

Pastiche making is not exact copying. (When we read Borges's story "Pierre Menard, Author of Don Quixote," we see where copying can lead.) But it does ask the new writer to make his or her way along the same path as a master, to walk in their shoes and see with their eyes. My friend Al Young sometimes asks his students to copy a page from a great writer, keeping only the sentence structure but substituting their own nouns, verbs, and other parts of speech. This helps. So does copying a technique, as in, say, a view of the land in *To the Lighthouse* or the prairie in Cather's *My Ántonia*, in which the student writer substitutes his or her own landscape for the master's. One exercise that worked with great success for my students was to make over the opening pages of a Steinbeck novel—*Cannery Row* served well as a model, as did *East of Eden*—using the material of their own youth.

Alternate points of view on great scenes in modern fiction also offer a good way to get students to use their imaginations within the firm boundaries established by a master. In one such exercise I ask students to read Chekhov's story "The Kiss" and write the signal scene—the soldier in the dark room receiving a kiss from a mysterious woman—from the woman's point of view. In another I ask them to write an alternative view of Chekhov's great story "The Lady with the Pet Dog" from the points of view of Anna's husband and her Moscow lover's wife.

All this has worked to stretch the students' sense of what they can attempt and what they can achieve with their own prose.

THE EXERCISE

Return to a story you love and replace the author's material with material from your own experience or imagination. Or return to a story you love and tell a different side of the story by experiencing and dramatizing the events through a different character's perspective.

Bret Anthony Johnston

HOW TO NAME THE WORLD: AN EXERCISE IN RESEARCH

I N GRADUATE SCHOOL, I WROTE TRAVEL ARTICLES TO PAY FOR food, rent, and books. Although other travel writers were sent to the Ivory Coast and Fiji, I wrote for a magazine that focused on domestic travel. My job was to write about South Dakota and Nevada and Pennsylvania; my most exotic assignments were Louisiana and Florida. I covered the Hershey factory—and its accompanying theme park—and the C. M. Russell museum and a giant Sam Houston statue, all of which are very pleasant, if comparatively unexciting, destinations. Still, the magazine paid well, and toward the end of my tenure on the masthead, I got to where I could write the articles within a few hours. Better still, I could write the pieces without ever leaving my apartment. I was a travel writer who never traveled. In other words, I was a fraud.

My fraudulence, though, was the decree of the editor. I would've been elated—especially during those long Iowa Januaries—to fly (or hop a freight train, for that matter) south for the winter, but such expenditures were not within the magazine's budget. More affordable was sending me monthly manila envelopes, pregnant with photos and statistical information and state-produced propaganda, and having me fabricate out of whole cloth a trip to the featured destination. To keep my lights and heat on, and to keep food on the table and gas in my truck, I had to convince the magazine's audience that I had seen firsthand the rare albino alligators through Louisiana's glass-bottomed boats and the streetlamps fashioned in the shape of Hershey's Kisses. I had to, in other words, write fiction.

And my fiction depended utterly upon my research. This was a new concept for me, one that changed forever the way I wrote stories. As a result, I can't remember a semester when I haven't required students in my fiction workshops to incorporate a research element into their fiction. Nor can I recall a story, mine or a student's, that the exercise didn't immediately and exponentially benefit.

But it's never an easy sell. Many writers have been weaned on the "write what you know" idea, and they mistakenly equate research with the antithesis of creativity. Personally and pedagogically, I respect and condone the "write what you know" approach because writers so often know more than they realize; however, research must be viewed as a component of imaginative writing, not its polar opposite. (It's interesting to note that students *expect* to incorporate research into projects for other classes; they think nothing of anthropology or psychology or literature professors requiring outside sources as tools to substantiate and expand their thinking and projects. When writing fiction, however, the idea of venturing outside their own sensibilities seems outlandish and somehow criminal.)

Often, how research manifests itself—or fails to manifest itself—in a project is the difference between a good book and a publishable book. Try imagining John Grisham without that authenticating legalese. Try imagining a Eudora Welty story divorced from her vivid and particular settings (the same for work by Richard Russo, Alice Munro, Toni Morrison, Chris Offutt, Jhumpa Lahiri, Cormac McCarthy, etc.). What if David Morrell's Rambo had just been a really brave soldier, as opposed to a Green Beret who'd won the Congressional Medal of Honor? What if the details of *One Flew over the Cuckoo's Nest* didn't ring so true? (Talk about research: Kesey bribed an orderly on a psychiatric ward to administer electroshock therapy to him so that he could render the experience in a believable fashion for the reader. And my students balk when I send them to the library or bookstore or Internet!) Such successful work depends on research, on buttressing the imagination with an unequivocal foundation in the material world.

Mark Twain said, "The difference between the right word and the almost right word is the difference between lightning and a lightning bug." And I would humbly submit that the same is true of details. Writers most often use research to find the perfect details, pieces of information that simultaneously ground a story and give it wings. Spot-on details elicit readers' trust while drawing them deeper and more completely into the narrative. Then, once the readers are immersed in the imaginary world, the research will work to keep them there, to sustain an atmosphere more real than reality. Isn't that what literature always aims to do? Your job is to take readers to places that they—and often you—have never been.

THE EXERCISE

Return to an unfinished project and ferret out places or ways to incorporate research. You want to strive for hard and fast information, for ways to authenticate and broaden the imaginary events and people you're trying to bring to life. Look for places to be ever more specific, more accurate, in your language. Occasionally you will be able to mine your own areas of expertise—write what you know—though other times will require you to venture outside your own experience; you'll be required to research and write what you don't know, to write what you want to know. Either way, ambiguity is the enemy here: your job is to name the world; your job, to paraphrase Joseph Conrad, is before all else to make the reader see.

The following is a kind of checklist that you might consider reviewing as you revise your fiction; it should help reinforce the strong parts of your project and it might open new avenues for you to explore. Of course, all of these criteria won't be applicable to every project, but the more you can check off—the more of them that you can logically and smoothly integrate into your narrative—the more affecting the work will be.

- Landscape and setting
- Flora and fauna
- Characters' occupations
- Characters' hobbies
- History and historical events
- Weather and meteorology
- Medical and biological information
- Architecture and apparel
- Technical and scientific information
- Culture and cultural events

Dorothy Allison

UNTOLD STORIES: AN EXERCISE
TO GENERATE FICTION

HERE ARE A FEW WAYS I GET MY STUDENTS TO START
stories.

Essentially, I make them write a piece beginning with the line
"I never told anyone . . ."

The trick is that I change how I set this exercise up all the time.

Sometimes I read some brief piece of fiction—first-person, self-
revelatory, strong voice. I change what I read as often as I can, trying to choose something they might not have read recently. (I love
to pull something from the back of my bookcase—there is a short
story taken out of Katherine Dunn's *Geek Love* that I used a lot for
a while, and a piece of James Baldwin's *Go Tell It on the Mountain*.
That is the quality of thing I use.)

Then I make them close their eyes, and I let this long silence
happen. *That is very important.* Make them a little nervous, so they
will focus. Then I tell them to take up their pens and write the first
line—"I never told anyone . . ."—and go from there.

They'll write for ten, fifteen, or twenty minutes. If they flag or
if I am feeling particularly irritable, I stop them, have them set
aside what they started, take up a new piece of paper, and begin
again. This time the line is:

"I did tell one person. God help me. She/he . . ."

That makes a completely different and interesting story, but I have been using it for only a couple of years, so I can't say it is as good as the other. It does, however, take the story away from memoir, so I sometimes like it a lot.

Sometimes I do a physical variation on this exercise. I get the participants to tighten every muscle in their bodies, just squeeze as hard as they can, and then release. If they are resistant or laugh, I make them do it a couple of times. Then I give them the line without reading anything:

"I never told anyone, but I'll tell you . . ."

Funny thing is that with the last approach, there is a strong tendency for someone to get weepy.

THE EXERCISE

Start a story or stories with one of the following lines:

"I never told anyone . . ."

"I did tell one person. God help me. She/he . . ."

"I never told anyone, but I'll tell you . . ."

C. Michael Curtis

BULLIES I HAVE KNOWN

M Y INTEREST IN WRITING EXERCISES IS A BIT COUNTER-intuitive, but it sits comfortably with my notion that *any* plunge into narrative is likely to prove fruitful, and that any writing, no matter how primitive or half-formed, is better than panic and paralysis. Many, if not most, exercises are intended to strengthen particular stylistic muscle groups—character, plot, dialogue, setting, and so on. This makes perfect sense, and it often works admirably. However, I like to postpone matters of technique until an idea of some sort hits the page running. I admire stories that have "moral weight," that have to do with difficult choices, life-changing catalysts, moments that force questions about "how to be." My sense is that once something potent begins to take shape on the page, a writer naturally turns to technique: What sort of characters are involved? What do we need to know about them? What do they sound like? Who is the best person to tell the story? How can language best be used to achieve a nuanced glimpse of these characters in action? And so on.

Some writers need only a nudge to get them going, and they are often surprised, and pleased, to find that an arbitrary assignment can open them up to a world of imaginative possibilities.

THE EXERCISES

1. SCENE OF A CRIME: I ask my students to describe a room an anonymous narrator has entered for the first time. No one is in the room, which can be in a home, an office, a warehouse, or anywhere. The given is that something dramatic has occurred there—or will soon. I ask that the narrator describe the room's furnishings, blemishes, oddnesses. Furniture? Status detail? (I will have pointed out how often writers use such matters as cigarette brands, magazines, artwork, and book titles to suggest income level, education, cultural tastes, hobbies, and so on.) Signs of recent activity? (Warm food on the table, blood on a countertop with Band-Aid wrappers, visible water stains on a wall or flooring, etc.)

The narrator is asked to adopt a voice of deliberate neutrality, observing but never interpreting. The trick is to note detail that, though seemingly of no importance, may lead to a reasoned conclusion about what has happened in the room and who has been affected by that action.

I tell students to pretend they're detectives investigating a complaint, or a report, or a request for assistance. In the absence of a human witness, they must draw what conclusions they can from the evidence available. The more subtle these connections, the less self-evident the dramatic context, the more successful the exercise. That is, I want them, if they can, to begin turning the exercise into a "story," to begin with a situation, then integrate characters, motivations, subsequent events, and consequences.

2. SHOOTING AN ELEPHANT: I invite, but don't require, students to read the Orwell essay of that title. I discuss the essay, however, to outline the moral dilemma it poses. (Shoot an elephant to satisfy Burmese villagers who expect a show of force from their British rulers and have been terrorized by a male elephant in the grip of mating madness? Or spare the elephant, now calmed, on the humane grounds that the animal is no longer a danger and has, in any case, done no more than follow its inner nature?) I ask students to imagine a situation in which he or she (or an imagined character) is under pressure to do something (e.g., share information on an exam, reveal private confidences) he or she would normally object to on moral or ethical grounds. The story or essay is meant to illuminate both the range and the inevitability of moral reflection and to provide "storytelling" with a weighty context.

In both of these exercises, I place emphasis on the "idea" of the story, rather than on the conventions of character, setting, dialogue, plot, voice, and so on. I do so in the belief that form follows function, that once you know what your story is about, you can then find the techniques best suited to your telling.

FOR FURTHER CONSIDERATION: With students who complain that they have no subject to write about or who simply wish for inspiration, I have asked for stories built around puzzling but arbitrary titles. Some have been more successful than others, but I've had luck with "The Perfect Dinner Party," "What I Do," and "Bullies I Have Known." In each case I've asked for *event, conclusion, moral weight,* and *distinctive characters.*

One of the most successful experiments occurred during a writers' conference, when I asked a group of student-writers to spend twenty minutes or so describing what they'd seen and heard in the previous hour. What emerged were mini-portraits of students, faculty, and guest speakers that were hilarious, informative, and sobering by turn. One of these "stories" was so stylish and so acute in its observations that the writer used it to win his way into an MFA program the next fall.

Tom Barbash

OUR EVER-CURIOUS MINDS

ONE OF THE HALLMARKS OF THE BEST LITERARY NONFIC-
tion is the intelligence and curiosity of authors like David
Foster Wallace and Susan Orlean. We read these writers in part to
spend time with their thoughts. In "Consider the Lobster," Wallace
considers not just the lobster but every aspect of his story, from the
setting to those who attend the lobster festival, to the history of lobster eating and catching, to whether or not lobsters feel anything
when we cook them, to larger questions about ethics and eating, to
the readership of *Gourmet,* the magazine that employed him to
write the article in the first place. He saturates us in the culture of
lobster, what period they date from (Jurassic), where they fit in
within the deep-sea pecking order, and how the high-priced menu
item was initially perceived as "low-class food" for the poor and in-
stitutionalized. Despite all the facts and information he provides,
we never feel bogged down in the writer's research, primarily because Wallace has preselected the most compelling and evocative
details and rendered them in lucid and entertaining prose.

In Susan Orlean's essay "Show Dog," the writer, a regular con-
tributor to *The New Yorker,* examines all aspects of the world of
show dogs, from diet to breeding to grooming to the fame some

dogs receive and the expense owners need to shell out. Orlean writes her piece with her signature sharp humor and satiric tone, and uses the traditional celebrity profile as its template. Orlean says she likes to write about those who are passionate about their pastimes. In order to capture her subjects in their ardor she tends to borrow their fervent natures, sharing their obsessions and their concern for the smallest of details. This technique brings us into worlds we'd otherwise never get to see.

Both Wallace and Orlean employ a great deal of research in their essays and yet both pieces read smoothly and effortlessly, more like short stories than reportage. Wallace occasionally inserts himself into the text, in part to examine his own moral culpability with regard to the questions he's posing. Orlean, on the other hand, keeps her distance. Though the authors approach their narratives differently, the effect is the same, a kind of unveiling of story and argument. A long essay or piece of narrative nonfiction should take its time arriving at meaning. This allows for the piece to read like an act of discovery, rather than a collection of evidence to support a preordained argument—as in your bread-and-butter newspaper column. How does one write in that fashion without creating a wandering, disorganized mess?

THE EXERCISE

Try writing about something you do every day and take for granted: driving a car, shopping at a convenience store, attending a movie at a multiplex. Then research several angles of this simple event. If, say, you go to a 7-Eleven, you might want to research the history of the franchise or consumption at convenience stores. Maybe you'll write about increased security (the four-inch glass the clerks sit behind), or about the products the store stocks and where they get placed (based on whose decisions), or about the effort to offer healthier items. An essay on multiplexes could tell us the history of that phenomenon, and how much income is derived from soda and popcorn sales, and how much a theater owner pays the staff, and how each theater determines which movies to show and for how long. You get the idea.

ADOPT A MYTH

MY FAVORITE EXERCISES GENERATE WORK DRASTICALLY different from what I've been producing. Structures, focused tasks, and prompts can send writers into their creative zones. Such exercises free a writer from working within familiar patterns or with the usual obsessions and set that same writer—with that same talent—off toward something less certain. The results are often impressive.

Let's say you're writing a story in which the protagonist thinks her boyfriend is cheating on her. Your story is rich in character and energy but lacks incident and *story*. You're having trouble with plot and form. Try borrowing a familiar structure from a fairy tale. Superimpose the existing draft over a fairy tale's structure, like so: the protagonist decides she must find three pieces of evidence before she confronts her boyfriend. She's on a quest! The protagonist now has three specific tasks to complete in order to achieve her ultimate goal: knowledge. And you have some structure.

Look for examples of stories or poems that draw on fairy tales, legends, or myths. Some examples are: "Cinderella" by Anne Sexton, *The Bloody Chamber and Other Stories* by Angela Carter, Alan Jay Lerner's script for *My Fair Lady,* and *Pygmalion* by George

Bernard Shaw. Margaret Atwood's subtle and subversive retelling of Goldilocks in "Wilderness Tips" is worth a look. By all means check out Janet Burroway's brilliant diagram of Cinderella's plot in *Writing Fiction.* For kicks, read Joseph Campbell's *The Hero with a Thousand Faces,* then watch *Star Wars* and identify the elements common to almost all mythic journey stories. The goal here is to gain a better understanding of how stories work: that one thing happens after another, that a story sets up its own rules and then characters struggle against them. You want your work to bust out of the humdrum by tapping into something ancient and perhaps universal.

THE EXERCISE

Model a scene on a fairy tale, legend, or myth. The tone can be humorous or serious.

CHARACTER

ON CHARACTER

Few of my characters are described externally; we see them from the inside out.
—Michael Ondaatje

You put a character out there and you're in their power. You're in trouble if they're in yours.
—Ann Beattie

Naming your characters Aristotle and Plato is not going to make their relationship interesting unless you make it so on the page.
—Annie Dillard

EVERYONE WHISPERS ABOUT THE PRETTIEST GIRL IN THE room. We despise the parents with the baby who starts walking and talking months early, and we sneer at the owner of the pedigreed dog that sits, heels, and has never once "messed" on the Oriental rug. On the other hand, we adore the woman who limps into her crucial business meeting four minutes late, carrying her broken high heel. We love the parents who pull out their hair because their child just upchucked applesauce onto the leather interior of the new SUV. We rally behind the frazzled, exhausted dog owner whose beagle jumps onto the dinner table, scarfs down the last slice of pizza, then an hour later "messes" on the Oriental rug.

The difference here is one of empathy. We can't identify, not completely, with perfect characters, so as readers we resist and retreat from protagonists with impeccable clothes, flawless skin, overflowing bank accounts, prodigious children. Regardless of genre, and whether you're writing fiction or nonfiction, the goal of the writer is to create likable, fully developed characters. (And even our villains and antiheroes must be likable.) The irony is that one of the most effective techniques for imagining such people is to focus on those aspects of the character that are least likable, least perfect.

Think about your favorite fictional characters. Why does Harry Potter wear glasses? Why is Indiana Jones desperately afraid of snakes? Why is Clark Kent—who also wears nerdy glasses—so bumbling, while Superman is so suave? Why does Owen Meany have that tortured voice? Why does Frodo steal, smoke, gorge—why is he so unapologetically lazy and cowardly? Why does Bridget Jones so remind us of Frodo? And what of characters from nonfiction? Why do the impoverished Irish children in *Angela's Ashes* remind me so thoroughly of the kids I grew up with in South Texas? How does Capote complicate our feelings for the murderers in *In Cold Blood*? Why do we find ourselves hoping they won't be executed? Why do we weep once the nooses are around their necks?

The answer, of course, is because we relate to these characters. You'd be hard-pressed to find a local gas station attendant who stands over six feet tall, with piercing blue eyes and thick, perfectly coiffed dark hair, and who, in addition to his überhandsomeness, can see through walls, deflect bullets with his chest, leap tall buildings in a single bound, and fly around the earth so fast that it reverses time. You might, though, be able to find a hapless fellow wearing taped-together glasses who blushes when a pretty girl drives up. Your readers are more likely to be afraid of snakes and to sleep too much, and, therefore, so should be your characters.

In my fiction workshops, writers turn in many more "perfect" characters than "imperfect" ones. This is neither surprising nor illogical. They want readers to love their characters, so they spend paragraph after paragraph, chapter after chapter, giving us every reason to do just that. Medals of honor, unconditional love for animals, perfect marriages, exquisite tastes in wine, literature, and art, physiques that Greek gods and goddesses envy. The only surprising thing about this narrative strategy is that it will—without exception—fail.

To forge a relationship between your characters and your readers, focus on what makes a character vulnerable, focus on their inconsistencies, focus on their flawed humanity. This is of the utmost importance. Your focus can be on physical or emotional vulnerability, but it has to be intimately tied to the character. What makes her sad, or what embarrasses her? What frightens her? What does she regret? What minor or major trespasses has she undertaken in her life? When addressing these aspects of character, work hard to make them meaningful. Think of Emma Bovary. We empathize with her not just because of her mistakes—though, again, many of us root for her because of those so-called mistakes—but because of how heavily those mistakes weigh on her, how her constant grappling with them leaves her so at risk. If your character is villainous, show the reader what redeems him. (Hannibal Lecter has a very refined palate, after all, and he's nothing if not eloquent and courteous.) If your character is saintly, show the reader what makes her human. Think of Jean Valjean and that loaf of bread, recall Sethe murdering her children to save their souls in Toni Morrison's *Beloved*.

Engaging such characterological complexity before and during the writing and rewriting process will also ensure that your readers meet your characters as fully rounded individuals from the first line of the story. The popular idea of "building" characters, of stacking trait upon trait onto a character, so that we fully know the cast only at the very end of the story, can be counterproductive. You want to *reveal* your characters throughout the story, not assemble them. By having fully imagined your characters from the first line of the story, you will achieve a deeper, more layered and sophisticated level of characterization, and you will take your readers *into,* not *out of,* your characters' hearts and minds.

The exercises in this section serve up a variety of approaches for rendering memorable and believable characters in prose. Although some of this character work will inevitably get left on the cutting room floor (or, better yet, in a file for your next book!), much of this material, this fleshing out of character, will find a way into your stories. Sometimes you'll need to include full-blown paragraphs of characterization, almost like character sketches unto themselves, and sometimes how deeply you know your characters will shine through in how they react within a scene or story. The result, however, will be the same: from the first word to the very last, your characters will be round and complex—living, breathing people with whom your readers will identify. We will empathize with your characters while we read, and we will miss them long after we turn the last page.

Debra Spark

WRITING AS PARLOR GAME

HERE ARE CARTOON BUBBLES OVER MY STUDENTS' HEADS. Cartoon thought bubbles, so I know what my students mean when they say, "Can we do a writing exercise?" The request always comes late in the semester. Gone are the classes that start with writing exercises and end with a general discussion about inspiration or knowing one's characters. We're into the serious business of the course—close analysis of assigned reading, workshops—and there's a student, hand raised, with a request for something else. "Can we do a writing exercise?" Meaning: "I haven't done the assigned reading." Or: "Can we play?" Hard to refuse. After all, I, too, have the most fun in the early weeks of the semester, when my classes begin with a game.

As in: Start a story with the words "She didn't want to go to _____, but . . ." (See Flannery O'Connor's "A Good Man Is Hard to Find" for inspiration.)

Or: Leave the classroom without a notebook. Tail the first person you see. Come back to class and write a scene from that person's point of view.

The idea of all this is to . . . well, there is no idea. Not really. If inspiration strikes, great. If not, fine. As a writing teacher, my job is to teach students the craft of fiction . . . and help them access their own best ideas, to learn something about their imagination. If the exercises themselves had a collective voice, they'd say, "Here is one way to proceed." They'd say, "Remember, this is supposed to be fun."

When I give writing exercises as take-home assignments—which I do, even in my advanced classes—I'm still using them the same way. Homework as parlor game. I don't like the more serious exercises I often see in writing textbooks. Write a scene in which two people are in conflict over an item but neither states what that item is. Ugh. Yes, I see the point of such an assignment from a craft angle, but what "real" writer ever started a piece of fiction from such a place? My favorite exercises start with the words "Imagine you're . . ."

At any one time, I have a few favorite exercises in my repertoire, and then I get bored and go looking for new ones. These two are currently my favorites, both because they are fun and because they produce such consistently interesting results from my students.

THE EXERCISES

The first one, called "The Truth, the Half-Truth, and Anything But the Truth," is from the novelist Monica Wood, the author of *Secret Language, Ernie's Ark,* and *Any Bitter Thing,* among other titles.

Begin a story or scene with a sentence that starts with a truth, proceeds to a half-truth, and then moves on to a complete lie. The example Monica Wood gives—although I'm not quoting her exactly, since I misremember the specifics of her life and the language of her example:

"When I was twelve, my father died. My mother was heartbroken and ran away with the mailman. Now, every few months, I get a postcard from Minneapolis."

All true till the word *heartbroken,* and then everything else is a lie.

———

For the second exercise, it's important to note that usually my exercises work because I'm the exercise master. I mean: I narrate the exercise for my students, and they have to do things, as I instruct them. No one knows what to do until I tell them to do it. There may be some loss of spontaneity for those who see the next exercise printed out on the page. But I like it nonetheless for its many parts, which guide one into constructing an entire narrative. I stole this exercise from the poet and novelist Donna Masini, who, in turn, got it from the writer Tim Tomlinson. It has several parts, as follows:

Imagine yourself as a character observing two people who are—for whatever reason—not where they are supposed to be. As an observer, you are not participating in the action of the scene, just watching. (An example: Tony Hoagland's poem "Mistaken Identity," which opens with the narrator saying, "I thought I saw my mother / in the lesbian bar," and continues to surprise by revealing that the narrator's mother is dead.)

After writing for a page, focus on one aspect of the dress or appearance of one of the people you are observing. Write about that single detail for half a page.

When you're done, write one of these two phrases on your paper: "What I've never understood is . . ." or "What I've always wanted to know is . . ."

Finish one of the two sentences and then continue writing for another half a page. When you're done, start a sentence with the word "Now . . ." Finish the sentence as you return to the action of the story. Then continue on to finish your scene.

In completing this exercise, students must write a scene, extended physical description, interior thought, and a transition back into the scene, all without really thinking (presumably) about narrative mode.

One of my favorite student responses to this exercise began with a young man returning to his car with some beer from a supermarket. From a distance, he observes his blind brother sitting in the driver's seat of a car, checking the rearview mirror and touching the steering wheel, as if he is about to start up the vehicle. Next to him is a hitchhiker to whom both the brothers have been lying (regarding their respective histories), ever since they picked her up earlier in the day.

———

Here's a third exercise—this one of my own devising. Early in the semester, I start a class by asking students to write about the nicest thing that happened to them that week. Their most pleasant experience. I warn them ahead of time that at least one other person in the class will see their work. (This is code for: protect your privacy; no sex scenes, please!) After the students are through, everyone divides up into pairs. The students read each other their experiences. Then they trade what they've written. The fellow student now has to introduce conflict into the pleasant experience. With this proviso: they are not now "doing" something nasty to their fellow student. Instead, they are using that experience as fodder for fiction and imagining where it will take them. This may not produce the same sort of imaginative pieces that the earlier exercises do, but it is often quite funny. (People love hearing what has happened to their pleasant experience.) And the exercise (I have students do it as a take-home assignment) starts students thinking not just about conflict, that old standard-bearer of writing classes, but about what makes life pleasant—a harder thing to imagine, in many ways.

R. T. Smith

OBJECT OF AFFECTION: PROSE EXERCISES

YEARS AGO I BEGAN ASKING PEOPLE I MET ABOUT PRIZED objects they own that have more symbolic than practical value to them. I was motivated by the conviction that even the most pragmatic of us invest objects with magical powers and believe they can somehow repay our attention to them. One painter I met carries, even when she leaves the country, a fiddle bow that belonged to her grandfather. A writer from Alabama travels with a gold-going-ocher ceramic vase he likes to say his genie lives in. I keep in my study and often haul around when I travel a pillow-sized Navajo weaving a recent acquaintance said must be my "blankie." Totems, talismans, fetishes—they all acquire emotional power and become ceremonial objects in the very private sacrament of *me*.

In this regard, both fictional characters and actual people we might write about resemble us. They own objects, some merely tolerated, others chosen and kept, still others cherished. Those latter ones are as haunted for them as for us and can provide keys to their tastes, interests, eccentricities, and even identities. Think of Frederick's butterfly collection in *The Collector* or Manley Pointer's swiped artificial parts in "Good Country People," Inman's copy of *Bartram's Travels,* Holmes's violin, Stella-Rondo's kimono in "Why

I Live at the P.O." And then there are Georgia O'Keeffe's skulls and Reagan's jelly beans, my maternal grandfather's map of World War I campaigns. When readers remember the pivotal characters in narratives, they often recall these charmlike possessions and use them to renew their acquaintance with the characters.

THE EXERCISES

Here is a fiction-writing exercise based on characters' relations to their treasured things.

- Choose an object that interests you enough to suggest it could be someone's centering symbol.
- List the reasons it might carry metaphorical force.
- Imagine how a character, perhaps based on someone you know, might acquire the object.
- Now write the character's explanation to himself as to why this item has taken on personal meaning. Some facets of the explanation might be logical, others irrational, still others a blend of the two. They may even involve a bit of narrative-within-the-larger-narrative.
- Finally, write a scene in which an acquaintance inquires about why the object holds such fascination for the protagonist and the owner tries to give a feasible and not wholly dishonest answer but without revealing to Character B the most secret ingredients of his attitude. Even as your character conceals much of his nature from Character B, he reveals it to the reader, which helps to develop both psychological complexity and dramatic tension.

For nonfiction writers, the exercise requires exploring one's own amulets or discovering and reporting, rather than inventing, those of other people. Observation replaces imagination. Documented accounts—ranging from correspondence to books to interviews—from the nonfiction subject will have to be tracked down, but they are probably there for the dedicated sleuth, and if your primary character is yourself, then memory is the crucial tool.

As you work at this exercise, you'll find you have to keep inventing (or discovering) history—both factual and affective—for your focal character, and pretty soon you'll realize you have to decide exactly why A doesn't want B to have ready access to this intimate information. Given this reluctance, why are they even friendly enough to have this conversation? What is A unwilling to risk, and why does it matter to B? As the questions radiate outward, so do the implications about their roles and attitudes toward each other, and there you have the kernel of the kind of conflicted and engaging relationship that makes any story, factual or imagined, compelling. Thereby hangs a tale, and you're too deep in to quit now.

Kyoko Mori

NONFICTION TIME-TRAVEL EXERCISE

USED TO PEEL MY SANDWICHES APART TO EAT THE FILLING
with a spoon. My favorite was egg salad. After the filling was
gone, I licked the mustard and then the butter, finished one piece
of bread and then the other, polished off the lettuce, the tomato, the
pickle. I liked every part of the sandwich so long as it was the only
thing I was tasting. Even now, at summer picnics with baked
beans, Jell-O salad, new potatoes, and corn on the cob, I'm happy
to be handed a plate with ridges. Food isn't the only thing I don't
like to mix. I won't listen to music while I'm running or talk on the
phone and wash the dishes at the same time. Multitasking is an
ugly new compulsion. Why not enjoy doing one thing at a time?
Egg salad sandwiches never tasted better than when I was a child
amazed by every salty or sour bite.

But life and work offer opposite pleasures. I try to keep things
simple and separate in my life; when I write, I love to mix and
complicate them. Every genre of creative writing relies on multiple
sensory details, time frames, place settings, shifts in voice, modes of
thinking and imagining, but nonfiction (because it doesn't necessarily emphasize storytelling and we get to explain the harder-to-

understand connections in prose) thrives, especially, on doing more than one thing at a time. The whole point of a memoir or a personal essay is the larger, freer perspective that the writer gains through the piece: we are not only encouraged but *expected* to move between fact and speculation, description and narration, what we saw and what we concluded, what we knew and what we imagined, what we understood then and what, years later, we would come to understand. Nonfiction is time travel. Through it, I can taste the whole sandwich—or maybe all the sandwiches I've ever eaten—without losing the pure thrill of each bite.

THE EXERCISE

Here is a simple stretching exercise to prove this point. Find a photograph of someone close to you from a time before the two of you met. This may be your mother as a young woman, your husband when he was a college dropout in the 1960s, your best friend in Kenosha, Wisconsin, from when she was married to her first husband in Brooklyn. The person may be alone in the photograph, or he or she may be part of a group. The setting could be indoors or out. The only important thing, really, is to choose someone about whom you cannot possibly be objective. You should have a close and complicated relationship so you feel entitled to take liberties and pass judgment.

Look at the photograph carefully and jot down the details you notice. Where is the person standing or sitting? What season is it? What is she wearing? Is he smiling, frowning, staring, or blinking? Next, describe your overall impressions. Is this a happy photograph or not? What do you make of the expression on the person's face? Is there something puzzling about what she's wearing? What feeling do you get from the setting? Finally, interview the person—you can do this formally with several specific questions or informally with just one or two openers—and get some background information. Make a list of the interesting facts you find out. If the person tells you his or her feelings about the photograph, you can include these, too.

Now write a portrait of the person in the photograph, using information from all three lists: what you see in the photograph; what you wonder, speculate, and conclude about it; and what the person told you about its background. Be sure to also add whatever you know and feel about this person from all the years of your acquaintance. Did the photograph or the interview change your perception of him or her or confirm what you already knew? Feel free to wander across time with flashbacks and flash-forwards ("Twenty years later, he will be an award-winning high school teacher in Minneapolis, but in this picture, he is a little boy who hates the smell of chalk and is crying to go home"). Use the present tense to describe the photograph ("He is standing in front of his grandfather's truck, which is parked in the driveway") so it's easier to go forward and backward in time without using the more cumbersome indicators (the past perfect tense, for example). You will find yourself shifting quickly from one list to the next and then back again, mixing and matching the various items in each. Words like *perhaps* and *maybe* and sentence constructions like *She might have . . .* will help you move easily from fact to speculation.

FOR FURTHER CONSIDERATION: The purpose of the exercise is for you to write with equal authority about what you know and what you imagine as you travel between your present relationship with the person and his or her past without you. In nonfiction, we can recount what we didn't see but heard about, what we might have done but didn't, what we can't prove but know to be true, so long as we draw clear distinctions where they belong. We can even explore why we are drawn to the gray area where truth and hearsay, reality and fantasy, science and faith all converge. Often, the goal of a memoir or a personal essay is to reconcile the facts and the fiction of our own lives without confusing them. In writing, we get to keep things separate and put them together at the same time.

Steve Almond

YOUR FIVE SECONDS OF SHAME!

THE YOUNG WRITERS I HOLLER AT FOR A LIVING SEEM TO face two central crises when it comes to their work. First, they have trouble forcing their characters into emotional danger, and second, they have trouble staying there. But of course this is the whole ball of wax, particularly when it comes to short fiction. Plot is merely the mechanism by which your protagonist is forced up against her deepest fears and desires. Danger. That's what the reader wants from you. Not your polite throat clearing, not your Big Ideas, and for God's sake not your indulgent experiments in style.

And the truth is—though writers are loath to admit this—that all of these fears and desires are ones felt by the author. They are not dreamed up and projected onto an imaginary character; they are summoned from within. Which is to say, writing a good short story is an act of profound exposure.

Unfortunately, most writers are scared to death of exposure. They don't want to experience all the scary feelings sloshing around inside them, and they especially don't want to reveal those feelings to the jerks in their workshop or, worse yet, to friends and family and ex-lovers, who will not necessarily understand, or believe, that a short story is an act of fiction, and will ask you if you're depressed, if you've considered upping the Paxil dosage, maybe even take umbrage at the piece, or entirely disregard it.

This reluctance tends to produce the kinds of evasive maneuvers noted above. What I'm suggesting is that most writers experience an *internal resistance* to producing their own best work, which is a matter of lacking not talent or imagination but the determination to lay themselves bare.

I should clarify at this point: I am not suggesting that you should empty your journals onto the page. A nasty prospect, we can all agree. In fact, fiction writers are fiction writers because we are not the sort of people who walk around saying, *Now, brave world, I am going to lay myself bare!* We get at the emotional truth indirectly, through sublimation, through the back door. In other words, we pretend we're not writing about ourselves.

We write about other people, and hopefully at some point in the process we start to care about them, to worry about their fate, in the best cases to actually love them. We don't have to be conscious of the hows and whys of this connection—in fact, it's best if we're not; we just have to allow ourselves to get emotionally involved. And then (the tough part) we have to put these dear surrogates through the ringer.

The result is often what I call the *scenus interruptus*. This is where the writer has managed to get his hero into a scene of actual dramatic valence but bails before anything too scary can happen. The best example I can provide came from a student named, if memory serves, Matt. Or maybe Kevin. Or Brendan. (When you teach at a Jesuit school, these are your three options.)

Whatever the case, this fellow turned in a story about a lonely widower raising his daughter alone. The story had one moment of genuine danger: the father sneaks into his daughter's room and finds the engagement ring she has received from her boyfriend.

The daughter comes home and catches him. The tension is exquisite. But Matt (or Kevin or Brendan) refused to stay in the moment. He kept bailing out. All semester, I pleaded with him to prolong the scene, to consider what the father and daughter must be feeling. This did not work.

As a result of experiences like this, I came up with an exercise called Five Seconds of Shame. It's pretty basic.

THE EXERCISE

Recall the most shameful moment of your life. This might be the first time you were caught shoplifting or saw one of your parents in a jam, or when you got caught naked in public. (One of the basic rules of life is that everyone has a most shameful moment.) You must now write about that moment for twenty minutes. You can do a little setup, if need be. But the bulk of what you write has to be the five seconds of purest shame.

The point here is to force some exposure, to establish that revealing a painful fragment of your past doesn't make you a reviled loser. And, just as important, to demonstrate that the most vivid, convincing prose emerges from a process of slowing down. Because when the action stops moving forward, the narrative has to turn inward, toward those deep feelings I keep mentioning.

Another wonderful thing happens when we slow down: we are forced to recognize how intensely we experience moments of great danger. So much can happen in five little seconds, if you're really there, paying attention. There are all the sensory details we might otherwise overlook (the smells and sounds and tactile sensations) as well as the fears and wishes and memories and fantasies that crowd our minds.

And, of course, this is precisely what we should be doing in our fiction. We need to be brutal enough to force our characters into the deep rough, and compassionate enough to stick with them as they struggle to hack their way out. This is an intellectual process, to be sure. But it is also an emotional one.

If you read enough fiction, you'll realize that most of the truly beautiful passages are the result of this process. The writer is not trying to impose style on the language. Instead, the effort to convey the truth of a charged moment causes the language to rise, naturally, into the lyric register, which is marked by a compression of sensual and psychological detail. In the common parlance: slowing down.

A great example: "Bullet in the Brain" by Tobias Wolff. The first half of this story takes place over the course of about five minutes. The second half takes place in a millisecond. It is a masterly example of all the dazzling stuff that can happen when you stop the action and turn inward.

Another great example: "Guests of the Nation" by Frank O'Connor. Notice, in particular, how the pacing slows in the last few pages, as the characters stumble into their given tragedy.

Of course, almost every compelling story or novel follows this same course. It's how most art gets made, actually: one shameful moment at a time.

So enough with the lecture. Get out there and shame yourself.

INTERVIEWING YOUR CHARACTER

MY CHARACTERS TAKE SHAPE SLOWLY, IN A PROCESS THAT might seem alchemical if it weren't so difficult. I start with an "idea" of a person—a very formal designation for the collection of images, words, and situations with which I begin—and over many hours I work to make sentences that start to collect, or capture, or animate that idea on the page.

Characters begin to feel real to me not the first time they speak (or gesture or think), or even the tenth, but only once my "idea" of them has given way to the volume of words that represent them in the text.

It can be a long, hard time getting there. Some characters are easy to write, but for those that are not, for the characters that seem dead on the page, or that slip away just when you think you have them, or that change in midstory into entirely different characters from those you intend or need, it can be helpful to step away from the actual writing and loosen up with an exercise.

THE EXERCISE

Simply put, you complete both sides of an interview as your character. Never mind that the responses may not figure in your story or novel; the value is in getting outside the text, outside your self-criticism, to where you can be playful and generative. A nice way to move past a roadblock, this exercise can also be helpful if you're having trouble getting started on something new. Whatever the reason you try it, be sure to write out your answers and to include as much detail as you can. Who knows? You might come up with the very linchpin of your book. And even if you don't, chances are you'll return to the actual writing with a renewed sense of optimism and purpose.

Needless to say, the questions you ask can be as varied as the characters you might invent to answer them. In fact, if you get stuck trying to answer the questions, you might take an additional step back and make up a dozen new ones.

Here are some that appeal to me:

1. On a winter afternoon I like to:
2. When I was a child, I wished:
3. My favorite dinner is:
4. The most painful thing a friend could say about me is:
5. I don't know why, but once in a restaurant I:
6. My mother/father was known for:
7. I have these ten things in my bathroom:
8. During the most boring week of my life I:
9. I have always wanted to go to _____, because:
10. I love the smell of:
11. I would be happier if only I:
12. The most annoying song of my high school years was:
13. When I'm alone in an elevator I:

14. It makes me so angry when people:
15. My family doesn't know this, but:
16. The person I'd most like to kiss is:
17. I've never seen:
18. If I could change one thing about my past it would be:
19. If someone gave me ten thousand dollars I would:
20. I always cry at:
21. On Halloween I usually:
22. In my earliest memory I:

FROM AUTOBIOGRAPHY TO FICTION

WHEN I WAS YOUNG, MY PARENTS WERE DERANGED AND self-centered, as all parents are. My mother was too busy frosting her hair and my father measuring the cheese to make sure no one in the family ate more than their portion. As a result, they let me watch too much TV, and for a long time I had trouble distinguishing between fiction and reality. One afternoon when I was six, I decided I was Mighty Mouse, and I pulled on my cape, opened the window of my second-story bedroom, and climbed onto the ledge. My mother was outside watering the sunflowers, and naturally she panicked. She raced upstairs and hauled me inside.

"You are not Mighty Mouse," she said. "Mighty Mouse is not real. Do you understand?"

I said I did understand when I really didn't, which is a habit of responding to life's challenges that has served me with mixed results for many years. My thoughts have always roamed into the fictional world, which is a good thing: a fiction writer has to dream outside his or her own experience. How do writers move from the nonfiction of their experience to the fictional world of their narratives?

Some writing teachers will say there is a danger in writing autobiographical fiction, and others will insist that beginning writers should stick to their own experience. Beginning fiction writers who write about their own experience sometimes find that they can't maintain objectivity about their material. They can't shape the material into art because they are blinded by their own emotional relationship to what really happened. As a result, the writer moves himself to tears as he writes, but the reader (who is not the writer's mother) is bored, puzzled, or confused. On the other hand, beginning writers who choose material that is too far from their experience sometimes find that they can't fully imagine the story because it didn't happen to them. They weren't there.

The following exercise will help writers transform their own autobiographical material into fiction.

THE EXERCISE

Identify a powerful and significant personal experience from your past and write an outline of the event. Now create a character whose biography differs from your own. The character might be a different age than you and a different gender; maybe she grew up in a different era or in a different part of the country. Write a brief biographical sketch for your character: include the larger details (gender, race, age) and the smaller details (breakfast cereal, clothes, gestures). Write a story with your fictional character encountering your experience. The details of what happens will be familiar, but your character's reactions should surprise you, and rightly so—he or she is not you.

Varley O'Connor

PUTTING CHARACTERS INTO ACTION

BEFORE I BECAME A WRITER, I WAS AN ACTOR. THE FOL-
lowing exercise employs methods actors use to make behavior
specific, lively, and communicative. Language, too, especially in
fiction, dies on the page if it is too generalized and static. The exercise works as a beginner's template, a guide to building observations about people into story. It can also be used as a revision
exercise for more advanced fiction students.

THE EXERCISE

The exercise is done in steps completed in three separate writing
sessions.

1. Meticulously describe—using concrete sensory details
   rather than abstractions whenever possible—a person who
   is vivid to you, either someone you know well or someone
   who has made an exceptional impression on you.
2. Write a monologue for your person or character. Do not
   write a soliloquy; in other words, do not write a "To be or
   not to be" speech in which your character is alone. Have

your character talking to someone, although the other person should remain silent. She or he could confess, tell someone off, lecture, or complain, for instance. Choose one. The *objective* is essential; determine the monologue's motivation: What is the character attempting to achieve with the monologue? What is driving her or him to speak? As an acting teacher would say, what is the *intention* or *action* behind the speech? And this should flow out of the character's confrontation of an *obstacle;* strong textured speech is propelled by something to overcome.

Showing is another principle important in both acting and fiction writing. *Show* who your character is and what she or he *wants* not only by what the character says but by *how* the character says it. Consider speech patterns, pauses, and figures of speech. Keep *who* the character is talking to, and *why,* carefully in mind as you compose the monologue.

Do not write any narrative; this is speech only.

3. Put your character in a scene. Choose a setting inhabited by your character that concretely reflects her or him. Write the scene from the third-person point of view of the character. Imagine her or him alone confronting the problem that initiated the monologue you wrote earlier, preparing to go see the person spoken to in the monologue. *Obstacle* and *intention* create the behavior. Or perhaps the character is about to receive the person with whom she or he is in conflict. Here you must put it all together. Write narrative, description, and actions springing from *tension* and *who* the character is. The character may mutter out loud at times, or even rehearse the upcoming speech. But *do not* put the person on a telephone. And *do not* use TV, music, talk radio, or the like.

As Revision

Editors have counseled me to recast into dialogue a bit of narrative that isn't working. For compression's sake, I have often revised scenes into monologues or description, particularly if a major change does not occur in a scene and it therefore requires minimal dramatization.

Revise a monologue into a scene, a description of a person into a monologue, an overwritten scene into narrative summary.

As a simpler revision exercise, apply acting vocabulary to a piece of writing: *intention, objective* or *action,* and *obstacle.*

Try not to explain much of this. Rather, *show* what is at stake and what is in the way through the tone and detail of your revision.

One of the pitfalls of story and novel openings is too much explaining and setting of scene. Readers need information to understand the world and situation of a story, but this must be fed in and shown as the story unfolds. I've learned that we can slip in a lot if only there are *actions.*

Always start *in medias res:* bring the reader into "the middle of things" at a critical point in the action. Put the characters themselves, right away, in action—doing, struggling, moving, persuading, *behaving,* as actors do.

In consideration of human psychology and verisimilitude, test it out for yourself: How often do you so much as cross a room without an intention?

SUBVERSIVE DETAILS AND
CHARACTERIZATION

'VE ALWAYS THOUGHT THAT ONE OF THE MOST IMPORTANT things—if not *the* most important thing—we learn at some point in our development as fiction writers is the vision that allows us to see more fully when we look at a character or a dramatic situation, allows us to draw out aspects of either that we never could have imagined we'd find. Often, this requires cultivating a talent for finding the opposites that coexist in nearly everything—a double vision of sorts, or the anagogical vision Flannery O'Connor talks about in *Mystery and Manners,* that ability to see more than one layer of truth at the same time.

I'm reminded of a story by Richard Yates, "Fun with a Stranger," about a prim, matronly third-grade teacher, Miss Snell, who's always lecturing her students about the importance of having the proper supplies necessary to their schoolwork. She's particularly fussy about erasers. Humorless and unforgiving, she often scolds her students until they break down and cry. The most dramatic part of the story takes place on the last day of school before Christmas vacation. The students are hoping for a party much like the one they know the younger, nicer teacher, Mrs. Cleary, is giving her students in the other third-grade classroom across the hall, but

Miss Snell insists on going through their regular lessons. Then, just before the final bell is to ring, she presents each student with a gift, the same practical gift: an eraser. She stands before them, a tremulous smile on her face, eager for them to give some sort of sign that they like and appreciate the gift. The children are forced now to see Miss Snell in a different light, and it's a complicated moment when this woman they've always thought of as inhuman tries to show a softer side of her personality, but in a very awkward way, presenting a gift that can only fall into the category of "Proper Supplies," and can be only a reminder of everything severe about her and not the sort of gift to be cherished at all. Her students are at a moment when they sense the contradictions that often make up a person. They're too young to do much with this understanding, but we, the readers, are quite aware of so much that Miss Snell hasn't heretofore been able to reveal about herself. We infer that she's always slightly resented the younger, more genial Mrs. Cleary, and that she is indeed, beneath her stern behavior, a woman who wants to be liked. All of this happens because of a ten-cent eraser.

In fiction, as in life, it's often the small detail that subverts everything we think is true about a character. A small, clear detail, such as the eraser, can open a character to us in a way that wouldn't be possible without that detail. If Miss Snell had gone ahead with the day's lessons and bid her students good-bye when the final bell rang, she would have remained the severe, unlikable Miss Snell, but because she gave them those erasers, she became harder to classify and, therefore, more interesting. She became more human because she became more than what she could usually bear to present to the world. She revealed a part of her interior life that she usually kept hidden.

Perhaps there's a way for us to learn to see more of our characters, and in ways that will surprise our readers—surprise them by giving them more truth than might initially seem available. Here's a writing exercise, then, that asks fiction writers to use a small, specific detail as an entry into character and an impetus for writing about the known and speculating about the mysterious—all with the purpose of complicating the people who populate our fiction and making them more multidimensional and memorable.

THE EXERCISE

1. Choose a character from a piece of fiction you've written, are writing, or hope to someday write. Then make a list of all the props associated with that character, all the things they touch, use, handle, and so on, in the story: blunt-tipped scissors, mechanical pencils, ten-cent erasers, whatever the case might be, anything that makes that character come to life for you and casts them in a certain light. You could also create a new character by constructing a similar list of props or possessions as a way of becoming intimate with a character by cataloging the things they own.

2. Now add another prop to the list, one you've just created on the spot, and make it a prop that doesn't quite fit in with the others.

3. Create a brief piece of exposition, the story of how this character came to own this anomalous prop. Perhaps you'll create the story of the day he or she purchased it, or the story of how he or she inherited it, or found it, or received it in the mail by mistake and couldn't resist keeping it.

4. Now begin a freewrite by entering your character's consciousness. If you're writing in a third-person point of view, begin with the phrase "What he or she couldn't tell anyone was . . ." Write about the secret aspect of the character's interior life suggested by the anomalous prop. Write about this deeper essence of the character that, like Miss Snell, he

or she constructs a facade to mask. If you're writing in a first-person point of view, begin with the phrase "I couldn't, for the life of me, let anyone know that . . ."

5. Then find a place to insert a curiosity, staying in the character's consciousness either in the third or the first person. Something like "So-and-so [or I] couldn't figure out why the such-and-such was so appealing." Continue writing, letting the character's own curiosity lead further into the contradictions and mysteries of his or her own interior life.

6. Think about what you want to know about your character. Come away from the story for a moment and jot down a few questions that you want answered, questions you'd ask the character if he or she were standing before you. You might even begin a freewrite with the words "I wonder whether . . ." Keep trying to imagine the interior life of your character more deeply than you have previously. Let your questions and curiosities suggest scenes and plot turns, and perhaps even a resolution. Let the anomalous detail lead you to further exploration of the character.

7. You've identified mask and essence—the face the character presents to the world and the deeper, contradictory truth generally hidden behind it. You've created a round character. Your last challenge is to construct a plot that somehow involves the anomalous prop and to find the right time to use it to force the character to open his or her interior life to the world. Timing, as the Yates story shows us, is everything.

FOR FURTHER CONSIDERATION: It's interesting to think about how the specific detail can simultaneously lead us to the vivid and the mysterious. How can something known lead to something hidden? As writers we're taught to trust in the specific, to rely on the things of the world to resonate with emotional and psychological significance, and yet it seems that the precise detail can open a world or a life in a way that illuminates while also pointing toward darkness that the writer must try to navigate. That's all to the good because it requires further writing, and in the process, if we're open to the exploration—if we'll only follow the details—we'll discover more of the truth of a character and his or her situation than we perhaps knew existed. All because we trusted in the details and how they could illuminate while also challenging us to uncover more.

COMPLEX CHARACTERS

Fiction writers, whatever their levels of skill and experience, start with nouns, verbs, articles (definite and indefinite), the odd adverb, maybe an adjective or two (but not too many of these, thank you), and seek to create from them living, breathing characters. What sleight of hand (or is it magic?) enables skilled writers to press the illusion of life into these otherwise inanimate parts of speech? Loving your creation, as the puppet master Geppetto discovered about his little blockhead Pinocchio, is a good place to start.

THE EXERCISE

The first thing I want you to do, as you prepare to create a complex character, is to find something to love about her, because if you love your character, there's a good chance your readers will, too. This is particularly important with an otherwise unsympathetic creation, someone whom, if you met her, you might not immediately be drawn to.

So pick a character, any character, and find something to love. Here are some suggestions. Give him or her:

Your mother's smile.

Your first love's shade of hair.

The loyal, loving nature of your family dog.

Or make it a treasured childhood memory—say, the day you caught the most fish on a party boat. Or the time your grandfather confessed—and made you swear never to tell—that he loved you more than any other grandkid, and gave you a dime to prove it.

Now take this character whom you can never hate no matter what terrible thing he or she does and splice in something loathsome. If this offends you, remember Jane Austen's famous remark about mixed characters in the Midland Counties. That is, in the places where we really live—for most of us live in the "Midland Counties"—there is, in most people, and certainly in those we are willing to know, "a general though unequal mixture of good and bad." Therefore, let this character, around whom part of your heart is twined, do one of the following:

Cheat on her husband.

Steal money from the tip jar.

Despise his best friend's child because he has none of his own.

Shave strokes from her golf score when she thinks no one is looking.

Or anything else that makes you really mad.

In short, let your character sin, because no one loves a plaster saint, either on the page or in real life. Now go off for a while.

Brainstorm. Make notes. Maybe even write a scene or two and see what you come up with.

————

Welcome back. You and your lovable, flawed character. Step two is to give that character something to do. If you've been paying attention, you may have noticed that just because you've joined something endearing to something all too human and perhaps even despicable, it has done nothing to successfully animate parts of speech. To achieve that, you must create the illusion of consciousness. One way is to force your character to process a great deal of sensory input simultaneously. Everyone knows it's impossible for words to remain words and nothing more than words if they seem to be thinking, feeling, and seeing all at once.

So here's an exercise for practicing the creation of a complex consciousness that I've asked many students to do, often with amusing results. I call it Two Spaces, One Time. (Two Spaces, One Time, by the way, is the inverse of Two Times, One Space, which is a flashback.) To begin, place your character in one physical space, but force that character to simultaneously process sensory input from two or more spaces. Here are some examples.

Your character is under a bed that he's been sharing with the right woman at the wrong time; her boyfriend came home and nearly caught them. So now your character has a view of underwear, shoes, and a pizza box. He's trying not to sneeze out the cat hair he's snuffled, while up above him the woman he's been snuggling (and whatever else) and her live-in fella discuss where to go for dinner. Maybe there's a television playing, so he's processing that aural input, too.

Or your character, a little girl with muddy shorts, is climbing a tree while down below her brothers, who are afraid to climb and jealous because she isn't, demand that she scoot back down. Above her, mourning doves coo. When she looks out through the tree's glossy leaves she can see the big house where her family lives, and the small house beside it, where the family's servants dwell. If she strains to shut out her brothers' voices, she thinks she hears someone, either their mother or their maid, calling them all home.

Or maybe your character sits on a Greyhound, which at any minute will depart the station. Outside, his parents and brothers wave, calling out farewells and encouragement. A row behind him, there's a woman giving him the eye; he just knows she is. Two rows back a baby cries; her parents argue, and the bus lurches slowly away.

If your character processes multiple sensory inputs at what *feels* to your reader to be the very same time, it creates the illusion of living, breathing flesh. Here's why this is so important. Your character's consciousness needs to feel complex, because even if he or she is a relatively simple character—say, a wooden puppet come to life—human consciousness is complex, with a million and one contradictory things going on all at once. For example: Wondering if you should attempt this exercise or skip to the next one. Hearing, with half your mind, the sounds in the next room. Or the sounds in the room in which I'm writing this, and trying to imagine if it's anything like the room in which you now sit. Wondering who is the puppet and who the puppet master, and what has breathed life into these words, and into the ones you are about to start writing . . . now.

TWO LITERARY EXERCISES

STREAM OF CONSCIOUSNESS

Creativity is linked to freedom of thought and the ability to play.

Party of Two

With another fellow writer or student, pair up and take a twenty-minute walk. The first ten minutes, Writer A simply talks, uttering aloud what the mind is saying to itself, remaining as faithful to the stream(s) of consciousness as possible, without editing, inhibiting, or conducting the mind's chaotic traffic into any organized or socially redeemable patterns. Writer B listens, nods, remains impartial and, above all, calm; Writer B must not betray any alarm, shock, horror, or ennui at what is being said. Writer A may respond to the walk itself, to sights, sounds, observations, or remain largely internalized in focus; it doesn't matter: the point is to unhamper the mind, letting it take whatever peculiar, mundane, and utterly unfettered course it will. Writer B, keeping track of time, lets Writer A know when his or her ten minutes is up. Then the roles reverse; Writer B becomes the Babbler, Writer A the Ear.

This exercise quickly and rather shockingly demonstrates how severely we edit our speech under normally socialized circumstances, how multifaceted and terrifyingly nimble the mind actually is, when unbridled. The exercise gives a slanted light into the workings of individual consciousness.

After twenty minutes, Writers A and B return to their classroom, rejoining fellow students who have been out rambling about in the same manner. Under the guidance of the teacher, each pair reports on the experience: what it was like to listen to a stream of consciousness, what it was like to be so vulnerable in speaking one's mind! Marvelous discussions ensue from this exercise, and the very nature of creativity and the mind's processes are freshly revealed.

Party of One

The stream-of-consciousness exercise can be adapted for one person . . . though I do not recommend that you wander about in public muttering to yourself. Instead, talk aloud for ten minutes or so in the privacy of your home or yard, wandering about, sitting or lying still, merely watching your thoughts without directing them in any manner. You can tape-record or write down what you hear. I find that my own consciousness, left to run free, naturally seeks patterns close to simple rhyme, musical rhythms, and poetic image by association. Memory is also surprisingly present.

OBSERVATION DRAWING

All strong descriptive power proceeds from precise observation.

Party of Two

Find a writing partner and take turns drawing first each other's profiles, then the full face. Ten to fifteen minutes is long enough for one person to agonize as the model and the other to anguish as the faux artist, before switching roles. Skill in rendering a likeness has nothing to do with this exercise; it is only about observing another person in an intimate but impartial way, something we rarely permit ourselves or are permitted to do. An essential point to remember while doing this exercise: the person drawing cannot look down at the paper; the gaze should never leave the model's face to judge the drawing's progress, for here the mind interrupts, criticizes, jeers, and the discipline of observation is lost. I strongly suggest that instrumental music be played as a means of absorbing the sound of scratching pen or pencil, scrunched paper, groans of irritation, curses, nervous giggles, and so on, all of which may occur in the first few minutes. Music helps calm everyone and gives a sort of elegance to the exercise. After the twenty- to thirty-minute exercise is complete, write about the experience: how did it feel to be the observer and the observed, what did you see that you might not have otherwise noticed, what emotions surfaced, what pleasures and disturbances? The point of this exercise is to slow down, really look, take time to see. By its very nature, drawing forces one to gaze openly and with a heightened precision. As this is an exercise for writers, the quality of the drawing isn't the point, doesn't matter, and is not up for critique. I have found students to be immensely moved by this exercise once they got over their initial discomfiture, and interestingly, those who were paired together often became close friends afterward.

Party of One

Practice drawing at odd moments, public or private. Draw your self-portrait, gazing in a mirror, or draw your nondominant hand, your foot or feet, other parts of your body, your whole body. See what memories or thoughts arise from such an exercise. Drawing, sketching, is one of the best ways I know to calm down enough, slow down enough, forget your own nervous mind enough to begin to actually see a thing, a person, a part of oneself with clarity and freshness.

GET CLOSER: EXPOSING YOUR CHARACTERS (WITH COMPASSION)

THIS EXERCISE WORKS FOR BOTH FICTION AND NONFIC-
tion writers. Imagine you are writing a scene in which two
characters are finally, after pages (or even chapters) of carefully
built tension and conflict, about to have a confrontation.

You are so immersed in the action of the scene, you don't even
notice that an hour has gone by, and suddenly the characters start
speaking and acting on their own, as if they possess a consciousness
separate from yours.

Of course, just as you realize this is happening, you fall out of
the fictional world and back into reality (the cramped corner of
your bedroom you call your "writing space"), realizing that you
have just spent an hour or more with make-believe people, the
grown-up equivalent of imaginary friends.

How will I ever get back there, you wonder, accepting that you
will just have to wait for another perfect moment in which you, the
architect of your story or novel, will disappear and the characters
take over.

How will you ever feel that confident again?

By getting closer to your characters.

Why, you may ask, must we "get closer" to our characters if they are not real?

Because this is how a writer feels confident in their understanding of what the character wants, needs, and fears. Not what *all people* want, but what *that character,* and absolutely no other, wants. It is the uniqueness of the character's desire (as revealed through specificity) that will make both you and the reader confident that the character is a genuine person with an urgent stake in the outcome of the story or novel. This uniqueness ensures that the reader will never dismiss your character, no matter how unlikable that character may be.

Just as it takes time to get to know the people in our everyday lives—our friends, lovers, coworkers, and neighbors—it takes time to get to know your characters. Writers must meddle, play Truth or Dare, ask busybody questions like *What's your most embarrassing moment?* or *What's a secret you've never told anyone?* in order to figure out what secret wishes, fantasies, phobias make your character unique among all others.

So much of successful writing has to do with manipulation. There is the manipulation of the reader, of course, the dropping of hints and subtle implications that act as clues in revealing the characters, the conflict, and what is at stake for them as they make their choices.

But writers must also manipulate themselves, convincing themselves that they do, in fact, confidently know their characters, specifically the traits their characters avoid divulging: the mother who loves one of her children more than the others, the husband who is unfaithful to his wife, the accountant who is embezzling money from his clients, the spinster schoolteacher who has never been kissed. This confidence is particularly important when writing a novel, a commitment that might span years—years spent with the same characters, years that require the writer to wait patiently as the characters gradually reveal their unique personalities, as shown by their distinctive desires and fears. There is nothing more frustrating than, after writing a hundred pages of a novel, realizing that you still don't really know your leading guy or gal.

Our writing workshop instructors tell us again and again to "get closer" to our characters. We nod our heads, but secretly we ask ourselves, *What does "closer" mean?*

Think about what it means to "be close" to someone in our own lives.

To be chosen as confidant, to be trusted with a friend's secrets that might reveal their flaws, their weaknesses, their vulnerabilities.

And then there is the knowledge you have discovered yourself: what your friend has *not* told you; the hints of longing, frustration, anguish, and distress that you are able to interpret from their gestures, facial expressions, and actions; the behavior that in today's psychologically aware world we call "passive-aggressive."

To be truly close to someone is to know what they want, what they need, and what they fear—even when they themselves might not know.

Sounds simple, right? And in some ways, it is.

We are *all* close to someone—usually several someones—and this makes us natural character experts. We spend much of our time analyzing our coworkers, judging criminals we see on the news, questioning *why* they committed their crimes. We scrutinize the people who sit across from us on the subway. We imagine what our lovers are thinking in the hopes that we will uncover what they truly feel for us. We imagine the day-to-day lives of the celebrities, filling in the blanks. What were they like as children? Were they popular in high school? Were they invited to their junior proms?

Your goal, as a writer, and in the exercise below, is to choose details that bring the reader closer to understanding your character. The reader should be able to take one look at the answers to the following twenty questions and *know* your character, believe that your character is unique among all others, that none of their traits are stereotypical. Stereotyping is a product of generalization and vagueness. Do not allow the reader to dismiss your character as a type. Prove to the reader—by choosing unique but concrete details—that your character is worthy of their sympathy, worthy of their investment in all that is at stake for your character.

THE EXERCISE

Take your time answering the questions below. Choose answers that create a sense of continuity in your characters' development. Try to make each answer enhance or develop the characters as unique individuals. Be as specific and as detailed as possible. (Obviously not all these questions will be applicable to your characters. For example, your character might not own a car, especially if he or she is a city dweller, so you would leave that blank.)

1. *Name* (Do they like their name? Hate it? If so, why? What does it mean to them?)
2. *Age* (What generation do they belong to? Baby boomers? Generation X? Y? Do they identify with that generation?)
3. *Marital status* (Married? Divorced? Engaged? Committed to one person? A swinger?)
4. *Home* (Renter? Owner? Living with parents? Sleeping on his best friend's pull-out couch? How is it decorated? Minimalist? Cluttered? Is there any art? Specific decorations that might reveal something unique about the character? Souvenirs from travels? Gifts from loved ones?)
5. *Fantasies* (Their "dream job"? Telling off that guy that dumped them their freshman year of college? Killing their boss? Making out with their favorite movie star?)

6. *Style* (Preppy? Hipster? Conservative? Hippie? Grungy? Mod? Does your character identify with one in particular? Why? How important is it to them that they look "good"? Why? How much time do they spend grooming and picking out their outfit each morning?)

7. *Demeanor* (How would the character describe him- or herself? Friendly? Shy? Outgoing? How would others describe the character? Standoffish? Abrasive? Aggressive?)

8. *Beliefs* (Do they believe in God? If not, why? Do they belong to an organized religion? Do they pray? If not, why? Are there religious icons in their home? Are they tolerant of others with different beliefs? What are their political beliefs? Do they vote? Do they donate money to a particular cause?)

9. *Most-used facial expressions and gestures* (Smirk? Frown? Wince? Do they use their hands when they speak? Shrug their shoulders a lot? Are they jittery? Do they make eye contact when having a conversation?)

10. *Hobbies* (Kayaking? Bowling? Barhopping? Traveling to exotic locations? Do they collect Pez dispensers? Do they make beaded necklaces? Do they practice the art of origami?)

11. *Relationships* (How often do they talk to their parents, siblings, grandparents? If they do not, why? Do they have a strong support system of friends? How much do they rely on their friends? How honest are they with their friends? Do they belong to a community or a close-knit group of friends? Are they "popular"?)

12. *Favorite story to tell* (What is the story their family, best friend, or significant other has heard a hundred times?)

13. *Obsessions* (Do they work out at the gym daily? Have they seen Bruce Springsteen in concert 150 times? Have they

memorized baseball statistics from the last twenty-five years? Have they ever stalked an ex-boyfriend or girlfriend? A celebrity? Or stayed home from work to watch all six seasons of their favorite television show in a row?)

14. *Personality flaws* (What would the character confess are his or her flaws? What would others list as the character's flaws behind the character's back?)

15. *Most prized possession* (Do they own a car? What would they rescue first if their house was on fire?)

16. *Occupation* (Do they enjoy their job? Despise it? What is their salary? How much responsibility do they have? How do they imagine their occupation characterizes or identifies them to other people? What is their dream job?)

17. *Desires* (What are their desires—especially concerning the other characters in the story or novel? Do they wish their husband or wife would love them unconditionally? Or that their unrequited love would ask them on a date? That their boss would keel over during a company meeting? That a modeling agency would discover them at the shopping mall?)

18. *Fears* (What does the character worry about at night when they cannot sleep? What do they imagine is the worst way to die? Are there places, people, situations they avoid? What are their phobias? Do they suffer from anxiety attacks? Depression? What triggers their worries and fears?)

19. *Needs* (What are they unable to live without? What keeps them going? What do they need to believe about their own personality, the other characters in the story, their most significant relationships, and so on, in order to survive?)

20. *Secrets* (What secret or secrets has the character kept from everyone, even their family and closest friends? Why?)

Michael Knight

THROUGH YOUR CHARACTER'S EYES

PICKED UP SO MANY BAD READING HABITS IN LIT CLASSES. It was my experience (and things haven't changed all that much, I imagine) that literature was generally taught in one of two ways: with an eye toward writing academic papers or with some kind of historical or social or political context in mind, both of which are mostly useless to a writer. That sort of reading tends to generate a kind of conditioned response. I'll ask a student what she liked about a story and get an answer like this: "I enjoyed this story because it sheds light on the plight of abused women." Which is baloney. The student liked the story because she wept when the wife was trying to cover her black eye with makeup. Or because she was scared to death when the husband was creaking up the stairs to give her a beating.

That's the honest response. Sure, if a piece of fiction is intellectually empty our response to it will most likely be empty as well, but emotion must come first. How does a writer generate emotion? Image and action. Show, don't tell. That's such an old saw I'm almost embarrassed to repeat it, but it's so easy to forget. Just this morning, I wasted three hours trying to describe how a character felt. Note to self: if you want your readers to have an emotional response to a piece of fiction, you must allow them to experience that emotion, along with your characters, rather than explaining it.

Below are two exercises I almost always use in class. I've been using them long enough now that I can't recall if I made them up or stole them from somebody else, but I imagine most teachers employ some variation of these regardless.

THE EXERCISES

EXERCISE 1: Describe the view from a window—any window, bedroom, barroom, bus, wherever—as seen by a character who has just received either some very good or some very bad news. Have some specific news in mind but do not mention it in the exercise. Don't even hint at it. The reader should be able to deduce if not the exact nature of the news, the tenor of it, whether it's good or bad, simply by the way you describe the view. The object here is to give the reader a sense of a character's internal life by relying on meaningful imagery alone.

EXERCISE 2: Write a scene, lots of dialogue, lots of body language, lots of concrete detail, and so on, in which one of the characters is keeping a big-time secret. She's pregnant. He's got cancer. Like that. Don't mention the secret in the scene. Instead, focus on how keeping such a secret affects your character's behavior, how he or she reacts to the environment and to the other characters. No, this is not an exercise in deliberately withholding information. The point is that the secret itself is less important than your character's reaction to it. Even if the reader isn't privy to the secret, we should be able to sense the tension it causes, its emotional effect.

———

In both exercises, try to avoid the obvious manifestations of a particular emotion. If, for instance, the character is sad, steer clear of storms, dark clouds, and the like. If the character is happy, avoid birds chirping, sun shining, all that. Also keep in mind that the reason we use imagery and action to capture emotion instead of explaining how a person feels or what he thinks—the reason we show rather than tell, the reason we dramatize in the first place— is that emotions are generally much more complicated than happy or sad. In a good story, the character's response, that original and particular and individual reaction, *is* the way he feels. It's the only possible way to make clear something that's more intricate than adjectives and adverbs.

Even talented writers—maybe especially talented writers—get into trouble when they make the mistake of imagining that readers care what they think. They don't. No matter what readers say. Remember, they've probably picked up all those bad habits in lit class, too. Readers care what you see and they respond to how your observation of the world makes them feel. And you can't make anybody feel anything if you aren't rendering real emotion on the page.

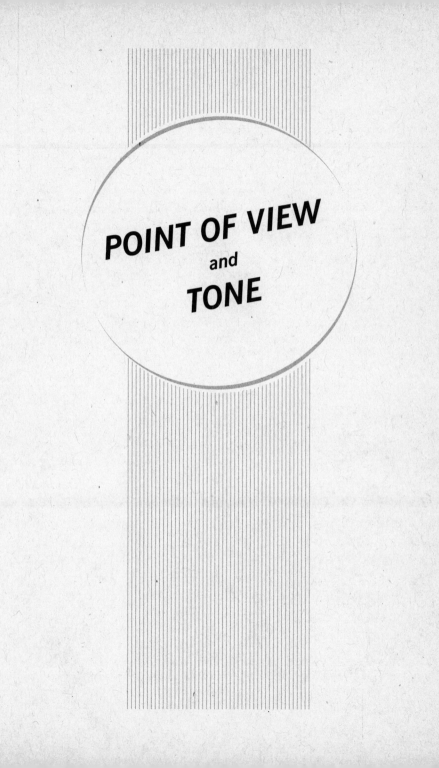

POINT OF VIEW
and
TONE

ON POINT OF VIEW

*I become the characters I write about. When I write about a thief, I
become one. . . . I become the characters I write about and I bless the
Latin poet Terence who said, "Nothing human is alien to me."*

—Carson McCullers

*Nothing is as important as a likable narrator. Nothing holds a story to-
gether better.*

—Ethan Canin

Caress the detail, the divine detail.

—Vladimir Nabokov

POINT OF VIEW IS THE ASPECT OF FICTION WRITING THAT
most regularly trips up my students. I'm never surprised.
Despite a profound and passionate knowledge about which point
of view is which—in graduate school, an argument over whether a
story was written in third-person limited or third-person omniscient almost came to blows—many writers lack a clear understanding of what point of view actually *is*. Every semester, I read
story after story in which there are no overt point-of-view viola-

tions, no unintentional second-person to third-person switches, but the perspective in each narrative is badly compromised. Take, for example, the middle-aged father and narrator who, during his son's burial, launches into an extended meditation on his bland prom date or, in a different story, the carjacker who, oblivious to the caliber of his pistol, prattles on about his victims' Ann Taylor blouses, Prada pumps, French-tipped nails. That the father might have other matters on his mind or that the carjacker would likely focus on different details never occurred to the authors. Those considerations, however, are tantamount to creating a believable and affecting point of view.

Point of view is arguably the most important decision for an author to make, since it determines—from the first word of the narrative—how the prose will be presented to the reader. Imagine *Moby-Dick* beginning with "His name was Ishmael." Or: "My parents named me Ishmael, not a name I liked very much, not until recently." Or what if Nabokov had written *Lolita* from Dolores's perspective, or the jury's, or the judge's? Would the reader still harbor those complicated, entangled feelings toward Humbert Humbert, or would we have written him off as a monster and immediately tossed the unread book into the garbage? Would Jane Austen's novels retain their whimsy and sublime insights and unexpectedly wicked humor if they were written in the second person; would McInerney's *Bright Lights, Big City* or Italo Calvino's *If on a Winter's Night a Traveler,* both of which are told through second-person narration, feel so immediate if they had more conventional narrators? Personally, I can't imagine Holden Caulfield calling everyone "imbeciles" or "knuckleheads" instead of "phonies," and I'm not sure Alice Sebold's gorgeous and heartwrenching *The Lovely Bones* would retain its raw formidability were it narrated by little Susie Salmon's murderer instead of the dead girl herself.

For the many vague and mercurial definitions of point of view (POV), the one that seems most helpful to my students comes from Ethan Canin. POV boils down to this:

Selection of detail
Ordering of events

What would this particular character think—recall, ponder, and so on—or do or feel at this particular time? In what order would *this* narrator tell *this* story? Which experiences from this character's life would she include to move the reader? In many ways, the goal of the writer trying to develop a compelling point of view is similar to that of a method actor: you want to become the character. Journalists write *about* characters; creative writers write *as* the characters. (Flaubert: *"Madame Bovary, c'est moi."*) The trick to becoming a character is to see through his eyes, to hear through his ears, to understand his unique desires, and to feel his individual memories. This section of the book aims to develop and sharpen those skills.

After my students get a basic handle on identifying the various POVs (first-person: "I robbed a bank yesterday"; second-person: "You robbed a bank yesterday"; third-person: "He [or she or they] robbed a bank yesterday"), we'll spend some time imagining a small room containing only a fireplace, a flickering fire, and four characters: a six-year-old girl, an elderly grandmother, a nurse, and a murderer fleeing the police. Then, writing from the perspective of the young girl, the class will try to perceive the fire and the other characters through her consciousness. What memories does the fire evoke for her? What have her parents told her about fire? To what will *this* character compare the flames, their color, their size? Will she want to touch them, will she be afraid of them? Our goal is to imagine fully the child's perspective, to experience the moment through her senses and her senses alone. Eventually, we will do the same for the other three characters.

The mechanism of the exercise is blatant—four different characters describing the same artifact in utterly different ways—but I'm always struck by how quickly and thoroughly it crystallizes the concept of deep point of view for students. Whereas before their methods of selection for what to include in a story were arbitrary at best, now, after the crash course in POV, they recognize the character as the sole organizing principle of the narrative. And the exercise inspires surprising and sophisticated observations: the nurse who thinks to douse the fire for safety or to start a bonfire outside the house to signal for help; the murderer who employs a burning log as a weapon or the instrument of his own excruciating demise; the grandmother who recalls the woodstove of her youth. And then there's my all-time personal favorite: the little girl who, despite her parents' repeated warnings, reaches into the fire. Does she pull back in time? Does she get burned? It doesn't matter. The image is characterologically correct, beautiful, and terrifying, but more than that, I love its implicit message: Question everything you've ever been taught, act boldly, trust yourself. This is a lesson unto itself, and it's as perfect a blueprint for the writing life as I've ever known.

STRATEGIES OF THE STORYTELLER:
POINT OF VIEW

WHAT MAKES FICTION WRITERS DIFFERENT FROM OTHER sentence makers is the sorcery of storytelling, the magic of the imagination, the invention of multiple voices, and the easy reliance on emotional truth. But before any of these writerly rabbits get pulled out of a hat, before the smoke appears and the mirrors reflect some human insight, the fiction writer must decide: Who is telling this story, and from what point of view is the story being told?

This is no small matter. Who gets to be the narrator of a story is neither a simple nor an arbitrary decision. All the potential narrators may inhabit the writer's mind, but only one (usually just one, but keep reading) will ultimately get called out of the creative bullpen to either command the reader's attention or lose his or her interest entirely. Some narrators are simply more reliable or sympathetic. Others are more engaging. There are, after all, many ways to tell a story, and various points of view from which to tell it. But the most satisfying stories read as though only one designated narrator could have successfully steered the tale. Only one voice was qualified, only one point of view was possible—even though the writer labored with many strategic options. In the end, it wasn't nearly as simple as moving a few personal pronouns around.

Certain stories require the narrator to be intimate with the events being told, because it is ultimately his story, and so he tells it in the first person—as in "I never did seem to get that summer out of my mind, when Emily rode sidecar on my Harley and the rolling suburban desert opened up as a mirage of romantic possibilities."

Other stories are better delivered by narrators who are not essential to the plot other than as observers to it—a neutral narrator, a peripheral character, someone with no personal investment or emotional connection to the story—as in "Who would have guessed that the neighbors next door never had sex. Their house was lavish but their body language was flirty, and fake. A For Sale sign announced that they were never more than roommates with a marriage license."

Many of John Irving's most successful narrators fall into this category of withdrawn detachment. The narrators are often in awe of far more charismatic protagonists. In Herman Melville's "Bartleby the Scrivener," the narrator is an aging lawyer looking back with regret and bewilderment over his incurably hollow but fabulously compelling former employee.

And, of course, there is the omniscient narrator—the voice so filled with insight, so in command of the story that it looms inside the head of the story's central characters. But there is also the indifferent narrator, a voice truly disembodied from the feelings and flesh of the book, a clueless onlooker who isn't any better at connecting the dots of the plot than even the most simpleminded readers. The narrative voice in Franz Kafka's *The Trial* comes to mind.

All these narrative strategies can ultimately complement and collide with the story's point of view.

For instance, in *To Kill a Mockingbird,* Scout narrates the novel as an adult looking back on her childhood and the momentous events that shaped her memories. From the point of view of a nine-year-old, she could neither have appreciated nor understood the complex dimensions of racism in the Deep South and her father's resistance to it. But distance and maturity now make her a more capable narrator, and she tells this story largely from the point of view of her father, Atticus Finch.

Harper Lee, the book's author, could have had Atticus narrate the novel himself, and from the point of view of his client, the doomed Tom Robinson. Calpurnia, the family's black maid, would have made an interesting narrator, too, since she inhabited both the black and the white worlds of the Jim Crow South and was surely aware of its multiple points of view. But then again, these would have been different books.

Sometimes a writer can cheat and have multiple characters take turns narrating the story, alternating the point of view and shifting the balance of storytelling authority. Stories that depict broken worlds are best told through such fragmented narration. Yet even within this poetic mix of musical chairs, a third-person narrator can surface and reassert control, reminding the reader that all these subsidiary voices and points of view belong to him anyway. Of course, as we know, even that third-person narrator is not fully in charge. All of these voices ultimately shriek and compete inside the cluttered head of the writer himself.

THE EXERCISE

1. Select a scene or a chapter from a story or novel on which you are working.
2. Identify all of the characters who could conceivably narrate the events being described. Don't forget the cat, the parakeet, and the fly on the wall. They make tremendous story-

tellers. Also consider an omniscient narrator and an indifferent narrator.

3. Alternate among the possible narrators. Give each one a turn, in their voice and from their point of view.

4. Now try it with the omniscient and/or indifferent third-person voice.

5. Finally, see if it's possible, by creating breaks within the narrative, to allow a number of narrators, with shifting points of view, to take turns alternating the narration without repeating one another or losing cohesiveness, so that the set piece, story, or chapter winds its way to some sensible conclusion.

Elizabeth Strout

EXERCISE ON POINT OF VIEW

HAVE ALWAYS BEEN INTERESTED IN THE FACT THAT IF SIX people are sitting in a room, whatever happens in that room, it is experienced in six different ways. Each response, of course, has to do with the character of the person involved, and this combination—character and point of view—is what interests me most in writing. If we think of character as how a person "acts" in life, the responses he has and decisions he makes, then it seems to me that a great deal of the plot of a story or novel will arise organically from the character and his point of view. Put a character in conflict, and all sorts of surprises will rise off the page. The quest is that of writing from the inside out, not the outside in.

In order to fully inhabit the character of a fictional creation, the writer needs to simultaneously leave himself and use himself, which is to say that whatever life experiences he has had will be the springboard for trying to imagine what it is to be someone else. And yet this is done most effectively if he can actually lose himself in the process. Another way of putting this is that it's essential for the writer to let go of any agenda he may consciously or unconsciously be clinging to.

THE EXERCISE

An exercise I developed that has proven to be at least interesting and at best quite helpful is to think back on the most recent intense altercation or disagreement you had with someone in real life. It should be an occasion where you were absolutely certain of the rightness of your position. After you ruminate on this experience of discord for a few minutes, write the scene from the other person's point of view.

Inevitably, this proves difficult. Right away you will scribble along, sometimes smiling, sometimes scowling, and yet when you reread the piece, it becomes evident that you are—not always, but quite often—still holding on to your initial point of view. You may be recording the argument from your husband or mother's eyes, but you have not truly inhabited what it felt like to be in that other's position. Often this exercise takes two or three revisions before the writer understands that he needs to let go—that it is all right, in fact essential, to let go—of his own personal sense of right and wrong. This is important because any judgment we bring to the page will dampen the freedom of the prose. And it is this freedom that the writer is after, the freedom to write about what it means to be human. The freedom to use his own experiences and emotions in a new and originally rendered way—through the eyes, body, and soul of another.

THE POINT OF POINT OF VIEW

POINT OF VIEW IS THE MOST IMPORTANT DECISION A writer makes. It influences every decision in a story thereafter. The most obvious example would be in Franz Kafka's "The Metamorphosis," where Kafka tells the story from the point of view of a dung beetle. Gregor Samsa must, at once, behave like a dung beetle, feel like a dung beetle, and move like one too.

The most frequently used points of view are first-person, third-person close, and third-person omniscient. This exercise is designed to teach you about these different points of view, their limitations and constrictions, and how to develop conflict—the primary element of plot—by cutting from one scene to another. This exercise should also help you to better understand the narrative voice and how it often fluctuates from one point of view to another.

In third-person close, the point of view is restricted to a chosen character; everything told to us has to be within the scope of the character's vision, hearing, touch, or thought. From the beginning to the end of this scene, we see exclusively through his or her eyes.

The first-person point of view is similar to that of the close third in terms of its narrative limitations; that is, we can know only what the character knows, sees, thinks, learns, or overhears. The advantage of the first person over the third close is that it offers a stronger sense of verisimilitude (the appearance of being real or true). The fiction unfolds as the narrator experiences it (the present-tense voice) or has experienced it and relates it to us from the past.

When writing in third-person omniscient you should imagine a long shot or an aerial shot where you can see everything that's going on in the scene. Third-person omniscient is often referred to as godlike or all-knowing. Describe the setting in detail for six or seven sentences before focusing on your character at the end of the paragraph. Your paragraph should be structured like a funnel, whereby the reader learns a good deal about the physical setting before the character enters the picture.

THE EXERCISE

Write three paragraphs describing the same character from three different points of view: third-person close, first-person, and third-person omniscient. Write each as a scene. Keep in mind that the location should not change with the different points of view, but the description of your scene will.

Once you've written three paragraphs from different points of view, all set in the same location, all dealing with the same character, and all set apart by a space break, you will use yet another space break and write one more paragraph. This final paragraph will be about another character, somehow related to the first, and will have a different setting.

For example, in the first three paragraphs, say you've described a woman waiting for her fiancé at the airport. Maybe she hasn't seen him in weeks. Maybe she is or isn't looking forward to his arrival. Now you could cut to the fiancé up in the plane. Maybe something happened to him during his trip and it has changed how he feels about his relationship with this woman. The point of view, in terms of the narrative, is your choice for the last part of this exercise.

FOR FURTHER CONSIDERATION: In a three- to four-page sketch, show one character from three different points of view but keep the same setting. Then write about another character, directly connected to the first, in a different setting. Developing conflict is the goal.

James Brown

AN EXERCISE IN WRITING MEMOIR

FICTION IS, MORE OFTEN THAN NOT, A MIXTURE OF TRUTH and invention. That fusion of the real with the imagined provides the writer with a kind of buffer. You can say, yes, that's how it really happened. Or you can say, no, I made it all up. No one, except yourself, can really know for sure, and that gives the writer a certain freedom, one that transcends the boundaries of literal experience. On the other hand, the memoir, by definition, requires the writer to recount or re-create his personal experiences with a minimum of manipulation. For me it is easier and far less painful to fictionalize parts of my life in a novel or short story than to meet my past head-on, undisguised.

In memoir you're obliged to tell the truth, both good and bad truths, and in doing so you must be honest with yourself and the audience. You'll worry about what others will think of you. You'll worry that you'll be judged, and you will be, because that's what people do to each other, but you have to accept this or you can't proceed. Our lives are inextricably linked to the lives of others, particularly those we love most, and there is an excellent chance that they won't exactly appreciate how you portray them in your work. But those are the costs. Those are the consequences. So be tough. Take some chances. Know going in that you can't write well and honestly about yourself and others with impunity and you'll be off to a good start.

THE EXERCISE

Write down three personal experiences that you might not want to share with your best friend, let alone a stranger. One could be about doing something to someone that you never should've done. One could be about the loss of a loved one, your mother or father maybe, and what you wish you'd done or told her or him but just never did. Or what about that car wreck you were in? The one you lied about that was really your fault?

Once you have three relative secrets committed to paper, choose one and write about it. Re-create the moment in scene. Recall the specific, most important emotions it conjures up and capture them in movement, thought, dialogue, and setting. Keep in mind that the way you describe a hospital room on the day you gave birth to your first child will be very different from your description of that same room had your father died in it. All you're after in this exercise is a single, well-visualized scene based on a personal experience that you've been unable to forget.

WHAT DO YOU WANT MOST IN LIFE?
A Point-of-View and Character Exercise

ORKS OF SUCCESSFUL FICTION—ESPECIALLY CHARACTER-driven fiction—have one thing in common: the characters want something, and the dynamics of their desires fuel not only their complex psychologies but also the dramatic energy of their story. Fiction, as Robert Olen Butler has said, is the art of human yearning. The world is real to us because we can see it, feel it, hear, smell, and taste it; and as humans in this sensual world, we will always yearn for something, whether it be love, understanding, revenge, or a glass of water. Since fiction in general is an effort to represent reality—and thus humanity—in some heightened way, it needs a sensual heart to breathe life into the story it tells. Start with a character who wants something, and you'll eventually find the heart of your story.

Good fiction, by the way, does not—and need not—always follow this template. It's difficult, for example, to feel the thrum of human yearning in the intellectual riddles of a writer like Borges or in a novel like *The Stranger,* where Camus's "white style"—stripped of all sensual perception—is intended to evoke the narrator's disaffected worldview. Nonetheless, looking at fiction writing from the sensual point of view can often be both useful and necessary.

THE EXERCISE

From a magazine, choose a photograph that is focused on one person, preferably someone who looks engaging or is doing something interesting—and preferably is not a celebrity. Study this person: age, sex, race, clothes, body language and facial expression, surroundings, and what he or she is presently doing. Now imagine that a complete stranger has just asked this person what he/she wants most in life. In a page or so, respond to this question using the person's voice (i.e., using the first-person point of view). Explain what he/she yearns for and why. Perhaps explain what he/she fears and hates. If you want, give some brief biographical information that might explain these feelings. As you write, consider things like the person's vocabulary and speech patterns, his/her tone of voice, personal attitude, present state of mind, what he/she is choosing to share, and what he/she is withholding. Be creative and consistent in how you imagine his/her personality and point of view. Be funny, be serious, be wildly imaginative—whatever you want, so long as the voice paints a vivid and convincing portrait of the person in the photograph and the desires that fuel him/her.

Susan Straight

POINT-OF-VIEW EXERCISE FOR
PROSE WRITERS

WILL TELL YOU A STORY. ONE NIGHT, MY FAMILY AND I were eating dinner inside our little dining room, which is ten feet from the curb of a busy street. We saw a blur, and a woman fell from the back of a motorcycle, hitting her head on the curb near where our street number is painted.

We called 911 and rushed outside. A crowd gathered quickly. The woman was very soft-looking, pale and plump, with cheap knit pants and short brown hair, about thirty. I picked up the tiny purse she'd dropped, hoping for an ID, but all I found inside were a flask of alcohol and a pocket comb. To me, she seemed like a too trusting woman who'd taken a ride with the wrong man.

To my eighty-year-old widow neighbor next door, she was a prostitute. "He probably picked her up at the bus station and didn't want to give her any money," she said righteously. "Look at her clothes. And there's nothing in her purse. Tramp."

To the arrived paramedics, she was a body. "Possible head trauma," they said, getting out the body board. "Female, about thirty, about a hundred and fifty pounds, no ID, not conscious. Okay, move her together. One, two, three. Lift. Load her up."

THE EXERCISE

Write about one incident, one day, one event, one gallery opening or wedding or murder or conversation or meal from three very different points of view. Sometimes, when you're beginning a story, the hardest part is to know whose story it will be, whose voice will be the best, whose point of view will be the truest and most plausible and most compelling. These three points of view about the same incident or event can be in three separate sections or in varying lines, as if all three people are thinking or talking at the same time.

TWO EXERCISES

'M NOT A FAN OF WRITING-WORKSHOP MANTRAS. IF YOU'RE in a workshop or have read other creative-writing exercise texts, you're certain to have come across the phrases "show, don't tell" and "write what you know."

The problem I have with the first mantra (or decree) is that when you write you're always telling a story, even if you're showing (by telling a reader) what various characters have said or done. It's as if by trying to become a "writer" you've forgotten a rule so elementary that even grammar school kids know it. They call it "show-and-tell." In workshops, however, the egalitarian conjunction "and" is replaced by the tyrannical "don't." As a writer, you show and tell; you don't limit yourself arbitrarily to doing one or the other.

As for the intimidating decree "write what you know," you would, if you accepted this totalitarian advice, surrender not only your imagination but also your freedom to deploy it however and whenever you wish to do so. Did Homer go to Troy? No. Did Pynchon fight in World War II? No. Was Faulkner black? Was Toni Morrison a slave? Was Shakespeare ever a king, queen, sprite, Moor, or ghost? If you write only what you know you voluntarily forfeit the possibility of telling stories that go beyond "what you know," and if you forfeit this possibility you undermine all of literature, as well as your own hopes for creating some of it yourself.

So: forget mantras. Instead, learn how to narrate, how to dramatize, and, more important, when to do one or the other.

Case in point: *Lolita*. Does Nabokov give us graphic descriptions of Humbert defiling poor Lo, or does he allow Humbert to narrate the story's sexually explicit episodes in a way that avoids any mechanical depictions of Humbert and Lolita's repeated couplings? Nabokov chooses the latter because he knows that in these instances telling rather than showing frees the reader to experience "aesthetic bliss," which Nabokov called the supreme response to a work of art. What Nabokov does dramatize is conflict: the snide and explosive arguments between Hum and Lo; the woeful seduction inflicted on brutally handsome Humbert by the bovine Mrs. Haze; and finally the confrontation between Hum and his doppelgänger and nemesis, Quilty.

THE EXERCISES

EXERCISE 1: Take a story you've written and convert all of it to narrative. Do not dramatize a single word of it. "Tell" all of it. Then decide whether anything is lost by your having done so. If nothing's been lost, then you likely don't have a story. I say "likely" because there are (in art there always are) rare exceptions, in this case the stories "Tlön, Uqbar, Orbis Tertius," and "The Approach to Al-Mu'tasim" by Borges.

Now try the opposite: "show" everything. If you can "tell" a story completely through dialogue you're either imitating some early Hemingway stories (or William Gaddis's *JR*) too ardently or you're writing a play.

This exercise will help you discern what in a particular story you need to narrate and what you need to dramatize.

For instance, consider how you might compress certain aspects of a story by narrating them rather than by dramatizing them. Take the example below:

> Sylvia picked up the phone. "Hi, it's me," Chad said.
>
> "Hi."
>
> "I'm going up to the country this weekend. Want to come?"
>
> "What day?"
>
> "Saturday."
>
> Sylvia drummed her fingers on her desktop. "I have yoga at seven that morning."
>
> "We can leave at nine."
>
> She thought of another way to put off Chad. "Will we have time for a latte?"
>
> "Absolutely."
>
> "I like to read the paper while I have my coffee."
>
> Sylvia listened, waiting for the long silence to end.
>
> Chad said, "Well then, maybe I'll go on ahead and if you make it, great. If not, I'll see you when I see you."
>
> "Wait, I'm not saying I'm committed to reading the paper *in* the coffee shop."
>
> "You're just saying you need news. You're a news junkie."
>
> "Yeah."
>
> "So, we'll go. We'll bring lattes, the *Wall Street Journal,* the *New York Times,* the *Washington Post,* and *U.S. News and World Report.*"
>
> Sylvia laughed. "Okay, but you're paying."
>
> "No problem. See you Saturday. Ciao."*

*(Never use "Ciao," even ironically.)

You can render this as a scene and thereby use 165 words (which is a lot of words for a short story), or you can narrate the episode: "After some indecision and flirting on the phone with Chad, Sylvia decided to go to the country with him on Saturday," which is 21 words. You save, if you feel you need to, 144 words, which might be put to better use in the story. Once you've tried telling this bit of the story as scene and as narrative, you can decide which technique better serves the story.

EXERCISE 2: As for "write what you know," the risk here is Updikeitis. If John Updike the person has a molar removed, John Updike's current protagonist has a molar removed, usually with "its yellowing outer shell, encrusted now with a brittle soot left behind by forty years of ill-advised smoking (his wife and his doctor had told him to quit on any number of occasions, hadn't they?)," after which Updike goes on to describe, quite beautifully, the meaty, inflamed red of his character's gums, the pulpy center of the tooth collapsing like a gumdrop, the final mortality-fraught crack, and so on for several hundred words. Another "write what you know" affliction, known as Roth's syndrome, is described in the *WDR* (the *Writers' Desk Reference: A Guide to Literary Maladies*) as a forty-five-year obsession with creating a perpetually enraged, relentlessly narcissistic, insufficiently loved, fantastically successful, handsome, macho, vengeful, empathetic (in the later books), dutiful, multiply divorced, paranoid, parent-loving, and Semitic alter ego so Rabelaisian in its excesses that it requires not one, not two, but three incarnations—Zuckerman, Kepesh & Roth (which sounds like a clothier or a law firm)—only to be in the end what? The same person.

So writing what you know can be limiting. On the other hand, writing (to paraphrase Wittgenstein) what "you don't know you know" can be more insightful, liberating, and artistically fruitful than living with yourself on and off the page for half a century.

As an exercise, take the dialogue above and reverse the gender. Then ask yourself: Does the meaning change if Sylvia is Sylvio and Chad is Chadetta? What if one of the characters is African-American and the other is, say, Chicano? Does that make a difference? What if both characters are fifteen and you, the writer, are, say, forty? Ask yourself questions like: Who's the narrator? Is he male, is she female? What's the narrator's attitude toward the characters? Loving, ironic, sympathetic?

The central question is, Can you write a story that goes beyond your personal experience; beyond your age, gender, political beliefs, and religious convictions; beyond the color of your skin; beyond your historical era; and, finally, beyond your identity? If you can't, quit right now, because you can't populate a fully realized fictional world by writing only what you know.

FOR FURTHER CONSIDERATION: As a last exercise, consider the implications of choosing a narrative point of view. Imagine a setting and then describe it through the eyes of six fictional characters, each of whom is not you. How does a courtroom, classroom, jail cell, cruise ship, bathroom, bedroom, or beach look, smell, and feel to each character? And remember this: every character perceives an utterly unique world, but you won't know what that world is like until, by using your imagination, you live in it. After that, it's up to you to decide how to show and tell a reader all that you've imagined.

THE CHICKEN CROSSED THE ROAD

POINT OF VIEW IS A TRICKY BUSINESS FOR FICTION WRIT-
ers. Whether a story is told in the first person ("I could not kill
the monster in the forest until I had slain the monster in me"), the
second person ("You are not the kind of person who would kill a
monster in the forest"), or the third ("He was a raging lunatic with
an obsession for monsters"), not to mention all the variants of psy-
chic distance ("He, Behemoth, would kill them all!" or "The monster in the forest seemed quiet now, but in eleven days he would
wreak havoc on Schenectady"), the right point of view is perhaps
the most crucial element in a piece of fiction. It encompasses almost
all of the other elements: voice, character, tone, scene, setting, time,
structure, and plot.

Because point of view is so tricky, such a complicated and arduous concept, it's best to approach it playfully at first. To convey the
intricacies of POV, I like to start with nonhumans. This is not entirely capricious; the differences between a chicken narration and a
human one are more cleanly delineated, allowing writers to see
more obviously what each POV requires.

THE EXERCISE

Why did the chicken cross the road?

1. Write a paragraph or two from the POV of the chicken. You may use first-, second-, or third-chicken. How would she or he answer this question?
2. Write a paragraph or two from the POV of anyone else who might know the answer to this question. First-, second-, or third-person. Anyone but the chicken.

Amy Hassinger

WALKING A MILE IN THEIR SHOES: DEVELOPING CHARACTER THROUGH ALTERNATE POINTS OF VIEW

L ET ME GIVE YOU THE BAD NEWS FIRST: YOU'RE GOING TO have to choose. Anytime you begin a new story, you will have to confront the sobering fact of limitation. When the page is blank, the options are wide open: your protagonist could be a worker laying the limestone bricks of a medieval tower in twelfth-century Provence, or she could be a quirky artist who builds medieval towers out of paper clips in twenty-first-century America. You could introduce a full-fledged villain, with blue-gray bags under his eyes and tracks on his arms, who seduces your protagonist and knocks down her medieval paper-clip tower, or, hang on a minute, you could write your villain's story—where did those baggy eyes come from and what spawned his addiction? The dreaming that happens before you actually set any words down on paper can be intoxicating: a new story is a fledgling utopia, full of the promise of perfection.

But, regrettably, there are the words. And the sentences. Each word you write forces a new boundary, each sentence an indelible line on the paper. You must make choices about your characters, and the choices you make will determine the trajectory of your story, which will be one trajectory, period. Likewise, your characters will have to develop qualities that make them one sort of person and not another. This is the tragic reality about writing and about life.

Now for the good news: you get to write more than one story. (Not true, you will notice, about life.) Not only that, but you can even write the same story from alternate points of view. You can do this not just because you have a pathological phobia of decisions but because it's actually a good idea, craft-wise. Writing a story—or even just a scene—from an alternate point of view encourages you to more fully imagine *all* of your characters' desires and motivations. Just why is your villain so destructive, anyway? And what is it with your protagonist and her obsession with building towers?

Whether or not the writing you do in your alternate point of view actually makes it to your final draft, it can be an effective way of helping you to understand your characters better. A new point of view reveals new details—some radically new, some just slightly altered—and teaches you compassion and broadness of mind, qualities that might just show up in your writing, if you're lucky.

THE EXERCISE

Start with a scene from a draft of a story. Rewrite it, transferring the scene's central intelligence to a different character. If your scene uses an omniscient point of view, limit it to one character and go deeper into that character's consciousness. The change should provide you with a substantially new vision of the scene. You may find that the exercise gives you one or two good insights into your characters that you can graft onto your original scene, or that you come away from the exercise with an entirely new story.

Alternatively, try retelling a scene from a classic story you know well using a new point of view. Jean Rhys did this to great effect when she retold *Jane Eyre* through the eyes of Bertha Rochester, the madwoman in the attic, in her novel *Wide Sargasso Sea,* as did John Gardner with *Grendel,* which retells *Beowulf* from the monster's point of view. The objective is the same: to come to a greater understanding of each of the story's characters by allowing the more peripheral ones to direct the action for a while.

THE GLORY OF GOSSIP:
AN EXERCISE IN POV

I'M NOT NECESSARILY PROUD OF THIS, BUT A WHILE BACK I attended my ten-year high school reunion. (I know, I know.) It gets worse: In the weeks leading up to the reunion, I bought a suit, shined my shoes, got a haircut. I'd been looking forward to the event for at least a year. (Truth be told, I'd bought my ticket the first day they were available, maybe the first hour. I seriously considered—but finally chickened out of—enrolling in dance classes. It's all wildly embarrassing.) I shaved for the first time in weeks, and arrived at the bar/restaurant/weirdly small venue an hour before anyone else. When my former classmates began filing in, they said things like "You're alive!" and we all laughed. (Long story, but suffice it to say my high school career wasn't one that would lead anyone to believe that I'd be in a state—breathing, say, or free on bail—to attend said reunion.) I shook their grown-up hands and kissed their grown-up cheeks, and wondered when we'd all grown up. I lied and told them I'd only learned of the reunion that morning. I bought them drinks and we toasted to being in the right place at the right time.

Here's my excuse: it was a reconnaissance mission, a blatant and shameless and *egregiously expensive* ploy to cannibalize their stories.

I'd known who these people were then and wanted to find out who they were now; what's more interesting than the passage of time, the trajectory of a life? I asked what they'd been doing for the last ten years, pressed them for juicy details about their jobs and marriages and children and vacations and houses; I paid explicit attention to what they were wearing and drinking, and asked them what they remembered about high school. After three hours, I'd gotten exactly zilch. Their lives and minds were boring, boring, and more boring. I thought the jig was up—*hoped* the jig was up—when people started asking why I was asking so many questions. I could've lied, but I decided to come clean for no other reason than that the stories I'd been hearing weren't worth the hassle. ("We got married after college, then once David became foreman, we had little Amber. She *loves* peas!" "I'm in insurance now. I sell peace of mind." "Seriously, if you tell them I told you to stop by, you'll get ten percent off a tire rotation. Simple as cake.") So I said I planned on putting their stories in a book, which plan everyone thought was a real hoot and probably delusional and maybe the result of certain substances that I may or may not have ingested en masse before graduation.

But which plan also, after a few minutes had passed, proved totally irresistible to the class of 1990. Once the deejay started spinning louder and more upbeat songs, which lured revelers to the laminated dance floor, people I'd never known—though I certainly knew *of* them, these former jocks and bullies and homecoming queens—began timidly approaching me to spill their stories. They detailed their every trespass and indiscretion. They surveyed the room behind me, checked over their shoulders, then leaned close and whispered, "Do you want to hear some gossip?"

Such as:

- The former star athlete and all-around most popular guy in our school was in prison for distribution of heroin. He maintained—via visiting hours and mail, I assumed—that he never used the stuff and that this was the first time he'd ever trafficked in it. He was doing ten years at best.

- At least three of the former cheerleaders and pep squad girls had married men who were forty to fifty years their senior. These men owned oil, lots of it. (This is in Texas, by the way.)

- One of the young women I'd known since grade school had been working as a barista when a "director" asked her if she'd like to be in the movies. She'd since done some local muffler shop commercials and a couple of movies that didn't require much in terms of "wardrobe."

- Another pep squad girl (or maybe one of the newly married ones; I couldn't keep the story straight) had an honest-to-God flask in her honest-to-God garter belt. Her husband hadn't accompanied her.

- One of our lowest-ranking classmates now worked for the government, most likely as an assassin. She wasn't able to attend the reunion, or she was there in disguise. (One of the oilmen?)

- A very, very nice and cool guy was doing life for murder. No joke.

- One of the most popular party girls had refused to attend the reunion unless another popular party girl sent her a substantive and *handwritten* apology for that thing that happened at the beach after the prom.

- A former choir student was now the bassist for one of the biggest, darkest heavy metal bands in the world. He was richer than God and worshipped the devil.

- See that woman in green? She slept with Mr. X while he was her teacher. See that bald man? He did, too.

Upon hearing each of these tidbits, I'd excuse myself and jaunt to the restroom to transcribe the information onto my little notepad. The frequency and urgency of my jaunts, it's entirely possible, created their own rumor mill: *Johnston can't control his bladder! He's snorting coke off the toilet! He's bulimic!* But the stories were worth it; they were worth all of it.

From a fiction writer's perspective, the glory of gossip is that it depends utterly on conflict, on a character acting unexpectedly. This doesn't necessarily mean acting "out of character" or acting like someone else; rather, it often means acting more "in character" than ever before. Gossip often results when people are caught being themselves. This is why it's so riveting, why we can't *not* pay attention. (I've never met a writer who could resist reading the tabloids in the supermarket checkout lines, nor can I recall a literary soiree—or any soiree—where intelligent, funny, well-adjusted, successful folks weren't huddled in a corner trading secrets, trading stories.) In an interview in *The Paris Review,* Updike said, "But no doubt, fiction is also a mode of spying; we read it as we look in windows or listen to gossip, to learn what other people *do.* "

If the glory of gossip is guaranteed conflict, the problem with it is the temptation of cruelty, of passing judgment. This danger carries over into fiction writing as well. Too often, emerging writers will stack the deck against their characters, specifically their antagonists; they'll write them in such a way that the reader finds it impossible *not* to judge them. That is, because the writers would never behave so badly, they can't help looking down on their characters who would, and that looking down corrupts the work for the reader. The problem very simply boils down to the writers' not trusting, or fully employing, their imaginations.

The judgment syndrome is a fast-moving, potentially terminal disease, but there is treatment. When my students start showing signs of infection, I tell them about my high school reunion. Then I paraphrase Goethe: I've never heard of a crime that I couldn't imagine committing myself. Then, just when they think I've completely lost it—*You went to your high school reunion? You're that dorky?*—I ask them to get out a piece of paper and a pen.

THE EXERCISE

1. Think of a piece of gossip you've heard recently, or a piece you've never been able to forget. Without flair or embellishment, write down the concrete details as a list or an outline or a few plain declarative sentences. (Simply: He stole money from the till. He lied to his boss and said the thief was the night manager. The night manager was fired.) This should take only a few minutes.

2. Once you have the skeleton of the event, put it away for a day. Work on something else until you return to your desk tomorrow. Try not to stew on the subject.

3. The following day, now that the gossip has been simmering in the back of your thoughts, turn the event into a short story or a scene in a story. The only caveat is that the subject of the gossip (in the example above, the man who stole from the till) must be your POV character. Your goal is to experience the event(s) through the consciousness of the so-called wrongdoer and to make the reader understand how this character would justify or substantiate his actions. You're striving to snuff out any hint of judgment. The scene or story won't work if the character is a monster or acting out of sheer malice. Readers always require a depth in your characterization and a cogency in your plot, and working to create believable motives behind the character's actions will usually satisfy these issues. As the author, you

know *what* happens; now, with this exercise, you're writing to find out *why* it happens.

FOR FURTHER CONSIDERATION: If this exercise clicks with you—either as a way to generate new work or a technique for shoring up drafts and characters you've been writing—you might consider taking it one step further. In addition to experiencing the episode through the so-called wrongdoer's perspective, add in the perspectives of other major or minor characters within the narrative. (This is similar to what Amy Hassinger urges you to do in her exercise.) For instance, in the above example with the man stealing from the till, dramatize the *same* events through the eyes of the night manager, the boss, *and* the thief, then alternate the perspectives throughout the story. By allowing the reader to see more than one version of the same event, and by dispensing the information little by little as the story proceeds, you'll find that you can create a lot of tension and further cut down on your tendency to judge your characters.

PLOT
and
NARRATIVE

ON PLOT AND NARRATIVE

If in the first act you say that a gun hung on the wall, in the second or third act it must without fail be discharged.　　—Anton Chekhov

I guarantee you that no modern story scheme, even plotlessness, will give a reader genuine satisfaction, unless one of those old-fashioned plots is smuggled in somewhere. I don't praise plots as accurate representations of life, but as ways of keeping readers reading.
　　　　　　　　　　　　　　　　　　—Kurt Vonnegut Jr.

I like to think of what happens to characters in good novels and stories as knots—things keep knotting up. And by the end of the story—readers see an "unknotting" of sorts.　　　　　　　—Terry McMillan

WHEN IT COMES TIME FOR ME TO BROACH THE SUBJECT of plot with my students, they freak out. It's adorable. First they launch into various highfalutin and complicated definitions of plot that they've memorized from their literature seminars. Then they climb onto their anti-plot high horses and bristle and argue that they're not interested in plot because they're striving to create

Art (with a capital A) and such pedestrian tactics and considerations are beneath them; they want to replicate the random meaninglessness of contemporary existence. (For about ten minutes, they wear themselves out belittling plot the way astronauts might belittle, say, paper airplanes or bottle rockets. So adorable!) Then, finally, the truth slips out: plot confuses and frustrates and roundly terrifies them. They have no idea what it is (various highfalutin definitions notwithstanding), let alone how to sneak it into their stories. So they write fiction where characters sit around talking or thinking or reminiscing; or, if the authors are starting to experiment with plot, they might throw in an earthquake at the end of the story (it's the climax!) or a nuclear attack or a winning lottery ticket. But those aren't plots, not even close, and hence the students' aforementioned adorable-as-could-be freak-out.

Simply put, plot is a succession of linked events that escalate in tension until they reach a point of resolution. For a plot to be technically sound, each event must predicate the next. (Though that doesn't at all mean the author has to arrange the events linearly or in chronological order.) That is, our plots must be characterized by causality and logic rather than coincidence and anecdote; our plots must be inevitable rather than possible. Think of Oedipus. He's been told that he will kill his father and share his mother's bed, and because he desperately wants to avoid that fate—often creating a successful plot is as simple as giving your characters believable, tangible desires and putting the right obstacles in their way—he sets out from Corinth and vows never to return. We know what happens next in the story, and next and next. More important, though, we know that the story could unfold no other way: Character is fate. Character is conflict. Character is, in a word, *plot*.

Writers get themselves stuck in something like narrative quicksand when they divorce plot from character. A very common malady is to cook up a brilliant plot and force-feed it to a cast of characters; the enterprise is usually as successful as juggling old, sweaty dynamite. (When you hear someone maligning a book or story as "plot-driven," this is what they mean. The plot, however solid, lacks substance because it has no bearing on or allegiance to its characters.) For example, if your narrator is a diehard Republican and you devise a plot that finds him transforming into a yellow-dog Democrat, you'll have to work overtime to prepare the reader for such a drastic change. Otherwise, the transformation will feel strained and phony; the change will feel contrived, unearned. (Incidentally, despite what your high school English teacher fed you, stories—fiction, nonfiction, short or long—are never, *never* about change. They are always about the possibility of change. If the reader believes that a character *can* change, but that character chooses not to, the story still succeeds. Often, in fact, it succeeds marvelously.) Plot should come from *within* the characters, not be thrust upon them. This is an important distinction. Flannery O'Connor famously said that she didn't know the Bible salesman in "Good Country People" was going to steal the fake leg until a few paragraphs before he did it, and it's this sense of surprise and inevitability that marks a solid plot for the writer. Instead of dragging characters toward the ending you've concocted, let them lead the way and you'll be as surprised and satisfied as the reader.

This is not to say that there's no craft involved, not at all. Plot is fundamentally a question of craft, of creating or arranging interconnected situations in such a way as to bring the most pressure to bear on your characters. Still, and unfortunately, crafting a successful plot isn't so simple as stringing together a series of events in chronological order; it's not so tidy as cataloging a character's morning, afternoon, and night, although many writers predictably make that "slice of life" mistake. Frank Conroy calls such plotting "abject naturalism," which translates to an author's including an event or scene in a narrative because it *could have* happened or, with nonfiction, including something because it *did* happen. Abject naturalism amounts to overburdening readers, weighing them down with extraneous material that relates to neither the cause nor the effect within the story; it bears no narrative, thematic, or emotional significance. (A good abject naturalism gauge is to consider whether shuffling the events or scenes in a narrative will affect the outcome. If, say, you can swap scene 1 with scene 6 or you can substitute chapter 3 for chapter 17 *without* affecting the narrative, your plot is probably suffering from abject naturalism.) To assuage this, Conroy suggests that writers imagine their readers carrying a backpack up a steep mountain. As the reader ascends the mountain—that is, as she proceeds through the story—every piece of information is a rock that the author is instructing the reader to pick up and place in the backpack. Upon reaching the end of the story, this backpack will be bulging with details and events and scenes and characters, and if the reader starts unpacking the bag and finds that she shouldered any unnecessary rocks, the story has failed and the reader no longer trusts the author. Read: She puts your book back on the bookstore shelf. Read: You're out of a job.

The exercises in this section outline various strategies for writing effective, cogent plots and fashioning compelling narratives. If there's a common theme here, it's that connections between events (and between events and characters) need to be *discovered,* not manufactured, not engineered. Your objective is to create tension, conflict, and suspense, to locate and dramatize those scenes and situations that will most truly and interestingly reveal your characters' souls to the reader, though another and equally important objective—Artists (with a capital *A*) forgive me—is to entertain the reader. Can you recall the last time you finished a piece of prose—story, novel, essay, or memoir—that wasn't entertaining, that didn't have you guessing what would happen next and why?

In its most basic and practical terms, plot is the storyteller's bread and butter, a tool to get the readers to turn pages. Without an interesting and well-spun yarn holding them together, all of your beautiful and dynamic characters, your brilliant and hilarious dialogue, that stunning description of the clouds on page 112, and your wise and gorgeous and heartbreaking last paragraph will likely remain unread and amount to nothing. The readers complete the narrative, and plots are often our first and best way of inviting them in, of entertaining and distracting them while our characters steal into their hearts.

Dan Pope

THE FIVE MODES

SOME YEARS AGO, WHEN I WAS WHAT YOU WOULD CALL A beginning writer, I was reading *Rabbit, Run* by John Updike for the second or third time, solely for pleasure, when I had one of those small moments of epiphany. It was like looking behind the curtains at the theater, seeing how the illusion of reality is produced. Everything suddenly seemed clear, just from the way the words *looked* on Updike's typeset page. Here were long strings of dialogue. Next came a thick block of prose consisting of description of a neighborhood. Next came a few paragraphs of action, of Rabbit driving his car. One could see, clearly, the organization, the method, the tools. The mysteries of the creative process seemed, all at once, less mystifying. This is what fiction is made of: a little bit of this, a little bit of that.

What I had seen so clearly on the page of *Rabbit, Run* were examples of the five narrative modes: dialogue, state of mind, action, description, and exposition. These are a writer's tools, and it seems to me that in teaching creative writing to beginners the first order of business should be to get students to recognize and practice these modes, just like a basketball player should practice the fundamentals of that game: dribbling, passing, shooting, and so on.

I sometimes challenge my students to find a snippet of writing that does not fall within one of the narrative modes. They try, try, try. What about *this,* they'll ask, but no—it's no exception. There are no exceptions. You have only those five modes of expression, and often you can be a great writer without even using all five. Cormac McCarthy, for instance, rarely if ever drops into state of mind. Joy Williams, in her early books, didn't much fancy traditional dialogue.

Of the five narrative modes, four—dialogue, state of mind, action, description—relate to *showing* (dramatizing, in scene), while the fifth mode, exposition, relates to *telling* (summary, not in scene), and this ratio seems about right to me. About 80 percent of a piece of fiction should be scene-based. "Dramatization," Frank Conroy used to teach in his workshops, "is a writer's strongest posture."

Now, of course there are exceptions. Many great works of literature are largely expositional, such as Proust's *Remembrance of Things Past.* Some novels, like *Vox* by Nicholson Baker and *JR* by William Gaddis, are made up *entirely* of dialogue. But, as any good coach would tell his or her players, work on the fundamentals first, and once you get that down, the fancy stuff can follow.

So the exercises I concoct for students of creative writing are generally quite simple, focusing on the five modes. Practicing the five modes individually may not be very sexy, but it gets the point across. These are your tools. Put them together, one block of prose at a time.

THE EXERCISES

Dialogue

Write a couple of pages composed entirely of dialogue between two characters. The conversation should involve a conflict of some sort—that is, an argument or a discussion of a dilemma.

State of Mind

Write a couple of pages composed entirely of a character's thoughts, elucidating the mental state of a character before he or she does something pivotal, like getting married, or shooting a penalty kick, or robbing a convenience store, or stepping off a bridge, or getting shot in the head.

Action

Write an action scene. Your character or characters should be in physical motion of some sort (walking, running, driving, etc.) and engaged in some sort of conflict, such as in flight from an adversary, or in a sporting competition, or at a casino, or in physical combat, or dancing.

Description

Write a description of a person you know very well: father, mother, sister, brother, spouse, or friend. Try to make the reader see him or her not through generic physical descriptions (à la a police sketch, "medium height, brown eyes") but rather through the idiosyncratic details that make up a person—say, his or her manner of standing or walking.

Next, write a paragraph description of what a certain character packs in his or her bag before going someplace for some purpose, without telling us where he or she is going. From what the character packs in his or her bag, the reader should have a pretty good idea of (1) where the character is going, (2) what he or she will do there, and (3) what sort of person he or she is.

Then write a description of a structure—a house, restaurant, office, barn, or toolshed—from the point of view of (1) a character who has never been inside this place and (2) a different character very well acquainted with the same place.

Exposition

Write a couple of pages of exposition about the place where you grew up, from your point of view, including your impressions of the place. This can be a suburban neighborhood, a town, or a city block, for instance.

Then write a couple of pages of exposition about some job you have had and the particular process involved in that job—the tasks and responsibilities of a summer camp counselor, chef, insurance investigator, basketball coach, taxi driver, or ski instructor, for example. "Process," as Frank Conroy used to say, "is always interesting."

THICKENING YOUR PLOTS

ORE THAN TWO THOUSAND YEARS AGO, THE AUTHORS of the Book of Ecclesiastes warned that "there is no new thing under the sun"—and yet somehow, year after year, the American publishing industry manages to produce tens of thousands of seemingly original novels and short stories. Does this mean we're being duped? That we're reading the same adventure, in disguised form, over and over again? Of course it does. The basic plotlines of nearly all contemporary fiction can be found in *A Thousand and One Nights,* of medieval Persia, and the one hundred tales of Boccaccio's fourteenth-century *Decameron* and Georges Polti's *The Thirty-six Dramatic Questions.* Sometimes it is claimed that there are only two plots: in one, a stranger comes to town; in the other, a person goes on a journey. Or even only one fundamental story line: somebody wants something. The task of the literary author is to transform "somebody wants something" into *Anna Karenina* or *Watership Down.* How is this done? By harnessing the power of "combination."

Consider the simple act of flipping a coin while pretending that the outcome of each flip is a potential plot. If you flip only once, you have two stories to choose from: heads and tails. But a second flip, combined with the first, gives you four potential plots. A third flip offers eight distinct stories. If you flip merely a dozen times, you have nearly five thousand different narratives at your disposal. Alternatively, think about a man missing one arm and one leg. A man missing an arm raises one immediate question: How did he lose his arm? That same is true for a man missing a leg. But a man missing an arm *and* a leg opens up so many more avenues of inquiry: Did he lose both limbs at the same time? Which one does he miss more? Are the lost limbs on the same or opposite sides of his body? This last question may at first appear trivial—but it is essential for determining whether he can walk with a crutch. Much as hybridization breeds hardier crops, combination builds more robust stories.

Creating an effective plot is often compared to assembling a jigsaw puzzle, but I think that analogy is rather incomplete. It is better to imagine that you have several million jigsaw puzzles jumbled together haphazardly. The first step in plot construction is to choose which puzzle pieces belong in the specific story you are writing. The second step is to assemble those chosen pieces into eloquence.

In selecting the pieces of your story—the individual conflicts, the background details, the particular turns of events—I urge you to explore the unfamiliar. Imagine yourself standing on the shoreline of a very large lake. The puzzle pieces of your story lie on the floor of that lake, the most precious and exotic ones farthest from dry land. Your responsibility as a writer is to gather these pieces. Doing so, of course, involves a complex assessment of risk. How far can you wade into the water before you drown? Nobody wants to read a story that clings to the safety of the coast. However, if you wade too far into unknown territory, you risk losing the moorings of your narrative.

Once you've gathered your pieces, your next step is to put them together. Here, obviously, the analogy to building a puzzle doesn't fit so neatly. The difference is that in writing a story, you have no template—there isn't one correct combination; many different combinations might work in different degrees and to varied effects. Much of the art of storytelling involves drawing the connections between these different elements. What is the link between a missing leg and a great white whale? Between tea-dipped pastries and childhood in a small French village? Between the green light at the end of a Long Island pier, an oculist's billboard, and an Oxford-educated veteran named Gatsby? Drawing these connections may seem like an overwhelming burden at first, but it's actually a tremendous opportunity. The trick is to keep combining—through trial, error, and instinct—until you have the makings of a story.

THE EXERCISE

1. Find a small group of people. This could be your class-mates in a writing seminar, members of a local senior citizens' group, or participants in an Internet chat room. More or less anybody will do. Ask these people to briefly describe the strangest thing that has ever happened to them. Or the oddest thing they have ever seen. Or the most unusual person they have ever encountered. The purpose of this simple research is to amass a collection of intriguing puzzle pieces as building blocks for your story.

2. Select three of the people or events described above and try to write a short paragraph about what they have in common. You can consider appearance, location, theme—any factor that seems to connect the parts. What you are trying to do is to uncover the latent bonds among these seemingly unrelated tidbits. The connections certainly exist—no episode is an island. It is just a matter of finding them.

3. Keeping in mind these similarities, try to write a short story incorporating each of these elements. If you "hit a wall" as you go along, discard one of the items and replace it with another of the strange people or events you have previously amassed. If you keep combining and recombining, eventually you are bound to hit upon a story line that works.

An ongoing philosophical inquiry asks whether a chimpanzee, typing indiscriminately for a long enough period of time, will eventually type *Hamlet*. At first, combining random, peculiar episodes may feel similarly futile. But be assured that we humans have an advantage over chimps: an uncanny knack for subconscious brilliance. From seemingly unrelated episodes, professional writers manage to cobble together coherent and compelling wholes. You can too. All that is required is a little bit of luck and a lot of resolute practice.

Josh Emmons

THE PLEASURE PRINCIPLE

SOMETIMES WRITERS GET DEPRESSED OR READ A BIOGRAphy of Gandhi or contemplate the fate of the planet and then ask themselves: *Why write fiction?* The question can be daunting, like trying to reconcile the theory of relativity with quantum mechanics. Give writers a few seconds, though, and they'll have the answer. Or answers. *To entertain. To edify. To create beauty. To make others feel less alone. To give people an emotional experience. To simplify what seems complicated. To complicate what seems simple.* There are a thousand reasons to write fiction, none of which disappear because we lose sight of them.

The first item in the above list, *to entertain,* is worth a moment's—or a lifetime's—consideration, because if a reader enjoys your writing she'll follow it anywhere. If not, she's likely to abandon it to that graveyard of barely begun or partially read stories that fills writers with terror. Your writing is in a way like Scheherazade in *A Thousand and One Nights,* and readers are like the sultan; they must be entranced by the unfolding narrative, drawn on to the end despite the myriad distractions offered by the world around them. Just as the sultan found the novelty of a different woman every night easier than committing to one person, the facile pleasures of watching television or shopping online exert a gravitational pull on readers; your fiction must exert an even stronger pull.

This is not to say that suspense should be your primary goal when writing, or that you've failed if the reader can guess what will happen next. It's possible to argue the opposite, as Flannery O'Connor did when she said that in good fiction, as in Greek drama, "you should know what is going to happen . . . so that any element of surprise in it will be transferred from its surface to its interior." Ultimately, as much discovery and revelation can happen through language and character development as through plot. Especially with literary fiction, good readers know that the journey is more important than the destination, that if a story makes them rethink a color or landscape or emotion or set of psychological conditions established between characters, then it has rewarded them for their efforts.

To entertain, therefore, does not necessarily mean to surprise. Nor does it mean to follow a certain successful narrative prescription, because, sadly, there is no such thing: Nabokov thought *Don Quixote* sadistic and cruel, Henry James called *War and Peace* a "loose, shaggy beast." The awful truth is that regardless of what you write, not everyone will like it. If you yourself are entertained by it, however, it's likely that a significant number of others will be, too, and a significant number, in our world and in this lifetime, is worth celebrating. Your permanent task is thus to write what you enjoy reading (modify this depending on how much you automatically love or hate your writing), be it comic mysteries, political thrillers, or paranoid first-person accounts of a badger keeping his burrow safe against enemies (it worked for Kafka). Just remember that only you can know what your story is and how to write it.

Given this freedom you have in conceiving and executing a story, the following exercise is designed to strengthen your writing by making it more real in a fictional sense, more compelling, more original, more—in a word—*entertaining*.

THE EXERCISE

PART 1: Think of the most frightening experience anyone has ever related to you—a carjacking, charging rhinoceros, or clown party, for example—and spend five to ten minutes imagining what it must have been like to be personally involved. When you've got a clear idea of the narrative trajectory and have felt a frisson of the fear it inspired, write out the incident in the third person, in fewer than fifteen hundred words.

PART 2: Wait a day and then look at your story. With twenty-four hours of perspective, draw a line through any clichéd language (this is a phrase you've seen before, like "the jaws of danger," "pale with fright," or "rolling thunder"). Cross out any hint of abject naturalism (this is the dutiful recording of real-life action—"The alarm rang and he turned it off. Then he stretched and rubbed his eyes before throwing back his bedcovers, sitting up, and feeling with his feet for the slippers he'd placed on the floor the night before"—that might be true but is certainly boring). Expunge any adverb that doesn't significantly advance the plot or reveal character. Look at sentence length and structure (if all the sentences are short and declarative, combine a few and add dependent clauses; if they're all snaky and multipartite, split some up), bearing in mind that healthy prose is defined by syntactical variety. Add a surprising detail to any character that feels stock or ready-made (the stern policeman might wear eyeliner; the mugger might have a small dog under his arm). Always use "said" for characters' dialogue, never "exclaimed," "ejaculated," or their ilk. Substitute specific adjectives for general ones ("cerulean" for "blue" or "cashmere" for "wool"), and insert an original simile. Make sure your metaphors are pure and unmixed. Unless you've written "Hills Like White Elephants," there should be more exposition than conversation.

PART 3: Compare what's left with what was originally on the page. The bad news is that you must repeat this process of composition and elimination and replacement at least a dozen times per story (and more for novels). The good news is that over time, almost by magic, you'll find yourself using fewer clichés, less abject naturalism, and more idiosyncratic sentences; you will make a great literary leap forward and feel relief and satisfaction to have worked so hard in the service of work that in itself will be able to answer the question *Why write fiction?*

Elizabeth McCracken

FROM ANECDOTE TO STORY

Our families, i think, are the first novels we know. That is: a complicated collection of people and anecdotes that adds up to more than the sum of their parts. Every story about an uncle in his youth is precious because it's what made him that *particular* uncle; a sad story of teenage love means something different if he's a cheerful old codger than if he ended up bitter and disappointed. It's that kind of pressure between event and emotion that fiction needs, and it's our early interest in that pressure that made a lot of us writers. Still, sometimes the family stories get plonked into short stories and novels and never become *fiction:* divorced from their people, they become only detail.

This is an assignment I sometimes give to writers who are just trying their hands at fiction, when they say they don't exactly understand what makes a story a story, and not a sketch.

THE EXERCISE

Choose a family story, an anecdote that you have no firsthand experience of. You can choose, for example, the story of how your parents met, the death of your great-grandfather, the disappointing love affair of your uncle's youth. Some people have many stories handed down like heirlooms; you need only one. It can be a significant story or a trivial one.

Choose two of the actors in this story and write down as many pieces of information as you know about them in list form. Feel free to make up the details. You're just piling up details that may or may not come into play in the story. If you're very close to the people in this story, you may want to start fictionalizing them instantly. Don't worry about the prose—you can do it in list form or in paragraphs, whatever helps you get the most on the page the most quickly.

Look at your anecdote. If there's a clear and sensible setting, again, pile up the details. If there isn't a setting, choose one. You may make the details up.

Put your characters in the setting on the day of the anecdote. Write a list that alternates a named action with an emotional response, one causing the other, and then write another action.

For example:

Ruth and Edna rushed ahead of Louis, eager to open the door to the museum by themselves.

WHICH MADE HIM FEEL: He was irritated by their slowness.
WHICH MADE HIM DO: He struggled to open the other side of the door by himself.
WHICH MADE RUTH FEEL: She was irritated by his bossiness.
WHICH MADE HER DO: She grabbed Edna and they rushed into the museum past Louis, nearly knocking him over.
WHICH MADE HIM FEEL: He decided that if that's what they wanted, he wasn't going to look after them even though he was the oldest and he was supposed to.

WHICH MADE HIM DO: He stuck his hands in his pockets and went whistling away in the other direction.

WHICH MADE HIM FEEL: Like a successful vaudevillian.

You don't need to alternate characters; you can have a character feel something, act on it, and then feel something again; or you can describe how what one character does makes another feel. The goal is to see the effect action has on emotion, and vice versa.

You should be able to see the first glimmers of a story: you have characters you know a lot about, in a well-described physical world, and at least the start of a plotline.

Now: Write the story based on your family anecdote. You should either start with the punch line of your family story or end on it. You don't have to follow your list of actions and emotions step by step or at all, really. Just keep in mind what you've learned from it and from your lists of details.

Adam Johnson

SEEING THE SCENE

WRITING IS ABOUT USING SCENES TO BRING PASSION AND
vision to bear on a character in the hopes that the writer's
deep connection will be transferred to a reader. While passion and
vision can't really be taught, good scene writing can. Prose fiction is
a linear form; it unfolds word by word, line by line, page by page.
Only one piece of information about a character can be disclosed at
a time, which makes revelation and withholding an important part
of the process.

The experience of being human, however, is a manifold one;
because we're able to do many things at once, a sense of simultane-
ity is part of being alive. For instance, while walking along the
beach (action) a person might speak to a friend (dialogue), see the
veins of kelp outlined in the turquoise curl of a wave (sensual description), avoid the Corona bottles and still-smoking logs of a de-
serted beach party (physical details), and wonder if youth is gone
for good (internal thought). In life, all these things can occur at the
same time, but unless you're James Joyce, you shouldn't try to put
them all in the same sentence: "Susan sank her toes in the sand as
she padded down the beach while she thought about Mike at the
same time she talked to Tina of the upcoming luau, as she tried to

ignore the sting of a sunburn on her shoulders, all the while attempting to avoid some beer bottles at the edge of high tide."

The technique of scene writing attempts to combat the linear tyranny of the fiction in a couple ways. By weaving together these basic elements of fiction—action, dialogue, description, detail, and thought—a scene can imitate all the ways in which real people experience life, making a character seem "three-dimensional" or "fleshed out." But it's not simply about deciding which character observations to make and in what order. Scene also tries to make characters seem rich within the confines of a linear form by making individual elements work on multiple levels. You can give only one line of dialogue at a time, but if the subtext is strong, it works as two lines. Only one action can be rendered at once ("Susan's eyes flashed toward the clock") but if charged with significance, even a small gesture can reveal emotion, desire, personality, and so on. Another way the use of scene wrestles with the linearity of prose is through pacing. Dialogue moves fast, as does action, and in a heightened state, relying on these elements of scene can convey an experience that's happening too quickly for a character to process. Description tends to be moody and atmospheric, and internal thought somehow timeless. While a car-crash scene might happen only in action and dialogue, the hospital-bed scene to follow might be deeply thoughtful, detailed, and descriptive.

When scenes weave together all the elements of life, work on multiple levels in an organic way, and reflect the characters' psychological states in their pacing, the reader begins to believe enough to apply to fiction one of the driving questions of life: "What the heck is going to happen next?" When this question has been asked, the reader forgets that a book is being read, forgets that his own life isn't being lived. And we all know the moment when we realize that our foot has gone to sleep, that the afternoon shadows have grown long, that we've been deep in a book while the world has gone on without us.

To get readers to experience a character's story in a moment-by-moment, scene-based way, I find I have to write in a moment-by-moment, scene-based way. When I have a character enter a house, I sniff the air for what dinner had been cooked earlier, and I scan the walls for family photos. I open the drawers, filling them with my imagination, and stare long and hard at what's held to the fridge by magnets. I touch characters' clothes, gawk at their teeth, guess what's in their pockets. I try to make connections, listen for subtext, and charge objects with history and gestures with nuance.

One of the difficulties I come across in the creation process has less to do with invention (which is always hard) and more to do with composing on a computer. In my opinion, word-processing programs have fused the creation and editing processes. Often, I'll write a sentence, then reread it in context with the four previous sentences, which I tune up; only then do I write another new sentence. Instead of looking for the next detail or listening to the next line of dialogue, I'm constantly moving backward. The result is that my scenes don't move forward as far as I like, things feel like they've been left undiscovered, and my sentences end up being way too overgroomed for a first draft, which makes me less likely to throw out a beautifully misguided sentence. I also find I get caught up in words, simply because I'm staring at them on a glowing screen, rather than getting caught up in what my character is feeling. Words are what I see, and I toy with them endlessly, making them pretty, counting them, cutting and pasting them. Long ago, when I used to compose on a legal pad, I thought more about a sentence before I lobbed it onto the page, and even if I scratched a sentence out, it was never truly gone. I meditated more; I closed my eyes and imagined more. I would return to longhand composition, but it's impractical, especially for a novel. I write too slowly, my penmanship is poor, and when it came time to rewrite, I'd have to type it all into a computer anyway.

THE EXERCISE

Turn off the computer screen during your next writing session. On my desktop computer, I call my document up, reread a page or two, find the home keys, and then hit the power button on my computer's monitor. (My Mac laptop has a screen that can dim to full black.) I find that instead of seeing the screen, I see the scene I'm imagining. It's weird to stare at a black screen, so right away, I close my eyes. I feel as if I get into the zone more quickly this way, and I definitely move much deeper into scene. When I forget where I am, I hit the Enter key twice and continue typing; this is the equivalent of flipping to a new page in a notebook, as it allows me to keep the flow going, but when rereading later I'll know that the section after the break is separate from the one before it. Sure, some of the lines are hard to read later, and the text ends up needing a major spell-check. But you'll be surprised by how easy it is to clean up. I often ask my students to try this exercise; some find it maddening (the ones who write too fast, usually), while others think of it as a weird, one-time experiment. And then there's that other group that makes a leap, that returns with a new gleam in the eye and stories in hand that are more surprising, more in the moment, and more revealing of character.

Michelle Wildgen

THE PARTICULAR GESTURE: WRITING SEX SCENES

A GOOD SEX SCENE DOES MORE THAN MOVE FROM FORE-play to penetration to mutual ecstasy—that's swell for the participants, but often rather boring for the reader. Two keys to a sex scene that moves us, affects us, and leaps off the page are emotion and novelty—but maybe not the kind of novelty you're thinking of at first.

Begin with two points. *One:* know the emotional complications behind your couple's coupling (or threesome or foursome; no one's judging here), and let them show through for the reader. It's whatever brought these two people to the bed in the first place, be it money, chance, boredom, love, or anything else. It's also whatever changes in the course of the scene. If nothing changes for them after the sex scene, it may not be serving enough of a purpose in your narrative. *Two:* worry less about conveying each clinical move than about including *at least* one unique, unexpected gesture, the intimate moment that illuminates the relationship or lack thereof between the lovers and makes this particular moment different. Often these two things, the emotional backstory and the particular gesture, will converge.

A few other dos and don'ts: The sex scene also demands especially careful attention to language and choice of detail. The writer must look for the unexpected detail, the detail of such intimate specificity that it's almost unbearable to write. This doesn't have to be some gynecological description, but it might be. It could be what someone says, what someone asks for, what someone cannot stand to do. (Don't confuse clarity, however, with humiliating your characters, pointing out their most hideous flaws and fetishes for their own sake.) Stay concrete. Forget sex scenes in which the participants leave their bodies and fantasize about meadows and sunlight. Think taste, think exact texture, think detail. Be vigilant against cliché and vagueness.

Lastly, be fearless. It can be as intimidating to get naked on the page as it is in person, and if you have to turn up PJ Harvey, shut your blinds, and pretend you're writing under a pseudonym, do so.

THE EXERCISES

EXERCISE 1: Write about the final time a couple has sex. One person knows this is the last time they'll be together; the other doesn't. By the end of the scene, both realize this is it. The catch? Try to write it without saying anything outright about the characters' emotional states. The couple is using body language to convey emotion; so should the writer. As you write, limit yourself to the most important details: the unexpected sensory and visual detail and the specific, emotionally loaded gesture. When you find yourself describing a fairly typical gesture, delete it. Write only the unique moments and let the rest remain in the white space.

EXERCISE 2: Forget the joyous union; write the unexpected sex scene. Try writing about an act that might be perceived as downright filthy—but make it as tender as you can. Write about extremely unfulfilling sex. Write a sex scene between the most unlikely partners you can imagine, and instead of heightening the absurdity of it, make us believe it and care about it.

CREATING THE MEMORY MAP
FOR YOUR MEMOIR

FTER THE PUBLICATION OF MY MEMOIR, THE QUESTION readers most frequently asked was, How did you remember your life so vividly? Human memory is a mystery, one that every writer—whether a poet or a fiction or nonfiction writer—grapples with. The question of memory, and how it is that we sometimes remember one situation in precise, perfectly ordered detail but cannot remember other events or circumstances, is a great puzzle.

The simple answer is: everyone remembers differently. Some people have photographic memories and can look at a page once and recite its words without the slightest mnemonic prop, yet have no ability to remember music or speech patterns or the details of people's lives. Still other writers have an uncanny ability to retain narrative—tell them a story with a beginning, a middle, and an end, and he or she will remember it forever.

So much of what I recall has to do with my state of mind, even my chemistry. When I was pregnant, my body pumped up with hormones, I could feel my ability to remember change by the month. In the first trimester, I began to recollect the smallest details of my childhood, down to the exact pattern of a tablecloth at a diner where I used to eat pancakes with my dad and the sandals he wore while mowing the lawn (rubber-soled, with thick straps of rawhide leather crisscrossing at the vamp). Then, in the second trimester, my memory softened and I could hardly recall my own name. As my chemicals changed, so did my memory.

One way to capture the slippery details necessary to write a striking piece of personal narrative is to attempt to nail down specific moments in time. There are tricks or techniques that will help the writer do this. One device I used in writing my memoir is something I call a "memory map." Like a road map to the past, a memory map guides the mind to the essential emotional truth of a scene by isolating details the writer may have forgotten.

For example, when I decided to write a scene about being in my father's favorite bar, a place called Roscoe's Vogue Bar in my hometown of La Crosse, Wisconsin, I knew that there was a lot of distance between the adult who was writing the scene and the child who had lived it. Of course, I had been inside the bar hundreds of times as a child, but I felt that parts of the experience of being in Roscoe's remained hazy.

My first step was to draw a representation of Roscoe's on a piece of paper, physically mapping it. I sketched in the wraparound bar, the jukebox, the bathrooms, the back door, the alley, everything I could recall about the physical layout of the place. This helped to bring my memory back to the physical space I was trying to inhabit in my mind, the setting of the scene. I then used different colored pens to write, in the various locations on the paper—that is, the bathrooms and the back room and the entrance—all of the details I could recall. For example, the bathrooms had carved wooden pig placards on the doors, bright pink with blue lettering that read, "Ladies and Gents." I wrote these details on the memory map. The back room of the bar had softball trophies and dartboards. There were taxidermy animals on a wall near the jukebox. The bar top was glossy and marbled with a tortoiseshell veneer. Next, on one side of the page, I made a list of sensory adjectives that described Roscoe's: smoky, dark, crowded, loud, hot, and so on. Once I'd divided up the space and made a mental journey though it, the details of Roscoe's came back with startling clarity.

Getting the physical characteristics of a scene into your mind is the first step to creating a vivid and engaging scene from your life. Revivifying and effectively conveying the emotional nexus of an experience, however, is often even more difficult to do. After writing a scene, I will sometimes go back to my memory map and try to get at this final (and more elusive) aspect by adding sensory experiences to the mix. For instance, I made a list of all the songs I'd heard played on the jukebox at Roscoe's and downloaded them onto my iPod, listening to them as I worked on the scene. I rented movies from the time period I was writing about (1984) and watched them to get a more intuitive feel for the mood of the era, the clothes, idioms, cultural concerns. I call this doing an "emotional wash" over the map. I've found that this final step in mapping an event from the past helps bring an emotional intensity to the writing that may not have been there before.

THE EXERCISE

1. Choose a scene or an event from your life that you would like to write about.
2. Isolate the main physical space where the scene (or the event) will be set and draw a map of the space on a piece of paper. Be sure to mark out all of the rooms and surrounding areas. Write down the characteristics and details you recall from each room. Note which people may or may not enter the scene. Be very specific.
3. List adjectives that capture the texture of the time and place.

4. Do an "emotional wash" over the map. Use music, photographs, movies of the period, diaries, taped conversations, anything that will give you the flavor of the real, lived experience of the event. Allow these sensory experiences to bring you back to the past. Write these memories, however fragmented, down on the map.

Robert Boswell

USEFUL LIES

ALL OF US IN OUR PRIVATE LIVES EMBRACE USEFUL LIES. Each lie permits us some kind of peace, and each also has its own expense. Fiction often examines useful lies, reminding us that we've made a compromise by accepting the lie. For example, Alice Munro's story "Royal Beatings" takes as its central moment an act that society had determined to be reprehensible (beating a child) and finds something else in it—something royal. The story does not excuse the violence, but it is not afraid to genuinely examine it.

Neither polite society nor pop culture permits genuine examination of our useful lies. Pop culture may be quick to grab at such matters, but only to reinforce the prevailing wisdom. Real scrutiny is left to artists.

And yet within the field of creative writing, we are also guilty of embracing useful lies. I wish to encourage, by means of the exercise that follows, examination of one such lie: that all stories are driven by conflict.

This is a useful lie because beginning students need to understand that peaceful days of bliss rarely make for good fiction. But many great stories are not driven by conflict. (I'm not arguing that they're without conflict, but that conflict is not the engine that makes the story work.) Often, such stories are interested in examining states of being. Munro has several such stories, as do Peter Taylor, Eudora Welty, William Trevor, Anton Chekhov, and many others.

This exercise is meant to serve as a hands-on introduction to the concept.

THE EXERCISE

Write a story that is largely without conflict. Instead, it should be about an identifiable type of human experience through which your character passes. While you must have two main characters and stick to those characters' (third-person) points of view, the story is not precisely about the characters. Rather, the story is about the human experience that one or both passes through. Therefore, the story is not about what the character "learns" as a result of the passage, or even how the character is changed. Create tension in the story by means of comparison and contrast at both the line level and in the characters' actions. Think of the plot as one of investigation and discovery.

Begin the exercise by selecting a human experience (see the sample list below).

Write down all of the conventional attributes one might associate with the experience.

Write the entire story in scene. Start not at the beginning but at some later point.

Make sure that your portrayal or enactment of this experience embraces irony and resists cliché. Irony and humor should alter or undercut passages that might otherwise become familiar.

———

Example: Let us imagine a story that is about an adolescent boy's first significant movement away from his family in the direction of a life of his own—and, specifically, a sexual life.

POV Character 1 is the boy. Let's make POV Character 2 his mother. What do we know about this human experience? What are the predictable attributes?

For the boy, it may excite an interest in sex that has been slumbering for some time, it may make him feel conflicting urges so that his pleasure will be mixed with guilt, it will likely be awkward for him, it will likely make him secretive (at least with his parents), and so on.

For the mother, it may make her evaluate the girl in question unfairly, it may make her jealous, it may make her feel her age more profoundly, it may make her nostalgic for her own adolescence, and so on.

Having made exhaustive lists, you should then see how you can give these attributes an ironic or humorous twist to undercut their familiarity.

So while the mother's surprise at seeing her son with a girl will be familiar (let's say she spots them in the school parking lot), you'll mitigate that by having this mother shocked at how lovely the girl is—how she seems above her son in the social caste. At the dinner table and throughout the evening, she compares and contrasts the current version of her son with the earlier boy. She compares and contrasts her son's behavior with that of the boy she loved when she was a teenager.

Meanwhile, when you move back to the boy's point of view, he exhibits much of the familiar awkwardness in dealing with this emergence of desire, but he copes with it in an odd and comic manner: he talks to the girl about his mother.

I can imagine a scene with the boy and his mother shopping together for groceries (as is their custom). While she is thinking that this might be the last time he'll deign to accompany her to the store, he's thinking about the party at the girl's house, how the girl's mother had intruded with a tray of fruit that no one touched. But

her appearance—and the way she pushed them to try the mango—
reminded the boy of his own mother, and that had finally given
him a topic and permitted him to talk to the pretty girl.

The story continues in this fashion, making use of the lists but
giving each item ironic torque. The boy does not have a traumatic
experience and neither does the mother, and while things are different at the end of the narrative, the story is not so much about
how they're different but how this transition is one that most humans in this culture endure; by describing it with clarity and insight you hope to shed light on the greater human experience. The
story will seem complete not because it shows how the character is
changed but because it evokes the experience so completely.

———

Here is a brief list of some human experiences to consider:

- Becoming serious about your ambitions
- Recognizing that you've aged
- Getting sober or clean
- Finding a lover who pleases you
- Becoming an adult
- Leaving home
- Going out on a limb
- Moving one's family
- Taking a stand
- Being duped
- Being rejected
- Being accepted
- Proposing marriage
- Having marriage proposed to you
- Losing your spiritual faith
- Discovering that you actually do or really don't believe what
  you've long espoused

- Recognizing that you've achieved something
- Understanding that your work has come to nothing
- Having an intellectual affair
- Discovering the truth
- Watching a parent or friend die
- Suddenly having an empty nest
- Getting cold feet
- Losing touch with someone
- Meeting someone new
- Losing a childhood friend
- Seeing (as an adult) the fallibility of your parents

The point of this exercise is not to produce a worthwhile story (although it may) but to introduce you to the idea of writing stories that are not driven by conflict. After you've completed this introductory work, you may wish to continue your study by thinking again about the useful cultural lies we all embrace. See if you can write a story that examines such a lie by means of the strategy described above. By resisting conflict as the driving force of the story, you may be able to investigate the useful lie with real insight and complexity.

Aimee Phan

REWRITING THE CLICHÉS

ONCE ASKED MY STUDENTS IN AN ADVANCED FICTION-writing workshop what they believed was the biggest cliché they found in fiction. Many of them stated that they were tired of reading about "love," especially the boy-meets-girl plot. I found their answer surprising, considering that many of them had addressed romantic relationships, either beginning or ending, in their workshop manuscripts. The next semester, I focused the reading list on contemporary fiction concerning romantic love. From reading the cheesy romance novel (*The Bridges of Madison County*) and chick lit (*Bridget Jones's Diary*) to literary fiction (*The Feast of Love*) and magical realism (*Love in the Time of Cholera*), the works challenged students to identify and determine how strong characterization, dialogue, and point of view elevated a seemingly familiar story line into something fresh and original for today's modern readers.

First, I asked students to list every cliché they could about love on the chalkboard. Here were some of their most popular choices:

1. Forbidden love (disapproving parent/warring families)
2. Dangerous love (bad boy or bad girl)
3. Love triangles

4. I hate you, now I love you
5. The exotic, mysterious foreigner
6. The rich bastard versus the poor but handsome neighbor
7. The Florence Nightingale syndrome (falling in love with your caretaker)
8. Adultery
9. Good looks versus a great personality
10. Misunderstandings keeping them apart
11. Some kind of bet
12. Innocent tickling that leads to an unexpected, intense attraction

Then I led my students through the following writing exercise, which requires at least two people.

THE EXERCISE

1. Freewrite a contemporary scene with two characters in any stage of a romantic relationship, using as many of the above clichés as possible.
2. Switch your scene with a partner. Read over your partner's cliché scene. Adapting as many aspects from the scene as possible, rewrite and transform the clichés into a believable, engaging situation. This will take considerably more time than the first scene because you should be focusing on developing character and plot.
3. Switch back and show each other your revisions. Discuss what changes you made in each other's scenes. What was necessary to convert the clichés into compelling characters and situations? How are the characters developed? What was altered in the plot and details? What aspects were unworkable?

In reading over and discussing the changes in the drafts with your partner, you should be able to determine the pitfalls and consequences of lazy, assumptive writing. For example, here's the cliché:

> Bridgitte was the most beautiful woman Gaston had ever seen, with eyes as blue as the brightest sky and wavy, shoulder-length hair as brilliant as the sun. He was in love.

This cliché may be a little over the top, but it's supposed to be: it gives the revisionist a greater challenge. Consider the readily romantic French names, the use of the tired words *beautiful* and *love,* the eyes and hair likened to the most common, obvious images of nature. What is the revisionist to do?

Here is one way to revise the passage:

> As Bridget walked ahead of him, Gary noticed how evenly her hair fell, a razor-sharp blond line that quietly swished along her shoulder blades. From behind, she could be mistaken for a schoolgirl, but he knew that once she turned around, those blue eyes, tired yet patient, would easily correct that assumption.

The French names had to go, clearly. The woman's name is Americanized and Gaston is killed, reborn as Gary. But Gary must notice more than just the hair and eyes of Bridget in order to indicate a romantic interest. The hair and eyes must demonstrate Bridget's personality. So now Gary notices the straight edge of her hair—this detail is particular and reveals an interesting viewpoint from Gary. He doesn't just want "a pretty face." Bridget's eyes now offer more than just a lovely shade, but also her life experience, and Gary's observation of these qualities make him a richer character as well. It's only a few sentences, but at least readers may be willing to find out more about Gary and Bridget than they initially would have in the first draft.

———

Clichés are possible in all types of writing, not just romantic fiction. Love is an easy topic to pick on because it's such a familiar and popular subject. Once you write out and become aware of the clichés and familiar phrases that are inevitably stored in all our memories, you can move beyond them and find your own voice.

Vanessa Furse Jackson

FROM IMAGINATION TO PLOT

'VE LOST COUNT OF THE NUMBER OF TIMES I'VE HEARD ONE writer in a workshop exclaim about another's story, "How did you *think* of that?" or "Where on earth did *that* idea come from?" These questions often stump the writer of the story quite as much as the questioner, writing being the mysterious business that it is. But let's ask anyway: Where do stories—or more specifically plots—come from?

What is it that enables and inspires someone to write not an academic essay, not a memoir, not a letter or a poem or a recipe for banana bread but a story—a piece of fiction?

Thinking about it, we'd probably start by answering, *Imagination,* but other possibilities crowd in as well: memory, knowledge, experience, dreams, something we've read or seen, a desire to tell others a tale we think is cool or amazing or freaky, a desire to get published, an urge to see what happens if we write, "Once upon a time" at the top of a blank screen or notebook page . . . but wait—we're in danger of traveling too far from the core of the question. Let's back up and look more closely at what we first thought of: imagination. Imagination, then memory, knowledge, experience. Interesting.

No one doubts that imagination is involved in the creation of a piece of fiction. But *imagination* is a slippery word that's tricky to pin down. Where are its heart, its lungs, its legs for running, and its wings for flying? What is it about the beast that allows us to harness it to the reasoning mind during the act of creation in order to bring forth a product that would not have existed but for the act itself?

Many writers before us have attempted to dissect the wriggling beast. Shakespeare, in *A Midsummer Night's Dream,* has Theseus suggest that "as imagination bodies forth / The forms of things unknown, the poet's pen / Turns them to shapes, and gives to airy nothing / A local habitation and a name" (5.1.14–17). In that definition, imagination seems fueled by an outside force (divine inspiration, perhaps) to provide writers with matter previously unknown to them, which they then shape into their own work. There have long been writers and artists who've believed that something beyond our conscious mind aids the act of creation. But are all the things conjured by our imaginations quite unknown to us?

Two hundred years after Shakespeare, another English writer, the poet William Wordsworth, would link imagination closely with memory. For Wordsworth, the imagination was in part a storehouse, in which memories are preserved not as static relics but as active contributors to our development as individuals, with the power to comfort us in dark hours, to aid our moral growth, and to allow us to see some way into the mysteries of life itself (read his poem "Tintern Abbey"). Imagination, in this definition, employs memory as a powerful tool that allows us to conjure up images from past experiences and "see" them as if they were still present.

A last English voice, Wordsworth's younger contemporary Percy Shelley, adds a further dimension to the concept of imagination. In his famous essay "A Defence of Poetry," Shelley begins by attempting to differentiate between reason and imagination. He conjectures that we use reason to analyze and make sense of the relationships between objects and ideas that are in themselves already known to us. Imagination, however, is what we use when we take objects or ideas and combine them, coloring them with our minds in order to make something from them that was not there before. This suggests that imagination employs preexisting knowledge, at least part of the time, which helps us form new perceptions and, if we are so minded, new representations or expressions of these.

So if we back up and lay out on the table our still slippery but at least partially pinned specimen, we might first say of it: imagination is the name we give to the human faculty through which we form mental images of things previously unknown to our conscious selves. But we might then add that it is also the faculty through which we retrieve stored memories, perceive relationships between things, and synthesize knowledge and experience we already have, all of which enable us to conceive creations unique to the individual maker.

If we now return to where we started and ask, "How are stories born from the writer's head?" we can see that our first answers might not have been so far off the mark—they spring to life through imagination, then memory, knowledge, experience, dreams, other stories, and so on—except now we can posit that these are not separate entities but are intriguingly interconnected. So how might this discovery affect the ways in which we search for plots and stories?

Many beginning writers are given the apparently sage advice "Write about what you know." This is good advice, but it raises the question, "If I'm to write simply about what I know, then what's the role of imagination in writing?" Good question. Some writers will run as far as possible from what they know, captivated by the idea of writing about unknown, imagined worlds and alien modes of living. Others will take the sage advice but stick so closely to what they know that their stories never escape the realm of the personal essay.

From my observations as both a writer and a teacher of writing, I've come to the conclusion that when we look for stories there's a vital balance to be found between staying too close to what we already know and rocketing too far away from it. Some of the best plots for stories come from the interconnectedness—and the *tension*—between what we already have stored in our minds and the transformation of that stored knowledge and memory into something original. If A + B = C, then C could not have existed without the combining of A with B. And both the retrieval of our material and its transformation are powered by imagination. It seems to me that if we fail to mine (think gold or diamonds) our own vein of riches, or fail to then take those riches and convert them into something breathtakingly *other,* we have failed to take full advantage of an extraordinary faculty we have been gifted with as humans and as writers.

Writing exercises can be wonderfully liberating, freeing us from familiar grooves and revealing roads we might not otherwise have discovered. Here is an exercise designed to both mine and transform your own experience.

THE EXERCISE

Make a list of events you've experienced that have particularly stuck with you. Don't be too picky at this stage. Just accept what your mind gives you. Graduation, falling off your first bike, a bad quarrel with someone you loved, a humiliation, a really funny episode, a funeral, a car wreck, having a baby, getting into big trouble . . .

When you have a good list, pick one experience you'd like to explore further. If it's hard to decide, be arbitrary. You can always come back later and try another one.

Write the basic outline of what happened. You could work this out in narrative form, telling us what happened, or you could just list the sequence of events as you remember them. You're employing your imagination to retrieve material at this point.

With the experience or event written down in words and playing in the forefront of your mind, you're now going to move to the second major stage of the exercise. This is more difficult, so tighten your seat belt.

What if something else had happened at some point in your event? What if a stranger had entered your scene and stood there staring at you? What if the event had happened in a different place? At a different time of year? What if you or another key player had been a different age? What if it didn't turn out okay after all? What if your worst nightmare had come true? Or, if your event was your worst nightmare, what if it had come out okay or at least differently? Write a list of possibilities. Try to find a minimum of five what-ifs. Think about them for a while (overnight is good), then choose one, or maybe two together, to try.

Now you're ready to write the first draft of a story that will contain elements of an actual event (A) *plus* purely fictitious elements (B) that will transform your personal experience into a story (C). The fictitious elements will most likely emerge from the knowledge of human nature you already have stored within you, but both they and the more direct personal experience will, with luck and perseverance, combine to form an original piece of short fiction. You will have taken something you knew and something you may not consciously have known you knew, and through imagination you will have combined them to form your own creature. Magic!

Bret Anthony Johnston

WHAT EVERY FICTION WRITER CAN LEARN ABOUT PLOT FROM THAT LOVABLE, FURRY OLD GROVER

YOU REMEMBER GROVER: LIVES ON SESAME STREET, LOOKS like—may, in fact, be—Cookie Monster's more svelte brother or cousin; his voice sounds like a barnacled version of Kermit's. When he gets excited, he pitches his head back in glee and does something akin to a fast, spastic waltz. He also has an alter ego, Super Grover. Super Grover sports a cape and an anachronistic knight's helmet; he flies pretty well but has significant trouble with landings—that is, he can't stop until he smashes into a building and slides, dazed and disoriented, helmet-blinded and cape-tangled, to the ground. He's complex and flawed, multifaceted and compelling. Grover is the thinking man's Elmo.

In 1971, Golden Books published the spellbinding tale *The Monster at the End of This Book.* Part character-driven autobiography (Grover is the narrator and only character), part page-turner, and part weird, second-person postmodern experience where the reader is the antagonist within the narrative, the book achieves that rare balance between art and entertainment. And in only twenty-four pages! The work is something like a minimalist *Anna Karenina,* if Anna were male and furry and bluish purple.

The premise of the narrative is that, well, there's a monster at the end of the book. Grover, good and timid soul that he is, takes it upon himself to protect you, the reader, from said monster. The task seems easy enough, but as Grover learns posthaste, you prove to be a very dim-witted and careless companion on this journey. While he trembles in fear at the thought of finishing the book and unleashing the monster, you dismiss his warnings and rush through the text. When he implores you to count your blessings and cut your losses and *stop reading,* you turn the page. He nails boards up to impede your cavalier progress; you rip them down. He erects a brick wall; you turn the page and bury him in a pile of rubble. Time and again, you read of another calamity befalling your lovable narrator—a calamity befalls or falls upon him on each and every page of the book—and although your heart breaks and you feel horribly complicit, you can't resist. You want to know what happens so badly, you want so desperately for the monster at the end of the book to be revealed, that you defy Grover's explicit and polite and *entirely wise* advice.

And thus Grover distinguishes himself as a true Monster of Letters, a narrator to emulate in your own work. His ultrasavvy storytelling style illustrates perfectly—deftly, smoothly, gorgeously— a strategy that writers of every stripe (or fur color) can use: When your readers want something, do not give it to them.

Or at least hold off for as long as possible before giving it to them. Whether you're writing literary fiction, mystery or romance or fantasy novels, or any kind of narrative nonfiction, Grover's plot example is one to follow. The relationship between the fiction writer and reader is, in some ways, tantamount to a seduction: the writer, via the plot, awakens a desire within the reader, and the longer that desire remains unsatisfied, the more intensely it burns. You aim to immediately introduce a source of tension and fan its flames (sometimes you'll need to squirt it with rocket fuel; other times you'll want to let it smolder) until the conflict is finally resolved. You want your readers aching to know who shot J.R., to know if Atticus wins the trial, if Elizabeth Bennet will marry Mr. Darcy. You want them to race through the pages, gobbling up the narrator's every word, to find the monster at the end of your book.

THE EXERCISE

The goal is to hook readers, then to keep them on the line, keep them reading. Work to introduce and cultivate a plot element that will keep the readers turning the pages. Try to engineer a concrete conflict through a character's desire—avoid abstraction and ambiguity at all costs—and put believable and formidable obstacles along the character's path. Grover introduces his conflict in the book's title, and from there, the tension mounts and mounts and mounts until the very last page.

For starters, brainstorm and write up a list of obstacles that would delay the resolutions to the conflicts below. You might, in fact, already have some version of these conflicts simmering in your stories or novels; if so, remember Grover's Golden Rule: As soon as the readers want something, withhold it. Try to find at least three (more is fine, especially for longer narratives) valid and vivid ways to sustain and evolve the readers' desire to find out what happens. Consider flashbacks, flash-forwards, subplots, and anything else in your writer's toolbox to help you seduce the reader. Grover goes from asking very nicely to screaming explicit orders to building brick walls, and as his attempts to hold the reader back escalate, so does the suspense. By withholding what we want, he makes us want it more. Follow his brilliant, furry model.

- Man wants to ask Woman out on a date. Woman wants Man to ask her out. What's stopping him? What or who gets in their way?

- A traveler needs to get to a certain place within a manageable but very tight window of time. What detours does he take and why? What problems impede his progress? How does the traveler try to make up lost time?
- A woman has found out something about her sister's fiancé and needs to get the information to her sister before the wedding the next morning. The groom wants to dissuade the sister from sharing the secret. How does one character work to circumvent the other?
- A young boy wants to find his lost dog before the animal control officer does. Where does he look? What clues assure him (and the reader) that he's on the right track? What impedes his progress?
- A teenage girl needs to sell two more raffle tickets before the end of the day in order to win a trip to Europe. Why is she having trouble selling these last two?

Michelle Wildgen

ON PLOT

PLOT SEEMS TO CONFOUND MANY WRITERS, ESPECIALLY AS one tries to involve emotional complexity with active momentum. New writers are often better at painting a still life than an action shot, and literary fiction often relies more on emotional consequences than material ones. Nevertheless, plot remains the motor that draws your story together and gives weight to characters' choices. This happens whether you're writing a large-scale thriller or small-scale family drama.

The old saw is that "The king and the queen died" is an event but "The king died and the queen died of grief" is a plot. Why? Cause and effect. Events happen *because of* other events rather than merely *in succession* to them. For my present purposes, however, I would change the second half of the saw to "The king died and the queen *killed herself* out of grief," because far too often what I see is a succession of actions rather than actions that happened one because of another. Look over your own stories and ask yourself, What if X had *not* happened? Too often, I find that the outcome is still the same; the initial emotions have intensified along the same lines but have not significantly changed. When readers talk about being bored, or about lack of momentum, this is often what they're saying: the story indicated that it was headed somewhere, and then it went there. The characters pondered their world with lucidity and humor, but that is all they did. (This said, an emotional response to events in a story is not wrong. But make sure the emotions are unexpected and have real weight—which is another exercise altogether.)

This exercise is a very simple one. It will help you push yourself to shove your characters into action.

THE EXERCISE

Examine one of your stories or someone else's. Make a list of the basics of action in it, keeping it simple and brief. For instance, I see a lot of stories that might look something like this:

1. Jane goes to the store to buy ingredients for homemade muffins.
2. There, she sees her mother canoodling with her boyfriend.
3. Jane goes home, makes the muffins in a daze.
4. Her mother comes home, and Jane watches her, notices some new facet or physical detail she hadn't seen before. She says nothing.
5. Jane thinks. Story ends.

Of course, once these events are wrapped in prose, they can feel far more substantive, but they may still leave you rather cold. The key to this exercise is to get at what's beneath the pretty prose wrapping and make sure it's really something. Try outlining a plot by filling in the blanks:

1. Jane goes to the store to buy ingredients for homemade muffins.

2. There, she sees her mother canoodling with her boyfriend.
3. Jane _____.

Go back to the big moment and have Jane do something, anything, that is real, directed action. Have her buy rat poison. Have her key someone's car. Have her make love to her boyfriend in some extremely disturbing new way. But when you feel yourself wanting to let your characters draw into themselves and be quiet, for this exercise, don't let them do it. Push them out there like a stage mother at an audition. And push them in a direction you don't foresee, maybe one that takes a little while to come up with. Because it is not enough to have Jane key the car, for her boyfriend to be angry, and for Jane to feel triumphant—this is pretty much what one would expect, right? There's anger, lashing out, then the natural angry response to said lashing out. Think of the book *Morvern Callar.* A woman finds that her boyfriend has killed himself and left his unpublished novel for her to send out. She sends it out as her own work and uses his money to go on a holiday. Her action happens because of his action, but it certainly isn't what one expects.

Finally, ask yourself what it all leads to, once your character has gone out and done the unexpected, the bold, the shocking. How is everything different? How does it change your character to have done what she's done?

Is this incredibly simplistic? Yes. Yes it is. But there are times when the simple framework leads you to the complex story. And sometimes it's easier to see the framework when you step away from your own carefully crafted passages and ask yourself, "What happens in this story?"

Nick Arvin

RECYCLING PROPS

THIS IS AN EXERCISE IN REVISION, AND TO START YOU NEED to look at a piece of fiction you've been working on and write down a list of five objects that appear in the story. These can be anything: big objects, small objects, objects that play a significant role, or objects that are only passingly mentioned in the setting of a scene.

Writers often talk about creating their fiction as if from within a waking dream—they speak of characters that take on a life of their own; they describe closing their eyes to look around an imaginary room and how from out of nowhere its contents emerge. Allowing the mysterious workings of the subconscious to take charge in this way is useful, even necessary, when drafting new material, but during the process of revision I find it helpful to occasionally remind myself that I am the author, that my characters are constructs of words I have put on a page, and that the objects in the rooms of my fiction have no reality except that which I choose to provide for them in my prose. When dealing with these objects in revision (the characters are a problem for a different exercise), I sometimes like to refer to such objects as *props*. Simply calling them props, as if they were items for use on a stage, reminds me of their artifice and helps me remember that as the author I have absolute control over my props—I can convey them and transmute them as I wish; they exist and relinquish existence at my whim.

Chekhov was talking about props when he said that if there is a gun on the mantel in the first act, it must go off in the third. The necessary discharge of Chekhov's gun in the third act is a matter of meeting the expectations of the audience: when a character puts a gun on the mantel, it creates an air of menace, it weighs upon the scene, and if the gun does not go off, albeit perhaps in a metaphorical sense, then the audience has a right to wonder why it was introduced at all. The converse of Chekhov's axiom is also useful: if a gun goes off in the third act, it's often best to put that gun on the mantel—so to speak—in the first act.

A gun that appears in a story gains immediate significance by the violence it threatens, but more innocuous props—a pair of socks, a tree, a tattoo, a shadow—can also gain significance through the course of a story. If a prop appears repeatedly within a story, it gains a history, and through its history it gathers layers of association, emotion, and subtext. At the same time, the unexpected reappearance of a forgotten object can create a happy thrill of recognition for the reader, and it also goes a good distance toward creating the sense that you, as the author, have crafted a world that is complete unto itself. So, for this exercise, you should think about the guns you have in your story, but I hope you will also consider the other, more obscure objects. Chekhov's mantel comes to mind. Everyone is preoccupied with the gun, but what would it mean for the mantel to go off in the third act?

THE EXERCISE

Look at your list, pick one prop, and write a new scene in which that prop is recycled into the story in a new and unexpected way.

Ideally you should give yourself only fifteen or so minutes; write quickly and creatively, and don't worry about neatly meshing this new material into all the demands of the story—you can go back and do that later. Try to repeat this exercise for each of the other props on your list. Some of what you write will never go any further, but with luck you will gain one or two ideas that will enrich the story you are working on.

DIALOGUE
and
VOICE

ON DIALOGUE AND VOICE

Dialogue, as much as anything else, reveals the character to the writer and, ultimately, to the reader. I don't have a very clear idea of who the characters are until they start talking. —Joan Didion

Dialogue is action. —Eudora Welty

Dialogue in fiction should be reserved for the culminating moments and regarded as the spray into which the great wave of narrative breaks in curving toward the watcher on the shore. —Edith Wharton

WHEN I WORKED ON THE EDITORIAL STAFF OF A NATIONAL literary journal, I watched an otherwise kind and gentle editor reject hundreds of stories based on dialogue alone. If the characters' conversations went on too long, the editor reached for the form rejection slips. The same with dialogue scenes that began in mundane or familiar ways—poorly rendered phone conversations, with all the helloing and such, suffered a lot here—and with conversations that went into a holding pattern of questions and answers. ("How are you?" he inquired. "Fine. And you?" she answered. "Where's Camryn?" he queried. "In her crib. Why?" she retorted. "Just askin'," he barked.) And dialogue tags! He'd go ballistic over flashy dialogue tags (inquired, answered, queried, barked, etc.), which some writers believe spice up their prose but really only shine a spotlight on flimsy language. He'd toss a story if the author tried to replicate speech patterns with a bunch of *uhs* and *ums,* or if the characters merely served as mouthpieces for the author's beliefs ("Crack is whack!") or for factual information about the story ("I'm going to the supermarket, then to the dry cleaner, then I'll rob the bank"). As harsh as this sounds—dialogue as litmus test for even *considering* a story—I want to stress again that the editor was an affable, charming, good-hearted, and intelligent young man, and he was genuinely rooting for every writer who submitted to the magazine. I'd also stress that of all the stories he rejected, I can't recall an instance where his instincts and decisions weren't dead-on right.

Whether you're writing fiction or nonfiction, dialogue is a crucial and revelatory aspect of dramatic prose because it's when the reader hears from the characters firsthand. How the author employs language in dialogue scenes often reliably mirrors how deftly or clumsily the other elements of the narrative will be negotiated—density of time, characterization, subtext, humor, conflict, and so on. Put simply, how a character says something is as important as what's been said. The writer's job is to use precise and original language to illustrate a character's truest emotions whether or not the character makes them readily available. Indeed, the best dialogue is made up of language that encompasses both what the character intends to reveal and what he intends to withhold. People rarely say what they mean, and the same is true for our characters; yet the author must find ways to convey that complexity to the reader. No simple task, that. What words will the husband who's just lost his job use to relay the news to his wife? To his son? To his bartender?

Will he use clipped sentences for one listener but longer, more rambling phrasings for another? How can you make the dialogue sound authentic without the repetitions and stutters that plague actual speech? How can you convey that he's worried or angry or relieved when your only dialogue tags are the bland but purposeful (and professional) *said* and *asked*? How could the completely kind and moral editor—okay, fine, *I* was that editor, and I'm sorry if I rejected your work, but hear me out—feel so sure that lazy or problematic dialogue always telegraphed deeper, more debilitating fault lines in the narrative? The answers are linked to the idea of "voice"—the characters' voices, the narrator's, the author's—and the exercises in this section address that seemingly ambiguous subject in a variety of practical ways.

To begin exploring dialogue and voice in my workshops, I give my students the I-rejected-stories-because-of-bad-dialogue spiel, and then I tell them to take out a clean sheet of paper and write down their five favorites words. The caveat is that for a word to be included on the list, its merits—meaning, why the student loves it—must be restricted to the sound or appearance of the word. If, for example, faith plays an integral role in the student's life, then the student is unceremoniously banned from writing the word *faith:* she doesn't love the piece of language; she loves its definition. To put a word on the list, a student must appreciate the particular arrangement of letters without concern for its lexical meaning: she has to love just seeing the word on the page, hearing or using the syllables in conversations; she has to be excited by the consonants, calmed by the vowels, struck by the glide of the diphthong. These can be words that illogically recall a pleasant memory, words that the students are proud to know, words that they find themselves trying to smuggle into discussions and stories. After about five minutes, volunteers share their lists. Off the top of my head, I recall: *cantilevered, accommodate, stuff, boo-honkey* (which is an ob-

scure southern term for one's *tokhes,* and which gained such purchase in our class one semester that the word stuck to the student as
her moniker: *I like what Boo-honkey said; Boo-honkey is really good
with dialogue,* etc.), *castigate, underbelly, imminent, chassis, verdad*
(Spanish for "truth").

Next, we do the same thing for words the students hate. The
same caveat applies: if the student despises racism, then she cannot
include the word on her list; she would hate racism if it were
known as *pizza.* Inevitably, someone asks about profanity—
occasionally we broach the subject in the first part of the exercise,
too—and I trot out the old (but sharp and true) saw that there is no
bad language, only language badly used. This part of the exercise is
more difficult and less fun, and could seem vaguely masochistic;
but it's no less important to illustrate that even the simple sound
and form of language has meaning, nuance, and power. I'm always
surprised by how few of the words shared in class are crude; there
are, to be sure, some predictable mainstays, but often the most interesting words are those that one wouldn't immediately assume to
be offensive: *auction block, cigarette, mealy, like, actually, facilitate,
bling.* Occasionally, more than one writer will have listed the same
word and an immediate sense of camaraderie will bloom; equally
as often, though, a writer will share a word she hates and another
writer will admit that he listed the same word on his list of
favorites.

Just as each writer has favorite and least favorite words, and
just as each of us has parts of speech and syllables that we employ
or avoid for highly specific reasons, so do our characters and narrators. While I've never suggested that a student make similar lists
of words for her characters—though maybe that could prove
beneficial—I do believe that voice (i.e., the cumulative effect of language within the narrative) often deserves far more attention than
it gets in contemporary prose. The inattention is doubly confusing

because voice is an element of narrative that almost everyone has mastered by the age of four. I ask my students to think of voice in basic, pragmatic terms: they speak differently to their pets than they do to their professors; they adjust their tones and vocabularies when addressing their parents, then adjust again when asking their bosses for a raise; they use different voices when trying to get out of a speeding ticket, when talking with doctors, when asking someone out, when bullying their younger siblings, when they're in chat rooms, when they're at a bar, when they're in church, when they're talking to themselves. Our voices, more than our clothes or cars or jobs, reveal and confirm our essences, so understanding whether a character would think of himself as fat or husky or rotund or Rubenesque or obese or portly is tantamount to knowing who that character is. Often the reason an editor or instructor will suggest that a writer cut a beautiful passage is because it reveals a lot about the writer—that she's got an ear for similes, an eye for lush language—but reveals nothing about the character or story.

The authors in this section explore how voice and dialogue relate to and differ from each other, and how the sophisticated prose writer can successfully navigate and employ them. The goal—the requirement—is for the narrative voice to enchant and enthrall the reader, to create such specific imagery in the reader's mind that she forgets she's reading, all without drawing attention to itself; Faulkner says, "The explosion must occur in silence." With dialogue, the writer aims to create the illusion of actual speech—both in form and content—while also honoring and embodying the characters' voices, personalities, and experiences. As with so much in creative writing, voice and dialogue boil down to desire: by using *these* words, *this* phrasing, *this* language, what does *this* character seem to want? (And make no mistake: every line of dialogue betrays—subtly or overtly—what the character is angling for.) What is her motivation for dubbing her small apartment "a palace"? What does the child hope to gain by telling his parents he washed the dishes while omitting that he failed his chemistry test? Why won't this character say anything, why won't that one shut up? Why does this one always curse, why does that one keep lying? Within such questions are your characters' truest identities and the hearts of your stories, and once you start to hear the answers, so will your readers.

DYNAMIC DIALOGUE: THREE EXERCISES

Good dialogue relies upon:

SURFACE TENSIONS OR UNDERLYING TENSIONS (SUBTEXT). There should always be the sense that what's being said, how it is being said, and what's being left unsaid are significant. Remember: dialogue isn't random but reflects your characters' emotional lives.

The real causes of conflict and tensions between characters may also not be immediately evident but may hide as subtext. For example, one character may know another is lying but never directly say so; nonetheless, the character's hidden belief that the other is lying affects what is said and how it is said. Sometimes subtext is social and political—racism, gender and sexual politics, nationalism, and the like can all potentially enhance underlying tensions in any conversation.

EMOTIONAL RESTRAINT (AND RELEASE). Characters, like people, attempt emotional restraint. (Subtext, by its nature, is a kind of emotional restraint.) Anger, fear, lust, or loneliness bubbling beneath the surface is more interesting than full-throttle emotional outbursts. When outbursts do happen, the prior restraint will make them all the more significant. Dialogue should be written with a sense of restraint and with the promise and fulfillment of releasing emotional power.

CHARACTERS' ACTIONS OR REACTIONS AND SILENCES. Engaged in dialogue, characters still have physical responses—facial gestures, stances, and so on. These actions and reactions reinforce what's said or being left unsaid. A character can say "I love you," but actions can prove the statement as truth or lie. Likewise, silences and hesitations can also convey the depth and truth of characters' emotions.

SPEECH AND RHYTHM PATTERNS THAT SUIT EACH CHARACTER. Characters' personalities, regional and class differences, educational backgrounds, and the type of community they live within all shape sounds and word selection. Abrupt, sweetly lyrical, or monosyllabic—the variety of speech is remarkable. Some characters will use simple words and be quite eloquent; others will use "fifty-cent" words to impress. Contractions, too, alter rhythms and are more common, colloquial: "I can't go" is more informal than "I cannot go."

SHORT SENTENCES AND SENTENCE FRAGMENTS. Lengthy, grammatically correct sentences make for stilted dialogue. Interruptions, sentence fragments, communication shortcuts, and dialect distinctions are more reflective of human speech:

> "Where you going?"
> "Church."

is better dialogue than

"Where are you going?"

"I am going to church."

A MINIMUM OF TAGS TO MAINTAIN PACING. Tags such as "he said" and "she asked" should be used only when absolutely necessary to avoid confusion about who is speaking when. Too many tags and readers will be reminded that they are reading rather than imaginatively participating in a story.

———

Writing strong dialogue is a skill that will serve you well in each and every story. Characters don't truly come alive until they *speak*, and their speech exposes conflict and advances plot. Every hour spent practicing dialogue will reward you with more readable and interesting stories. As you become more sensitive to the sounds and speech about you, your characters will whisper, holler, and sigh new emotions and new stories.

THE EXERCISES

Exercise 1: Talking Solo Voice

Spend two days listening for a person whose speech interests you. It can be a FedEx driver from the Bronx, a Wall Street financier, or a Jamaican immigrant. *What is it you like hearing?* Is it the rhythm, the word choices, the dialect lilt? What sentence pattern do you hear most often? Is the tone emphatic? whiny? measured? aggressive? blunt? hesitant and shy? Ask the speaker if you can tape-record her dialogue. If this is impractical, rely on transcription and memory.

Next, selecting *one* of the situations below, write a monologue using your newly captured "voice":

- Imagine a suspected bank robber pleading innocence and fabricating an alibi for a detective.
- Imagine an abused wife trying to explain to a social worker why she won't leave her husband.
- Imagine a clerk at a convenience store trying to explain to a fellow employee his infatuation for a customer who comes in every Monday and Friday for a quart of milk, two beers, and a carton of cigarettes.

Spend an hour writing and revising a monologue. How well does your creative version compare with the original voice? How well does the voice suit the situation and character you created? Does your monologue have tension? Emotional restraint? Are there any actions, reactions, or silences in your monologue? If not, why not? Is the speech credible? Consistent? Are there any weaknesses in your monologue? What are its strengths?

Exercise 2: Dialogue at Odds

Building on the previous exercise, expand your monologue into a dialogue. For example, if you created a monologue of a bank robber lying to a detective, you now need to expand it to create a two-person dialogue. To do this you need to:

1. **Imagine the second character.** Who is she (or he)? How long has she been a detective? Does she like her job? What needs and motivations does she have? What does her voice sound like?
2. **Add more tension and subtext.** Does the detective suspect that the robber is lying? Does she have only circumstantial evidence? Is she trying to trick him into a confession? Is she

secretly sympathetic to him? Does she find him attractive? Does she have money problems? Has she ever dreamed of stealing? Is the robber attracted to the detective? Is the robber carrying a concealed weapon? Is the robber especially anxious because a new conviction will mean life imprisonment? Did the robber recently discover that his wife is pregnant?

3. **Establish setting.** Where are your characters? In the downtown police station? At the robber's home? In a probation office? Has the robber been run aground in a suspected crack house?

Once you've imagined the new character, established a setting, and increased surface and underlying tension, you're ready to imagine a good dialogue scene.

Write a dialogue between two people based on your original monologue. (Remember: characters do not speak in a vacuum but within the context of who they are, where they are, and the purpose or goal they need to achieve.) Don't censor your words. Write quickly for at least thirty minutes, trying to create interesting and credible dialogue. (Don't worry about a resolution. The bank robber doesn't need to confess.)

Next, read your dialogue aloud. Are the speech patterns and word choices of the two characters distinct? Does the dialogue seem stilted or natural? What types of sentences did you use? Are they effective? Did you use any sentence fragments? One-word responses? If not, why not? Could you use more sentence-rhythm variety? Do any of your lines sound awkward, stilted?

Have you added enough tension and subtext? Do you need to add more character responses, actions?

Spend another thirty minutes revising your dialogue. Reread

your dialogue aloud again. Is the second version better—easier to follow, alive with sound and substance?

Exercise 3: Practicing Subtext

Underlying tensions rule much of human conversation. Polite society usually discourages direct expressions of strong emotions: outrage, anger, love, desire. We learn to dissemble, bury our emotions as subtext within our speech. A teenager struck with romantic passion may blandly say, "She's okay" while his heart more eloquently speaks of love.

People often avoid saying what they mean or say less of what they mean, which creates subtext and conversational tension. This sense that another conversation underlies our dialogue or that meaning is found "between the lines" makes conversation interesting.

Pay attention to how you and those around you argue. How many times have you and your loved one argued over the toothpaste cap when you're really fighting about how each other spends money? How many times have you criticized your children's clothing or hairstyle when you were really arguing about the suitability of their new friends?

It is important to remember that subtext as a form of emotional restraint can't last throughout your story. Eventually, what's at the heart of the conversation has to be confronted—it is this confrontation that your readers anticipate.

For the next twenty minutes, using *one* of the ideas below, write a sequence of dialogue that has subtext, underlying tensions. Ideally, you will want the reader to be able to tell that there is something lurking beneath the surface conversation. Leave clues: unfinished sentences, unexpected silences, emotional responses that don't fit the conversation, or more emotion than the surface situation would warrant.

- Two characters argue about the unequal distribution of household chores.

  The subtext: One partner believes the other is unfaithful.
- Two characters argue about whether the Chicago Bulls will win the play-offs.

  The subtext: One friend has started to deal drugs.
- Two characters argue about whether a diamond is an exploitation of black labor or an expression of love.

  The subtext: Both partners are reconsidering the engagement.

Read the dialogue you produced. Have you established a sense of tension? Of something to be revealed later?

Write for another twenty minutes, adding to the scene and allowing the subtext, the hidden tension to break through. For example, the wife finally accuses the husband of infidelity or the young man directly confronts his friend about his drug abuse.

In your dialogue, there may or may not be a resolution of conflict. Possibly tensions will subside, becoming subtext once again. One partner, still not sure if her lover is unfaithful, may conclude the conversation with "It's your turn to clean the bathroom."

The best thing about subtext, however, is that hidden tensions always rise to the surface. Just as in plot development, it is this rising and release of tension that will excite readers to continue reading more.

Read your entire scene aloud. What can you do to make it better? Is the language and diction credible and engaging? Are there enough clues about the subtext? Is it emotionally dramatic when the subtext is revealed?

HE SAID WHAT?

I AM A SHAMELESS EAVESDROPPER. WHETHER WAITING IN A grocery checkout line or perusing bestsellers at a bookstore, I am always straining to overhear other people's conversations. I'm at my worst in restaurants with tables grouped inches apart, an eavesdropper's dream. Once, while vacationing in the southern California desert, I was sitting in just such a restaurant, a tiny Mexican joint. My friend and I were practically bumping elbows with the man and woman seated next to us; they were so close I could see the grease under his nails and the blusher caking her laugh lines. I managed to ignore them until my friend excused herself to make a phone call. Then I couldn't resist listening in. They were obviously on a first date, exchanging basic getting-to-know-you information: where they lived, whom they knew in common, how many failed relationships between them. She was a recent divorcée and waitressed at a local bar; he was a die-hard bachelor, a mechanic with a penchant for Harleys. He had other passions, though. "Welding's my true love," he told her. "I can weld anything but the crack in your ass and a broken heart."

So what does eavesdropping have to do with writing fiction? A lot. Not only has it gained me some great tidbits for stories (Mr.

Ass-Crack Welder has shown up more than once in my work), it has also taught me how people really talk to each other, which is essential to creating believable characters. The cadence of people's speech changes with their audience. Formality sets in with strangers or acquaintances; casual shorthand takes over with loved ones. No matter how familiar their audience, though, people rarely state every bit of information an outsider needs to completely understand the conversation. Everyone makes assumptions about a listener's knowledge of the event under discussion. In addition, people often communicate just as much through body language as they do through speech. A mother who laughs as she tells her child drawing on a wall, "Stop that right now!" will spur a different reaction than a mother who scowls and takes away the marker.

To write good fictional dialogue, however, you can't simply reproduce the way people talk. Instead, you have to mimic real speech. Everyday conversations are often rambling and repetitive; they contain lots of filler ("Hi, how're you, how was your weekend?"); sometimes they're just plain boring. Fictional dialogue can't afford such pitfalls. It should be used sparingly and with purpose, to engage the reader, move the story along, reveal characters' true natures as well as some essential conflict between them. All this can be accomplished not just through what is said but also through what is not said, through characters' reactions to each other, and through accompanying gestures and actions. Using a combination of these tools, you can create a fictional conversation that engages the reader and evokes vivid, exciting characters whose stories demand to be told.

THE EXERCISE

1. Keep a notebook with you for a week and listen in on people's conversations wherever you are—a doctor's office, a

coffee shop, a grocery store, anywhere. Transcribe, *verba-tim,* as many conversations as possible without getting caught (for those of you new to the art, we eavesdroppers are an unappreciated lot). Also note people's gestures and reactions to each other. (E.g.: Man [scratching armpit]: "I can weld anything but the crack . . ." Woman [frowning]: "How interesting.")

2. Pick a conversation and describe, in a few sentences, the conflict between the speakers. If the conflict isn't clear, make it up. Better yet, even if it is clear, make it up. The conflict could be something simple and obvious (like a father and daughter arguing about a curfew) or something complicated and unspoken (like a man and a woman having different expectations for their first date). The point is to ensure that you have a clear conflict in mind before you rewrite the conversation. Defining the conflict will force you to start imagining each speaker as an individual with unique thoughts and desires, likes and dislikes. A defined conflict will also immediately add tension to even the most mundane conversation. For instance, without a clear conflict, the conversation between Mr. Ass-Crack Welder and his date becomes a routine, rather dull exchange of information interesting only to the speakers. If you consider, however, what the conversation means to each individual, its significance heats up considerably. Mr. Ass-Crack Welder could be out with his date as a favor to a friend and wants to get rid of her as soon as possible so he can meet his buddies at a Harley show. His companion, on the other hand, could be on her first date since her divorce and is determined to get him to ask her out again. Or flip their roles. He could be the recent divorcé looking for a second date and she the one who can't wait to ditch him. Consider how

these desires, and their reversal, would change the conversation.

3. Next, write a scene consisting only of dialogue based on the transcribed conversation and the conflict you devised. Don't use every bit of what you overhead verbatim, and make up dialogue as necessary. Use your understanding of the conflict between the speakers to shape your selection of how much of the actual dialogue to keep and how much to make up. Also, keep in mind that people often don't directly discuss a conflict. They can express just as much through what they avoid saying as through what they do say.

4. Next, rewrite the scene, adding in the specific setting (e.g., a restaurant, a coffee shop, a bedroom). Include your characters' reactions to each other using gestures, actions, physical descriptions, and so on. Consider how the setting affects what they say and how they say it. Also, avoid describing the characters' emotions ("He felt bad when she laughed at his love of welding, so he said . . ."). Let what they say and how they behave convey their feelings.

5. Finally, change the setting of the conversation. Consider how the change affects your characters, not just in their speech but also in their actions and reactions. What if a certain someone takes his date to McDonald's instead of a tiny Mexican joint with closely set tables and an eavesdropping writer sitting nearby? Depending on the conflict between them, their conversation could go in a strange and unexpected direction (maybe involving blowtorches and tattooed asses), resulting in a whopper of a scene that could, in turn, lead to a whopper of a story.

CHARACTER AND SITUATION
THROUGH DIALOGUE

CHARACTER IS FATE. CHARACTER IS ACTION. CHARACTER IS nature. Character is nurture. Character is the sound of a voice, a gesture, the color of the eyes, the hair, the texture of the skin. It is a matter of imagining, even when you are using a model, and it involves the marvelous *reasonableness* of the world's fictional people—that is, we understand Jay Gatsby's behavior, we are privy to his "romantic readiness," and we have full knowledge of what he felt standing at the end of his dock, his fantastic mansion rising behind him in the night, while he gazed, arms outstretched, across the sound, at Daisy's green light; we know why Quentin Compson commits suicide, and why Emma Bovary does, and Anna Karenina, too. We know these people, therefore, better than we ever really know anyone in life.

And so one of the first things to learn is that fiction has more to do with itself than it does with life. You are not putting life on the page, because life is confusing and random and constructed of a mess of unknowable and conflicting forces, and fiction is organized and shapely, and arises out of a passion to *make sense* out of experience. A fictional man or woman has no more substance than a *painted* man or woman. The shapes and shades of color, or light, are used by the artist to *deceive* the eye into believing that what it is seeing is flesh and blood—but of course it is not flesh and blood; it is paint.

You are making a *picture* out of words, a portrait. And fiction is a magic act.

Obvious enough—even elemental—but you'd be surprised how many inexperienced writers forget that.

How do you create characters? By refusing ever to think about people as types. By imagining yourself into the *body* of a character, into the *senses,* that is, of a created someone *in context.*

Context is situation. And situation involves that most elemental part of the fictive world: conflict.

If you think of conflict merely as an argument, you're badly limiting yourself; but even an argument is preferable to the indefatigable rendering of dailiness that I often get from inexperienced students, aiming to put life down on that page as it really, really is. Life as it really is turns out to be boring on the page. (It is even, to some extent, boring in the reliving of it: notice, those of you who have video cameras and record family celebrations, how much of the time, during replay, you have your finger pressed on the fast-forward button.)

If one of the elemental ways to deliver conflict is through an argument, there are also many ways to deliver a sense of tension—an argument that may or may not happen. In any case—in every case—you must, while considering the facets of your conflict or about-to-happen argument, work into your portrayal all the other aspects of the art. That is, while delivering a scene that presents one character in conflict with another, one also has to pay attention to characterization, plot, theme (the aboutness of the story), increasing complication, history, setting—all of it.

No matter what element of the writing of fiction you are concerning yourself with, *all* of the elements of it must eventually come into play in any given scene.

I have concocted an exercise using dialogue, by itself, to demonstrate this to students, and to help them teach themselves about the use of dialogue in fiction—which is, in fact, far different from the use of it in movies or films. (In movies and films it's the camera telling the story, and the dialogue is quite often secondary, or even rather dull. Quentin Tarantino has a reputation for writing "realistic" dialogue in his films, but the fact is, it's awfully dull to read: two men discussing laundry in the front seat of a car, after having blown the head off a man sitting in the back seat of that same car.) In a story, the dialogue is never there for space, or for any rendition of "reality." You have two people waiting for a train on a station platform, and your instincts may tell you that they would talk about the weather or whatever's in the news—but if their talk is not about the story's central matter, then they say nothing that you bother to report.

THE EXERCISE

This exercise is limiting in the way most exercises are. And it is also simple in the same way virtue is simple—which is to say that it is extremely difficult, too. The idea is to concoct a circumstance where two voices are to be heard. And to allow yourself no lines of summary, no attribution, no descriptions of tone, no characterizing of voice or the words. Just the two voices.

Now, it would be easy enough to produce the circumstance and plenty of tension:

> Suppose you open that cash drawer, bub.
> Don't shoot. Please. I have a family.

But it is another thing altogether to produce character, and all the other requirements of a good story, simply through what the two people say, what words they use. That is, you must give the reader a sense of the character of the two people, along with whatever is at issue between them, along with something of their history and their motivations, and all the rest.

Because you have no attribution, no "he said" or "she said," you must portray those silences and pauses by the use of ellipses. So when one person fails to respond to the other and there's a pause, you put an ellipsis on the following line, thus:

> That was good.
> Mmmm.
> So good.
> . . .
> I've been so miserable lately.

And it is understood that the person who said, "So good" also said, after a silence, "I've been so miserable lately."

With only their exchanges, then, you must deliver who they are, what sort of people they are, the nature of their trouble, and where they are in time and place, *without* ever letting it seem forced or contrived. Remember that the first three letters of the word *artificial* are ART. It's a magic show, and this is just teaching yourself one of the tricks. One way to help yourself in revision of such a piece—actually, in revision of any story you write—is to read through and try to make sure that every single line of it is accomplishing more than one thing: it's giving character *while* advancing the plot *while* enhancing the reader's sensual experience of the whole *while* foreshadowing the eventual outcome. All that. Remember that writing a good story is at least as hard as learning how to play a musical instrument. If it feels overly difficult and complicated to you, then you are probably a writer.

ON DIALOGUE

HOW WE SPEAK TO ONE ANOTHER REVEALS MUCH MORE about ourselves than the words themselves. The effective use of dialogue in fiction allows our characters to hoist themselves with their own petards. We, as narrators, need not intrude very far to get our readers to understand much of what they need to know through what our characters say.

Most writers lean too heavily on exposition to help them delineate character or advance plot. They mistrust their characters' own voices. I find it helpful, therefore, to have students err on the other side. They go from writing a scene in play form, without the benefit of stage directions, to gradually incorporating action and description to support the interaction between two characters.

THE EXERCISE

1. A married couple is speaking. The woman wants a divorce. The man does not. Write a page of dialogue between them. At the end of the page, one of them convinces the other. Use dialogue only. No description, action, or thought.

2. Now write the same scene in exposition. Use no dialogue.
3. Take your original scene in dialogue and judiciously add some of the description, action, and thought that might fill out the scene. Make sure that the dialogue is still doing most of the heavy lifting here.

Bret Anthony Johnston & Robert Torres, Illustrator

THE THING ABOUT DIALOGUE

. . . IS THAT IT NEEDS TO SOUND LIKE REAL SPEECH WITHOUT being real speech. That was the mantra from most of my teachers in graduate school, and like a good student, I've been parroting it for years in my own classes. Here are a few more hints my teachers gave me or that I've discovered on my own:

- *The shorter, the better.* Dialogue reads very quickly to a certain point—I've found that that point is right around three lines per speaker at a time. After that it drags and its spell on the reader wavers.
- *Focus on conflict.* Dialogue is a fantastic place to introduce and develop conflict. Ethan Canin has a great example for this; compare these two versions of a line:

  "I love your dress," she said.

  "I love your dress," she said. "Did I see it on the sale rack at Goodwill?"

In the first version, we learn nothing. The dialogue has provided no valuable information about the dress or its owner or even the speaker. It's short, which is good, but it's also flat. In the second version, however, the author is introducing conflict, as well as some dark humor that absolutely characterizes the speaker and ratchets up the tension.

- *Focus on humor.* As in the previous example, humor can work very well in dialogue. If you or, better, your *character* has a funny bone, dialogue is the place to use it.
- *Lies are good.* Anytime a character lies to another character, the tension soars. I can't count how many times students have come to me with a problem in their dialogue scenes and I've encouraged them to have one character lie to another. Often this will thrust the conversation (and sometimes the whole story) in an unexpected and rewarding direction.
- *Beware of questions in dialogue.* A lot of times—maybe most times—when writers use questions in dialogue, they're only doing so to elicit the answer that follows. Often, the stronger posture is to skip the question and cut straight to the answer. Compare these three versions of a conversation between a wife and her husband, whom she fears is having an affair:

"What time did you get home last night?" she asked. "I thought we were having dinner."

"I'm sorry, honey. Work ran long. Some of us ordered a pizza, then I went for a drink with the guys. You were already asleep. I didn't want to wake you."

"I thought we were having dinner last night," she said.

"I'm sorry, honey. Work ran long. I didn't want to wake you when I got home."

"I'm sorry, honey. Work ran long. I didn't want to wake you," he said.

"I wasn't asleep," she said. "I thought we were having dinner."

The difference between the first version and the last two is one of agency. In the first exchange, the wife is more submissive, more passive in her dialogue, whereas in the next two, she's more assertive and direct, which makes her a more interesting and compelling character. Also, in the last two versions, you can see how the ordering of speakers affects the tone and meaning of the exchange, as well as the characterization. In the first two versions, the husband is responding to his wife's inquiries—more than likely he would have never broached the subject if she hadn't—but in the third version, he tries to preempt her questions. One character waits to respond; another starts making excuses before the question's been raised: the difference in characters is profound.

• *Finally, avoid mundane dialogue.* Beware of words and phrases such as: Hello, Hey, How are you?, How's it going?, Fine, Never better, What's up?, Take it easy, Talk to you later, and Good-bye. The list goes on and on, but you get the idea. Often we include such dialogue to give the feeling of real speech—the defense in workshop is always *But that's how people really talk!*—but remember: dialogue needs to *sound* like real speech without *being* real speech. Both in life and in fiction, such talk is often just a kind of throat clearing before the true conversation, and the true conversation is what we're after. (It's also true that *because* that's how people really talk, the reader anticipates this kind of speech in the text and her expectation renders it unnecessary.) One very easy way to avoid including mundane dialogue is to steer clear, as often as possible, of scenes that begin with characters entering rooms or answering phones. Start in medias res and most of the mundane dialogue will have already happened.

THE EXERCISES

EXERCISE 1: Study the illustration on the following page and pick the exchange that looks the most interesting to you. Using the above points about dialogue, write a scene in which two strangers talk to each other.

EXERCISE 2: Same as above, but now write a conversation in which the characters know each other but have not seen each other in a long while. What is their relationship? How does the conversation begin? (Remember, avoid mundane dialogue.) Try to reveal why they've not seen each other in so long without actually spelling it out.

EXERCISE 3: Same as above, but now write a conversation in which the characters are traveling together but are having a disagreement over something. Would they be the kinds of people who shout and allow everyone at the bus stop to hear their argument, or would they try to keep it down? Is this a big argument or a small one? Where are they coming from? Where are they going? Try to reveal all of this without explicitly stating it.

EXERCISE 4: Same as above, but try to write a comic dialogue exchange. (Here, the robot might really help out.)

EXERCISE 5: Same as above, but try to include as many characters as possible in the conversation, without losing or confusing the reader.

FOR FURTHER CONSIDERATION: By choosing which conversation to focus on, you are also choosing the story or scene's POV character. To further hone this skill, you might consider picking one character at a time and having him describe the others, the situation, the setting, and so on. Try to write a page or two of interior monologue, stream of consciousness, or exposition for each character, or try to write a scene without dialogue from the POV of each. What the characters choose to focus on—and how they describe and consider it—will ultimately and essentially distinguish them from everyone else. Obviously, the robot will process information differently than the skateboarder does, but the other characters will also likely have some drastically differing observations.

Robert Rosenberg

USING SUMMARY, INDIRECT, AND DIRECT DIALOGUE

THE PLIGHT OF TRYING TO TEACH ANYONE TO WRITE FIC-
tion is such that, whatever useful craft advice an instructor offers up, its strict adherence brings with it new problems. One of the
simplest and most powerful lessons Henry James offered the aspiring writer was the dictum "Dramatize, dramatize, dramatize." It
is, perhaps, the primary lesson any writer must learn, and with it
the young writer takes a great leap forward in his storytelling. But
no sooner does the zealous writer start dramatizing than suddenly
everything's getting indiscriminately dramatized: bathroom scenes,
sex scenes, the making of a character's bed in the morning.

And, inevitably, dialogue becomes bloated as well. A strict
fealty to James's advice too often results in scenes in which the dialogue seems either inert or rushed.

Take, for example, the extremely hackneyed "breakup scene" I
often see in my students' stories. A couple whose relationship is on
the rocks enters a restaurant. We read:

"Hey."
"Hey."
"You look nice tonight."

"Thanks."

"Would you like some wine?"

"I'd love some."

"Red or white?"

"What do you prefer?"

And so on. This is a case of overdramatization, the use of small talk in an effort to replicate the way we actually speak. It attempts to mimic, as accurately on the page as possible, the way people slowly broach a subject. It might ring true enough, but the combination of tediousness and lack of plot relevance makes it the death of compelling dialogue.

Sometimes the beginning writer errs in the opposite direction: the same fictional couple will sit down at the table in the fancy restaurant and the woman will blurt out, "It's over between us." For a reader it will seem as if they've been sitting all of fifteen seconds, that they haven't even unfolded their napkins, before the fight is on. Of course, this almost never happens in real life, and as such it is difficult to believe. More likely, there'd be a slow buildup to the breakup, a hesitation, a beating around the bush. Without this, *or without at least a hint that it went on,* the scene won't be convincing. It's a case of not providing enough of an illusion of time passing before a character leaps into the heart of the confrontation.

The problem with writing dialogue, then, is essentially one of pacing. A reader will be bored to tears with mimesis but will not believe the skipping of actual conversation.

To encourage control of these typical exchanges of dialogue, I ask students to pay attention to the way published authors use a combination of *dialogue summary, indirect dialogue,* and *direct dialogue.* Take a look at this example:

He was complaining the whole time about his utter exhaustion in Chiang Mai, about the steamy afternoon rains, about the exhaust-filled air. [Summary.] The heat was killing him. He said his throat was permanently sore. He'd give it five more days, and then he was out of here. [Indirect dialogue.] "You'll regret leaving so soon," she warned him. "I don't think so," he said. "I don't think so at all." [Direct dialogue.]

Dialogue summary is something writing students are urged to avoid. ("Show, don't tell!) But in the opening moments of dialogue, it can be effective to simply "tell." An entire fictional hour of conversation might usefully be compressed into a line or two this way.

Indirect dialogue does not use quotation marks. It imitates speech using the narrative voice—not the actual voice of the characters. In this way it still compresses a conversation while giving the illusion that two characters are speaking. It is a technique few beginning writers are aware of, though many use it accidentally. (García Márquez, who has famously touted dialogue as one of his weaknesses, uses a great deal of indirect dialogue to compensate for what he considers a craft shortcoming.)

Direct dialogue is just that: characters' words in quotation marks, using dialogue tags. I warn my students that it is so powerful a device—for plot, for characterization, for theme—that it cannot be squandered on small talk, trivialities, or irrelevant issues.

THE EXERCISE

Choose a section of dialogue from your story in progress or one you still need to write. Our goal is to transition more smoothly into dialogue.

1. In your head, consider these questions about the scene: What will the ultimate goal of the scene be? How and where have the characters come together? What does each of them want at this moment in the plot? What are the characters battling over? Why is it necessary that they have this conversation?

2. When this is all clear to you, ask yourself how the characters actually begin speaking. What is the nature of the small talk that will lead up to the vital issues in the conversation? Now, get writing. Write out a page or two of this preparatory blather. Get it out of your system. Don't be afraid to put it on paper (you'll be cutting it out of the final draft.) Think of it as a warm-up, an exploration of voice. Once the characters start wandering into the heart of the conversation, stop writing.

3. Go back over all this small talk, noting its triviality and how it's most likely unessential to the plot. In its place, write a new paragraph of a few sentences, *summarizing* this early part of the conversation. ("He was complaining the whole time about his utter exhaustion in Chiang Mai, about the steamy afternoon rains, about the exhaust-filled air.") Essentially you are explaining what the characters are talking about. This will serve as an introduction, a path leading up to the stuff that matters. It will also give the illusion of time passing, while in reality allowing the reader to skip the tedium of the unessential remarks.

4. Now you want to transition from this summary into the direct dialogue. This is an effective place to use indirect dialogue. Ask yourself: What is the *turning point* of this small talk? What subject is raised that will lead the conversation toward the real issue you want your characters arguing about? At the end of your summary paragraph, give us this

turning point using a sentence or two of *indirect dialogue.* ("The heat was killing him. He said his throat was permanently sore. He'd give it five more days, and then he was out of here.) This sets up the direct dialogue, focuses it on the subject at hand. It is the gateway to the critical speech you want to present.

5. You have eliminated all the small talk and transitioned, naturally, into the heart of the matter. Now write out the *direct dialogue, eliminating all narrative for now. Focus only on what the characters say.* (" 'You'll regret leaving so soon,' she warned him. 'I don't think so,' he said. 'I don't think so at all.' ") Make sure you follow certain standard practices: Is every line doing more than one thing? Is there conflict or humor in the exchanges? Are they short? Do you make effective use of silences? Prefer *said* and *asked* as dialogue tags. Vary the dialogue tag placement, or eliminate it when the speaker is clear. Make your dialogue at least a page long. Read it aloud to hear if it's natural or wooden, if it's excessively casual or formal.

NOTE: You can use a similar technique—returning again to summary, then transitioning with indirect dialogue into direct dialogue—to skip over later parts of the conversation. Not all dialogue needs to follow this pattern, of course. (You can, and should, weave setting and action within and throughout, but that is a matter for a different exercise.) Still, the effective use of summary and indirect dialogue is a craft skill to add to your repertoire, especially useful as you begin editing, recasting, and compressing your drafts.

Kate Myers Hanson

DIALOGUE: MASTER OF MULTITASKING
AND SLEIGHT OF HAND

AS AN EXPERIMENT AND PART OF OUR EXPLORATION INTO what makes good dialogue, a handful of graduate students gave me permission to record *their* dialogue as we discussed Tobias Wolff's short story "Bullet in the Brain." We recorded every sound, the interruptions and odd pauses in "real" speech, complete with *um*s and *ah*s and *you know*s and *uh-huh*s and expletives. Keep in mind that what these students had to say about Wolff's story was insightful and reflected a sound knowledge of the foundations of writing fiction, in particular how well-crafted dialogue characterizes through precise language, syntax, and sentence rhythms, how it creates a specific atmosphere or mood, and with an eyedropper gives the reader an immediate sense of the conflict and theme, what Edgar Allan Poe calls the *single effect.* "You know on so many levels that someone is going to kill this guy," one of my students said, referring to Anders, the central character. In addition, they discussed how the dialogue works in concert with setting, the confined space in the bank, to create tension, advance the action, and even, with references to Vietnam and the killing of villagers, foreshadow. As William Sloane, in *The Craft of Writing,* says, "Dialogue must do more than one thing at a time or it is too inert for the purposes of fiction." Wolff's story more than satisfies that dictum.

But back to the recording of our discussion of "Bullet in the Brain." When we read aloud our transcribed dialogue, it was confusing, interruptive, and at times barely intelligible. This was "real" dialogue, wasn't it? Why did it seem so clunky? The truth is, as fiction writers our goal is not to *record* or *reproduce* actual speech, with all of its clumsiness, dissonance, and rhythmic missteps. Dialogue has its own reality, but it is not "real" speech. It should be used for a specific purpose and therefore crafted to meet that purpose. Consider "The Cutting Edge," a short story by James Purdy. A son reluctantly returns home to see his parents after a long absence. The mother argues with her husband over their son's beard, his rudeness, but the father is reluctant to become involved. As readers we wonder what is really going on. Our allegiances are divided at the beginning of the story, but as the story progresses dialogue unravels the past and deepens the characterization. We begin to ask questions. Is the son really the victim here? Why doesn't the husband stand up to his wife? What's at stake? With sleight of hand their dialogue becomes revelatory, and we eventually learn that the wife holds currency in the relationship—the father's infidelity—which she uses to control both her son and her husband. Dialogue, the master of multitasking and sleight of hand, again serves the story, revealing a truth that works against the expectations of the reader.

THE EXERCISES

1. Develop the beginning of a story, no more than one page. Establish a setting that you believe might work in terms of conflict and theme. Place in that setting two characters who have known each other for a long time and give one a secret

that will change their lives. Give them room to talk and act, but don't allow the character with the secret to reveal it; only allow the reader to intuit it from their dialogue.

2. Write a page of dialogue between two students who come from very different backgrounds. For example, one grew up in a wealthy suburb in Atlanta and the other grew up on a farm in Iowa. Do not *state* where they are from, what their experiences have been, or what each of them wants. Use only dialogue (language and level of diction, sentence rhythms, and you can also include syntax; characters' gestures) to reveal and to differentiate the voices of these characters. Use an objective point of view, without sinking into either character's consciousness. Read Hemingway's stories "Hills Like White Elephants" and "The Killers" as examples of an objective point of view.

3. The following is an example of "packed" dialogue, an effort to give the reader too much information. Therefore, the focus of the story is unclear and this overload disengages the reader. At this point, the dialogue is trying to do too much.

> "Oh, Shirley, it's so nice to finally meet you. Of course I've seen you getting off the downtown bus at five every weekday. You always look so tired."
>
> "You're right about that, Linda. I have a boss who has me running all day at the Grinder, a new coffee shop near the Greyhound bus station, and then I have to come home to this run-down apartment building and deal with my mother. It's depressing."
>
> "You don't sound like you're from around here, Shirley."
>
> "No, I'm from Texas, down around Brownsville."

"I thought I detected an accent. Well, maybe you'd like to come up and have a drink with me and my husband, who just got promoted to foreman over at Westwind Industries. We could have some wine. What do you think, Shirley?"

"That would be nice, but first I have to check up on my mother, though that might take a while since she's a real hypochondriac. Yesterday she said she couldn't stand up because the bottoms of her feet were too hot, called me at work in the middle of the day and insisted I bring home a bag of ice so she could soak her feet in the bathtub."

"You seem to have a lot on your plate, Shirley."

"You have no idea, Linda."

Write a page of dialogue between these characters. Consider adding other elements to work in concert with the dialogue to move the story forward, but allow dialogue to drive the story.

José Skinner

THE FOREIGN VOICE

Language is an instrument for ordering the world and society," wrote the linguist Émile Benveniste. "It is applied to a world considered as 'real' and also *reflects* this 'real' world. But in this sense, each language is specific and asserts the world in its own peculiar way."

This becomes obvious during the process of translating one language into another. In translating a text from a foreign language into her native tongue, the translator realizes how each language works to order and control its particular reflection of reality.

As the Russian formalists pointed out nearly a century ago, the aim of literary expression is to make things "new and strange" and in so doing reveal the contingent and constructed qualities of the realities we take for granted. (Marilynne Robinson, a fiction teacher at the Iowa Writers' Workshop, tells her students right off that she will be looking for the unusual and the strange, no matter how subtle, in each piece they write.)

The following exercises do not actually require knowledge of a language other than one's own. There is only one tool required: an online translator, which you can call up using Google or another search engine. There are many of these free services, and they are all laughably bad, which makes them good for these exercises. They use what's called machine translation, computer programs that have been tinkered with since 1954 but still can't handle the semantic complexities of language or the elements that make literary language what it is: wordplay, ambiguity, contextual meaning, cultural understanding, and so on. In short, to use language the way we humans do, you have to understand the realities reflected in our languages, and computers don't have the life experience to do that (they don't have sentient bodies, for one thing, or culture).

THE EXERCISE

1. Using the online translator, type or paste in a passage from a text written in a foreign language by an author you admire. Choose a text you know has been professionally translated into English; the translation should be available to you but one that you haven't read yet. It's best to select a passage you know or suspect is written in a colloquial voice and contains at least some dialogue.

2. After you've had your laughs at the machine translation, rework the translated passage into the best English version you can. If you're working in a group, compare your work with that of the others. Your group may be able to come up with a consensus version, or not.

3. Now try the reverse. Ask the machine to translate your version(s) back into the foreign language, and then have it translate *that* version into English again.

4. Finally, consult the published human translation of the text. (If you are fortunate enough to know someone familiar with or a native speaker of the foreign language being translated—many of my creative-writing classes have been blessed with students whose mother tongues aren't

English—that person can make his or her own translation of the passage.) In what ways does the published translation diverge from the machine translation and from your own revisions?

5. Try the exercise using different languages and see which are more comprehensible in the machine translation, which less.

6. As you're putting the texts through the online translator, make collections of the strange and interesting words, turns of phrase, and syntactical twists that the computer, in its linguistic innocence, has come up with. You might need to run a number of passages through the machine to generate a nice, workable cache of oddities—ones that you could put in the voice of character who isn't a native speaker of English.

7. Using this material, write a monologue in the style of, say, Jonathan Safran Foer's Eastern European taxi driver in *Everything Is Illuminated*. Next, try writing a third-person scene, using the nonstandard usages in the dialogue of one or more characters. You may, of course, add to any of this what you already know about "foreignisms" in English (Spanish, for example, doesn't stick to subject-verb-object syntax as strictly as does English, which can lead to some interesting constructions). You can also get a dictionary of idioms and colloquialisms in a foreign language, and instead of using the definitions there, translate the idioms literally, looking up the words in a regular dictionary. (For example, the idioms dictionary might blandly define *Aquí solo mis chicharrones truenan* as "I'm the boss here," but your literal definition would read, "Only my cracklings crackle around here!") Conversely, your speaker could struggle with colloquial English and the ensuing malapropisms

("When the other shoe falls, we'll wear it!"). But I'll stop now with the examples; I don't want to pour too much cream on the tacos.

Many writers struggle to render into some kind of English the speech or thought of nonnative speakers—Hemingway, for example, produced some notoriously stilted passages. Cormac McCarthy, on the other hand, doesn't even try—he just plugs in the Spanish, unitalicized at that, and lets the reader deal with it. But others, like Foer, have risen to the challenge and created whole, book-length characters from the problem, with felicitous results. This exercise is useful for creating such characters, and for exploring how nonnative speakers go about mapping the realities reflected by their own language onto the realities presented by the new language. It can teach a lot about how different languages fragment the world in different ways.

A DIALOGUE EXERCISE

THIS EXERCISE MIGHT BE DONE BY JUST ONE PERSON, BUT it can be more productive with two people trading found conversations with one another. To complete it you must go to an area where people are talking freely on their cell phones: a coffee shop, the mall, the line at the grocery store. You are looking for a conversation with a bit of substance to it—not just "Hi! How are you?" Instead, you want something where you can detect an edge of some sort, perhaps the sneaky furthering of some agenda. I happen to teach at a university, so such edgy conversations aren't hard to find. (Hint for college students: your commons area can be a gold mine!) Obviously this edge will vary, but it's nonetheless essential; the edge is the conflict, and without a sense of it the exercise will flop.

A tape recorder can be handy here, though, depending on the site, you might be able to use shorthand. (Hint: it's easier to write in a notebook in a coffee shop; it's tough to power walk through the Montebello Town Center in pursuit of your subject, scribbling on a clipboard the entire way.) Once you've found a juicy conversation, the goal becomes writing everything down verbatim, precisely as it is said to the other person on the telephone. Include all the pauses, the *umm*s, and the *like*s. (While the days of the Valley Girl are long over, *like* still tends to be, like, common around here.) Also take note of any mannerisms that your speaker—let's call her "Subject A"—exhibits as she speaks. Does she stomp around? Does she look disinterestedly at the things in her purse? Does she seem to mimic the voice of the person speaking to her? You should try to have enough for an eventual page or maybe a page and a half of typed material.

Go home and transcribe the one-sided dialogue as you would for a scene in a story, starting a new paragraph for each new statement:

> "I don't know what you want to eat."
> "No, really, I don't know."
> "Uh, if I knew I would tell you."

THE EXERCISE

With this raw material on the page, you should find that a sense of character has started to emerge, both for the speaker and for the unseen person on the other end of the line. Their personalities, their characters, will be suggested by the way the conversation goes. If after five minutes someone is yelling into her cell phone about hating sushi, odds are that sushi is the least of that person's immediate worries.

At any rate, the goal is to imagine this real-life person in a room with another imagined person, who will provide the second half of the conversation. Where you place them is up to you. What the other imagined person says is also up to you, so long as it follows the template set up by Subject A.

"I don't know what you want to eat," he said.

"You don't?" she asked. "Really?"

"If I knew I'd tell you."

"If you were paying attention, then I wouldn't have to tell you."

At this point you might modify the *umm*s and the *like*s if they don't seem germane to the scene taking shape (odds are that they won't).

The conversation should also begin to take on some more fictional qualities. You might add some description, maybe a flash of interiority.

"I don't know what you want to eat," he said.

"You don't?" she asked. She twisted her napkin into a tight white ball. "Really?"

He tried to recall what she'd said but came up empty. "If I knew I'd tell you."

"If you were paying attention, then I wouldn't have to tell you."

Combining the real with the imagined can be a quick way to illustrate that dialogue in fiction does not have to be the same as that in real life. This can be a tough principle to accept, particularly for the enthusiastic novice. Nevertheless, to have a productive conversation on the page, the writer will have to trim away the odds and ends. I've found that comparing the original transcribed material to the finished draft of the exercise drives this point home.

It may seem ironic that I'm advocating this idea, since I'm probably the last person in southern California who doesn't own a cellular phone. But with so much information floating around out there, we might as well put some of it to productive use.

DESCRIPTIVE LANGUAGE
and
SETTING

ON DESCRIPTIVE LANGUAGE AND SETTING

She would also remember the blood-soaked shoe; the exact detail of the shoe would always lead her to remember the leg.

—John Irving, *A Widow for One Year*

When you depict sad or unlucky people, and want to touch the reader's heart, try to be colder—it gives their grief, as it were, a background. . . . Yes, you must be cold.   —Anton Chekhov

Words set up atmospheres, electrical fields, charges. I've felt them doing it. Words conjure.   —Toni Cade Bambara

IMMEDIATELY, I CAN RECALL THE TODDLER'S JESTER HAT from Tom Perrotta's *Little Children,* and the Apache warrior cresting the hill in a woman's bloodstained wedding gown in Cormac McCarthy's *Blood Meridian.* And there's the drive-in movie speakers, originally and heartbreakingly mistaken by the narrator for grave markers, in Denis Johnson's *Jesus' Son,* and that single whisker on Zoe's chin in Lorrie Moore's "You're Ugly, Too." I remember growing hungry—famished, actually—upon reading how the narrator in Haruki Murakami's *The Wind-up Bird Chronicle* prepares spaghetti. (And, thus, the power of literature, of perfect description: despite my having not read the book in years *and* my having eaten less than an hour ago, my stomach literally—*literally*—just growled and I've decided to have spaghetti for dinner.) There's more, instantly accessible: the blue parrots on Bailey's yellow shirt in "A Good Man Is Hard to Find," the unrelenting sunlight and omnipresent electric fence in Cynthia Ozick's devastating story "The Shawl," the fog that envelops Dickens's *Bleak House,* the green overall buckles in Alice Walker's "The Flowers," the desolate Sahara of Paul Bowles's *The Sheltering Sky.* With each of these snatches of memory and image, my mind slides into the contours of the narratives themselves: the story arcs, the characters, the tone, and even how each image made me *feel* upon my first reading; it's all there, fully and suddenly formed by the recollection of a single telling detail.

This palliative response is, of course, what Proust so stunningly renders in *In Search of Lost Time,* and it's what each of us has encountered at various unexpected moments in our own lives: on a crowded subway, you smell the cologne of a long-gone lover and it leaves you weightless with nostalgic desire. Or you happen upon a radio station playing a song you've not heard in decades and suddenly you're back in the carefree, sun-dappled days of childhood. Or you pass someone wearing the plaid shirt your father used to wear and you long to hear his voice, or you remember where you were the exact moment you learned he'd died. Or, despite his death, you pass the person wearing his plaid shirt and you hear his voice for the rest of the afternoon. Stated another way: the route to a reader's heart is through her senses.

This argument makes theoretical sense, but in practice writers often defer to reason and declaration rather than trust the subtleties of sensuality. To affect us, though, to *move* us, you must make us feel, not *think* about feeling. Don't describe the wine-dark sea; drop your readers into the middle of it. Show us those heaving waves and the gulls hovering like kites and the ocean spray that feels more like sand than water. Which is not to say that the key to creating setting or to writing sharp, dynamic descriptions is to heap on adjectives and adverbs. In fact, the goal is often to locate the solitary detail that will instantly open up the narrative universe and then to move on; you want to find the exact song that will recall the reader's childhood without forcing her to listen to the jukebox's entire catalog. No small task, that. And it's just as mercurial whether you're writing fiction or nonfiction, whether you have memories to consult or whether you're making up the story (and characters and setting and aforementioned universe) with each word.

The problem is that the relationship between writer and reader is far more complex and fragile than many of us think. It's not, this relationship, a dry and impersonal transaction whereby the author simply deposits an indelible and absolute image into the reader's mind. The most affecting descriptive writing results from an author's providing not a linguistic blueprint of a library but the raw material (the air tinged with the scent of old pages, the shafts of dusty light diffused through window slats, the whispers, like trickling water, of the librarians behind the oval reference desk) from which the reader can erect her own library. Appeal to our senses, and we, your readers, will complete the story.

This active collaboration in the creative process is what distinguishes reading from, say, watching the boob tube—that epitome of a dry, impersonal transaction—and it requires that authors trust their audience as unconditionally as the audience trusts the authors. Such trust is born from a sense of inevitability, as opposed to indulgence, within the writing, and a kind of tacit assurance, from writer to reader, that neither her time nor her attention is being squandered by lyrical window dressing or throat clearing. That is, don't give the reader laundry lists of images—at best, she'll skim pages until she sees some dialogue; at worst, she'll close the book and reach for the remote. Instead, give her prose that evokes the strange beauty of lived life.

Whether you're describing how a character boils spaghetti or a child's silly hat or the long midday shadows over a field, the aim is to create what John Gardner famously called a "vivid and continuous" dream in the reader's mind. This work requires that your language and imagery be neither vague nor trite nor flashy; what's more, the prose cannot be—and this is exceptionally difficult to swallow—so exquisite that it impedes the reader from proceeding to the next sentence. Tempting as it seems, the goal is never to make the reader stop and marvel at this gorgeous simile or that perfect analogy; rather, the challenge—the fundamental imperative—is to create such fluid and truthful and seamless prose that the reader can't *stop* reading.

In practical terms, descriptive writing introduces and sustains the physical world and emotional tone of a scene or story; it establishes when and where the action happens, and through carefully chosen details, the setting and imagery usher the reader into the narrative locale. The details create the atmosphere, both thematic and topographical, and they implicitly promise either to deliver the reader to a physical and/or emotional place she's never visited or to shine a surprising and authenticating light on those places she most keenly knows. Description and setting, like plot, cannot be divorced from the particular characters within a narrative: each is an extension of the other. If a story would unfold in Costa Rica just as it would in Siberia, then the author hasn't yet fully developed the characters or their environs. Try imagining Huck and Jim floating down the Rio Grande or the Amazon and the novel *not* being changed. What if it were, say, Gatsby's massive baseball card collection, rather than his beautiful imported shirts, that brought Daisy to tears? What if the Red Tent were the Purple Guesthouse?

The exercises in this section lay out a variety of techniques that will draw the reader into the specific world of your story. Because the biggest traps within descriptive writing are a lack of precision in the language and an authorial tendency to arbitrarily include details rather than letting imagery evolve from the characters, many of the following exercises work to ensure that your descriptions are integral to the narrative itself. The authors here offer practical ways to weave imagery into dramatized scenes (as opposed to always relying on those easily and often skipped long paragraphs of descriptions), to evoke settings that form and inform your character's internal lives, and to use the odd and unexpected detail to gain the reader's confidence, to move them, to leave them hungry for more.

Sarah Shun-lien Bynum

DESTROYING WHAT YOU LOVE:
AN EXERCISE IN SETTING

I OFTEN FIND MYSELF GAZING AT MY ONE-YEAR-OLD DAUGHTER and dreaming about the many ways she might fulfill my own un-realized hopes (she will play the electric guitar! she will have a lightning-fast metabolism!), and as a writing teacher, I have a ten-dency to regard my students with the same wistful and expectant air. I want very much for them to become adept in precisely the areas where I am most lacking.

One of those is setting, the necessary matter of when and where. As a young writer, I couldn't be bothered with all that com-monplace information! Time, locale, weather, geography, histori-cal period—it seemed a tedious bit of business to get through. Why describe those things when you could rely on the miraculous process of osmosis instead? The reader should *intuit* the setting, without the writer's dwelling on the dreary facts of time and place like a newspaper reporter.

And so, repeating this questionable logic to myself, I neglected a wonderful element of fiction. It languished and rusted in my proverbial toolbox. My characters moved about in blank apart-ments, nameless towns, and indeterminate eras; they occupied a landscape without discernible seasons or features. Certainly one can argue that the absence of setting may act as a compelling environment in and of itself. But I wasn't avoiding setting as a bold aesthetic choice; I simply lacked the confidence and discipline to identify the physical surroundings in which my stories were taking place.

A revelation for me was the idea that setting isn't merely a practicality, a means of conveying dull yet essential information—setting also does the thrilling work of conveying *emotion*. Nowhere is this better illustrated than in Denis Johnson's novella "Train Dreams." Absolutely particular with regard to time and place—it spans one man's life, from 1886 to 1968, and occurs around the Idaho Panhandle—"Train Dreams" is a story where setting proves more riveting and more dynamic than even plot or character. Every description is alive, shot through with wonder and yearning.

A passage that is especially poignant to me describes the small cabin where the main character once lived with his wife and daughter. While he is away building bridges for the railways, his family and home are lost in a terrible fire. Years after the fact, he has a vision of his burning house: the moss on the roof curling and smoking, the logs in the walls popping like cartridges, the pages of a magazine spiraling upward, the cabin's one glass window shattering. The curtains begin to blacken at the hems, the wax melts off the jars of tomatoes, beans, and Canada cherries. He imagines all the lamps alight, and a metal-lidded jar of salt exploding, until finally the whole structure ignites.

The density of historical detail here astonishes. With this single image we understand what life was like in one of the last remaining corners of American wilderness in the early twentieth century. The cabin is spare, rough-hewn, isolated, and most likely dark, yet the small, determined gestures toward comfort—window curtains, preserved cherries, a magazine resting on the table—make it unmistakably a home. And though the passage's tone is perfectly straightforward, the choice of detail moves us as we watch these objects go up in flames. Everything is animated. The power of setting lies, perhaps, in this alchemy of action and emotion. If we saw this world in stasis, would we feel as keenly how dear and hard-won this home was, and also how precarious, how contingent? This description does more than tell us about the Idaho Panhandle in 1920; it tells us about the experience of loss.

THE EXERCISE

Describe a place you love by detailing its destruction. Or describe, as Denis Johnson does, a place your character loves. Nature could be the destructive force—fire or flood or the ravages of weather—but feel free to interpret the idea of destruction broadly. Consider the erosion of neglect and poverty, or the damage that comes with discovery, or the harm that's done in the name of improvement. Your setting could be anything from a hurricane-torn backyard to a city block that's being gentrified. My hope is that the parameters of the exercise will offer—even for those who, like me, are tentative writers of setting—a foolproof means of generating descriptions rich with both movement and feeling.

A STRANGER COMES TO TOWN

FICTIONAL SETTINGS ARE NOT SIMPLY PAINTED CANVASES in front of which the actors move: setting can be *action*. A character whose story is taking place in a familiar setting is going to behave differently from a character who finds himself far from home. I'm thinking of a story like Alice Munro's "The Jack Randa Hotel," in which a woman follows her ex-husband and his new wife to Australia. There she moves into an apartment and, disguised as someone else, begins sending him angry letters. The strangeness of the setting (and yet it's a perfectly ordinary neighborhood in Brisbane) allows the main character, Gail, to say things to her husband she never dared say before. She is a stranger there to everyone, including herself.

This is an exercise I give to students who seem to have difficulty with settings that are very familiar to them—their hometowns, their suburbs, their neighborhoods. The idea is to make the familiar as specific as possible, and then make it strange.

THE EXERCISE

1. Draw a diagram of a major town or street in your story. Include as much detail as possible: the styles of houses or

apartment buildings, the types of trees and flowers, the species of fish swimming in the lake. Don't worry about whether or not it's an authentic detail; if you're not sure about something, make it up. Mark the places on the diagram where important or interesting events occurred. Choose the most interesting event and write a paragraph describing the event from the point of view of someone native to the town.

2. Choose a house in that town or on that street that will be of major importance in your story. Draw a diagram of it, again including as much detail as possible: the pictures on the walls, the dishes in the sink, the items in boxes in the attic. Mark the places on the diagram where something interesting or important occurred. Choose one event and write a paragraph describing it in detail from the perspective of someone living in the house.

3. Choose a room in the house that is of particular importance to your story. Draw a diagram of it, again including as much detail as possible: the clothes in the closet, the items in a drawer, the secret compartment where a diary is hidden. Describe one important event that occurs in the room from the point of view of its occupant.

4. Now introduce a stranger into the story, and describe the town, the house, and the room from the point of view of someone seeing it all for the first time. How does this person look at everything differently? What does he or she see that a native resident does not, positive and negative?

5. Finally, introduce the native resident to the stranger and write the conversation between the two.

At the end of this exercise you are likely to have the beginnings of a story: setting, characters, and conflict. From this point the story can progress into action: What do the characters *do* as a result of their conversation? If each person we meet is a new place we've been, then both characters will have just been somewhere interesting, and nothing will be the same for either of them again.

Jonathan Liebson

THE MONSTER IN THE ATTIC

EVEN LESS EXPERIENCED FICTION WRITERS SEEM TO KNOW that the use of description depends largely on an individual writer's style. Anyone who's dabbled with Hemingway recognizes easily enough his flatter, more straightforward descriptions and how they differ, for example, from the elaborate landscapes of such writers as Annie Proulx or Cormac McCarthy. To illustrate, just compare the beginning of Hemingway's classic story "Big Two-Hearted River" with the opening of Proulx's "The Unclouded Day":

> The train went on up the track out of sight, around one of the hills of burnt timber. Nick sat down on the bundle of canvas and bedding the baggage man had pitched out of the door of the baggage car. There was no town, nothing but the rails and the burned-over country. [Hemingway]

> It was a rare thing, a dry, warm spring that swelled into summer so ripe and full that gleaming seed bent the grass low a month before its time; a good year for grouse. When the season opened halfway through September, the heat of summer still held, dust lay like yellow flour on the roads, and the perfume

of decay came from the thorned mazes where blackberries fell and rotted on the ground. [Proulx]

What's immediately apparent here is the greater simplicity of Hemingway—his lack of extra words to describe—as compared with Proulx's plentiful adjectives and her use of figures of speech ("dust lay like yellow flour"). But if younger writers are capable of identifying these distinctions, they may not as readily notice an all-important similarity. In each passage, despite their differing styles, the role of description still serves a common purpose. The external landscape acts as a mirror for the internal life of the characters in the story. Take Hemingway's Nick Adams, a young man returned from war and trying his best to shut out all emotions and memories that might be painful or complicated. Thus the stripped-down descriptions of northern Michigan, which seem perfectly suited to someone who finds little or no meaning left in the world. By contrast, in the above as well as in other of Proulx's stories, the wilder, more exotic impulses of her characters always seem to correspond with—if not get fed by—the exotic surroundings they constantly inhabit.

Here's another way to think about it: every character has a lens through which he looks at the world. That lens is a two-way viewfinder: to the outside world itself—but also to their inner soul. Thus, to the degree to which a writer understands those emotions, he'll not just identify *what* his character sees but *how* those things actually look to him (simple and unadorned for Hemingway, lush and untamed for Proulx).

THE EXERCISE

To appreciate this concept, describe your least favorite room in your childhood home. Take about ten minutes and write a good paragraph's worth. After you've finished, read on.

———

The trick of this exercise is that you're already starting with an emotion. The words "least favorite room" should provoke dislike, or remind you of some place you find distasteful, and the fact that it is in your childhood home should put you in touch with feelings your adult self might not admit to. When I ask my students to perform this exercise, here's what usually happens: regardless of what room they choose, they tend to put down on paper their impressions of this room—that is, their feelings toward it, as opposed to what the room actually looks like. I have no doubt that, in their own minds, my students have a vivid picture of that room; probably, they have at least three or four crucial details tattooed on their brains. However, what they write most often looks like this:

> I never liked going down to the basement. It was a creepy place, cold and dark and awful. Every time I walked down the stairs a shiver ran down my spine, and I always dreaded whenever I was forced to run some errand for my mother. . . .

Perhaps this is a reflex in the young writer. It is easier to convey how they feel in that basement than to show us the basement itself. But think about yourselves as readers: it's one thing to believe a character you read about is creeped out; it's another thing for you, the reader, to be creeped out as well. As writers, the latter is what we aspire to. We want our readers to experience what our characters are experiencing; we want them to feel as if they're looking right over our characters' shoulders, as if they're right there in the basement with them.

Look back at your own paragraph now. Try to identify how much of it is dedicated to your feelings about the room versus what actually reveals the room itself. In the above passage, the only physical words are *cold* and *dark*. Clichéd or not, they still give the writer a starting point. Consider the rest of the paragraph a throat clearing. In your own paragraph, try to highlight whatever words appeal to the five senses: sight, sound, smell, taste, and touch. Then put a line through all nonsensory (nonphysical) words. You may be left with only a couple of sentences, or even just a few descriptions, but it still may surprise you how much work these sensory words actually get done by themselves.

If, however, you have only one or two words, as in the example above, start a new paragraph entirely. This time, don't use the first-person "I." Think of yourself as the camera operator now, not the narrator. No voice-over; no direct thoughts. All you're allowed to do is describe what the lens sees, or what the microphone (or your nose) picks up. Do this, then come back again and read on.

This time you probably came up with a greater physical sense of the place itself. For myself, remembering my own childhood basement, I picture the island of brown water stains on the ceiling tiles. Between the washer and dryer there's an inch of dust impossible to sweep out with a broom; in the corner sits an old charcoal sofa with loud springs, while the closet door opens forbiddingly upon a row of weathered old coats, guarding the pull chain to an out-of-reach fluorescent light.

Just for fun, I also tried this exercise with my childhood attic, but it turns out I had less to say about it. And it's no wonder: I was always too afraid to go up there.

DeWitt Henry

SIMULTANEOUS ACTIONS IN FICTION

HERE IS A PRONOUNCEMENT BY A CRITIC: "LANGUAGE cannot convey non-verbal experience; being successive and linear, it cannot express simultaneous experiences; being composed of separate and divisible units it cannot reveal the unbroken flow of the process of living. Reality cannot be expressed or conveyed—only the illusion of it" (A. A. Mendilow, *Time and the Novel,* London, 1952).

In fact, English does have the resources to express simultaneous experiences. For instance, the Middle English Arthurian poem *Sir Gawain and the Green Knight* is structured to counterpoint the lord of the castle's hunting and the lady of the castle's attempt to seduce Gawain back in his chamber. Note how the verbs begin in definite past tense, then subtly change to continuous past tense, distancing the lord's action and freezing it in dynamic stasis; then how we slide back to continuous past, and from that to definite past describing Gawain's perspective:

Hunters after them HASTENED with horns
So loud in their sharp burst of sound as TO SUNDER
The cliffs. What creatures ESCAPED from the shooters,

HUNTED and HARRIED from heights to the water,
WERE PULLED down and RENT at the places there ready;
Such skill the men showed at these low-lying stations,
So great were the greyhounds that quickly they got them
And DRAGGED them down, fast the folk there might look
        At the sight.
    Carried with bliss away,
    The lord DID OFT ALIGHT,
    Oft GALLOP; so that day
    He PASSED till the dark night.

THUS FROLLICKED the lord on the fringe of the forest,
And Gawain the good in his gay bed REPOSED,
LYING snugly, TILL sunlight shone on the walls,
'Neath a coverlet bright with curtains about it.
As softly he SLUMBERED, a slight sound he HEARD
At his door, made with caution, and quickly it opened.
The hero HEAVED up his head from the clothes;
By a corner he CAUGHT UP the curtain a little,
And GLANCED out with head to behold what had
   happened.
The lady it was, most lovely TO LOOK AT,
Who SHUT the door after her stealthily, slyly,
And TURNED toward the bed . . .

Compare the simultaneously actions in these sentences by Bernard
Malamud from *The Fixer* (he is deliberately imitating Russian syntax, of course):

A butcher HOLDING up by its thick yellow feet a
SQUAWKING hen BEATING its wings SAW the wagon
GO BY and SAID something witty to his customers. One of

these, a young woman who TURNED TO LOOK, CALLED to Yakov, but BY THEN the wagon was out of the market-place, SCATTERING some chickens NESTING in the ruts of the road and a flock of JABBERING ducks, AS IT CLAT-TERED ON.

THE EXERCISE

Imagine two lovers parting in a crowded, public place such as a train station. The leave-taking is all consuming to the lovers, but is counterpointed by surrounding actions that they are indifferent to. Think of ten or fifteen typical actions, such as: (1) a blind woman whose dog is being teased by a child; (2) a mother scolding the child for teasing the dog; (3) porters rolling carts of luggage in and out; (4) a team of Irish clog dancers performing; or (5) food vendors cooking everything from pizza to chow mein. Now portray the blur of these actions, in prose, centering on the lovers' parting.

Imitating the passages above, look to *verbs* (including the full conjugation of tenses, definite and progressive); *adverbial conjunctions* (e.g., *as, meanwhile, while, during, when, still*); *punctuation* (e.g., semicolon, dash, parentheses), and *gerunds* (participles used as an adjective or noun). Also note as verbal conditions: alternating focus, cross-references, vivid contrast between actions, and emphatic unity of time.

The implicit lessons here are (1) that theoretical or descriptive "rules" about art ought to provoke writers to a kind of "oh, yeah?"; (2) that all art brings reality to mind, rather than presenting reality; and (3) that students need to explore the resources of grammar and punctuation in the complex English sentence.

Mark Winegardner

LEARNING TO LIE:
AN EXERCISE IN DETAILS

FICTION WRITERS MUST BE, OR LEARN TO BE, GOOD LIARS. Specific, definite, concrete details are, as every good liar knows, the stuff of persuasiveness. They are also the lifeblood of fiction: proofs, actually, like those in a statistical argument or a geometric theorem. If you write in abstractions or judgments, you are writing an essay. If you let us use our senses and do our own generalizing and interpreting, we will be participants in your story—and then you'll have us. Fiction writers *must* deal in details that come from the senses, and those must be details that matter. "Significant detail" Janet Burroway calls it in her landmark textbook *Writing Fiction,* referring to the sort of detail that means both what it says and also *more* than what it says. If you want to write fiction, you must not merely say what you mean (a big job, actually) but mean more than you say (easier than it sounds, if you can get out of your own way).

THE EXERCISE

Below is a bit of inept fiction writing. Revise, using significant detail, so that the passage shows rather than tells, dramatizes rather than summarizes. As you do so, strive to avoid clichés and stereotypes. Make sure that your revision of this is no shorter than two hundred words and no longer than four hundred. Once you've completed the revision, read the note following the original text below.

> When Mr. and Mrs. Stillwell got to the rural doctor's office, there was only one chair left. This made Mrs. Stillwell angry, although she considered herself too much of a lady to let on. She and Arlen were white, middle-class, and in their early sixties. She was a very fat and extremely self-satisfied woman who believed that life had certain rules which well-bred people follow and who, though she was genial enough not to be unlikable, was very judgmental and condescending to everyone. Also, though she was somewhat unaware of this, she had a tendency to henpeck Arlen.
>
> Anyway, she looked for another seat in the waiting room, but the only possibility was a couch where a little boy was lying down. His parents must be very irresponsible, Mrs. Stillwell thought, or else they'd ask him to make room. So, since it was Arlen who was the one that needed to see the doctor, she told him to sit down, and he did. That was a good example of how henpecked he was.

The above passage is a mangling of the opening of Flannery O'Connor's brilliant story "Revelation." When I go over the students' revisions, I discuss several—making sure there are a few good ones—before my, um, revelation of the source of this passage (and the terrible things I did to it). The point isn't to show that there's a "right" answer to this exercise, of course. O'Connor's opening is a wonder, but it's a mildly unorthodox wonder, one that gets away with things like calling Mrs. Turpin "very large" because of the rhythm of the sentence and the joke created thereby in also calling the waiting room "very small." O'Connor also had a way of writing expository prose at the beginnings of her stories that allows the reader to hear what the characters sound like before they ever open their mouths: a dazzling and surprisingly stealable signature technique, but surely an unorthodox one, too. The point is that O'Connor's stellar opening is only one path to excellent writing; the students will have come up with a few more (a confidence builder for the class, even those students who bollixed this). I typically use this exercise very early in the term, often during the first week. Thus one of its other virtues is that it gets them thinking about revision from day one.

Feel free to rewrite and constructively mangle other masterly passages of fiction. I've done this with several other stories, and the task always teaches me something, though the means are admittedly perverse.

Nick Arvin

ARTISTIC PERSPECTIVE

OVER TIME I FIND MYSELF TURNING MORE AND MORE often to the other arts for ideas I can carry into my writing. Geoff Dyer's book about photography, *The Ongoing Moment,* was particularly helpful in this way, and I'd recommend it to any writer looking for a jolt of creative energy. Here is an example: Dyer discusses three photographs of picket fences. The first, a black-and-white photograph taken in 1916 by Paul Strand, is a simple, straight-on view of a weather-beaten fence. It is considered, Dyer says, one of the central images of photography as art, described by one critic as the "locus classicus for the subsequent development of the main tradition of American photography." The second is a black-and-white photograph of a picket fence by Michael Ormerod (this photo is undated, but it was taken sometime after the Strand photo). The obvious difference between the two photos is that this second picket fence is broken. Because of the stature of Strand's image within the world of photography, when Ormerod created his photo he must have been aware, on some level, of Strand's. Thus, while Ormerod's photo is only a photo of a broken fence, it is also a commentary on Strand's photo, and Dyer notes some of the questions raised by it: "Is Ormerod suggesting, therefore, that the photographic tradition initiated by Strand has been broken? Or that the tradition is resilient enough to accommodate all manner of internal ruptures and revolutions?" Because of its historical relationship to Strand's photo, Dyer says, "the photo raises these questions without even asking them." The third photograph of a picket fence was taken in 1976 by Joel Meyerowitz, one of the pioneers of artistic color photography. In this photo the viewer's position is inside, or behind, the fence, and this, too, can be read as a commentary on the Strand photo. "By photographing the fence from behind—from the opposite side of the fence to Strand—Meyerowitz declares that there is now another way of looking at what makes a photograph."

What does this have to do with writing? Well, any number of things, probably, but what it caused me to think about is how these photos provide a visual illustration of a problem that writers face all the time, which is that a story line and its elements will always elicit comparisons to other, previously told stories. (The most reductionist view that I have encountered is that there are, at root, only two types of stories: journey stories and stranger-comes-to-town stories. And one can see that even these two are merely opposite sides of one thing. Very quickly, then, every story becomes a variation of every other story.) Readers inevitably interpret their reading in the light of what they have read before, and whether we like it or not, on some level our stories will always be read as variations of and commentaries upon other stories. And, as writers, we have a responsibility to find a viewpoint (as must a photographer, aiming a viewfinder) that is fresh, that offers something new. It is in this way that we join into the centuries-spanning conversation of literature (and, more broadly, art). It is also one of the reasons why we should read as widely as possible.

Thus, how a character's journey (for example) works as a reflection of and complement to *The Odyssey* is a real problem for a writer. This can be intimidating, but it can also be inspiring. It worked out great for James Joyce in *Ulysses,* and Shakespeare seems to have stolen practically every story line he wrote from someone else.

THE EXERCISE

For the purposes of this exercise we need to simplify the problem somewhat. Read and consider the passage below by James Agee, which is about overalls. Imagine that this is the definitive statement in prose about overalls, the writing about overalls to which all other writing about overalls will be compared, and then try to write a short, descriptive passage about overalls, thinking about how you can write about them in a way that might be considered a commentary on or reaction to Agee's passage. For example, what might be implied if the overalls described are broken, torn? Or what might it mean to write about overalls from "behind"? To write them in "color"?

From *Let Us Now Praise Famous Men* by James Agee:

They are pronounced overhauls.

Try—I cannot write of it here—to imagine and to know, as against other garments, the difference of their feeling against your body; drawn-on, and bibbed on the white belly and chest, naked from the kidneys up behind, save for broad crossed straps, and slung by these straps from the shoulders; the slanted pockets on each thigh, the deep square pockets on each buttock; the complex and slanted structures, on the chest, of the pockets shaped for pencils, rulers, and watches, the coldness of sweat when they are young, and their stiffness; their sweetness to the skin and pleasure of sweating when they are old; the thin metal buttons of the fly; the lifting aside of the straps and the deep slipping downward in defecation; the belt some men use with them to steady their middles; the swift, simple, and inevitably supine gestures of dressing and of undressing, which, as is less true of any other garment, are those of harnessing and of unharnessing the shoulders of a tired and hard-used animal.

They are round as stovepipes in the legs (though some wives, told to, crease them).

In the strapping across the kidneys they again resemble work harness, and in their crossed straps and tin buttons.

And in the functional pocketing of their bib, a harness modified to the convenience of a used animal of such high intelligence that he has use for tools.

ALL ABOUT RHYTHM

Style is a very simple matter; it is all about rhythm. Once you get that,
you can't use the wrong words. . . . Now this is very profound, what
rhythm is, and goes far deeper than words. A sight, an emotion creates
this wave in the mind, long before it makes words to fit it.

I CAME UPON THIS QUOTATION FROM ONE OF VIRGINIA Woolf's letters a few years back. I circled it, came back to it again. I typed it out and found myself quoting it, days later, to the students in my fiction workshop. Woolf seemed to say something I'd been trying to articulate to myself as a writer and teacher of writing for years: what exactly happens on those very rare and heated occasions when it feels as if the work's coming from some source outside us, unbidden? I don't think we're talking about latching onto a vocabulary of interrelated, idiosyncratic details, though that may be part of it. I don't think it's simply about coming to know one's characters so fully that they begin to take on independent lives, though that may be a part of it too. It seems to me that that sense of supreme immersion might have something to do with matters of rhythm—or, more precisely, finding a rhythm that matches the meaning of the drama. A rhythm that is not decorative or distracting but crucial—the crucial music that makes a piece of fiction sing. Of course this is something that can't be willed into being. Talk to any poet and she'll assure you of that. (Which is probably why poets, unlike fiction writers, might be more sporadic creators than we are—we poor, poor fiction writers, with our chair-bound work ethic. I wonder what the interrelationship is between rhythm and the condition we typically describe as "inspiration.") Still, how can we bring one of the central tools of the poet to our work and be more deeply aware of pauses, sentence length, stops, even alliteration and assonance in the prose we read and write? Not to will the mannered into being, but to open ourselves up to our own rhythms—the patterns of our everyday speech, the quirkiness of the way we move and walk—and to carry those over to the lives of our invention.

THE EXERCISE

Take a paragraph by a writer whose work has been important to you. Type it out once. Then type it again. Once you've done that, substitute your own noun for each noun, your own verb for each verb. Replace all the adjectives and adverbs. Play with it for a few days. Then do another version. If you're lucky you might have the beginnings of a story. Or, at the least, a more intimate sense of that writer's rhythms.

EMOTION IN FICTION

ONE OF THE MAIN AMBITIONS OF ART IS TO DEPICT AND evoke emotion. By the end of a story or a novel, we hope that both characters and readers will have felt something: pleasure, sorrow, amazement, curiosity, awe, humility, fear, trepidation, intellectual satisfaction, humor, the delight of solving a problem or of understanding how this particular world works, whatever we call that emotion summoned forth by beauty. But how to do this in the twenty-first century is a challenge.

Two ferocious dragons guard the source of true feeling: sentimentality and frigidity. Sentimentality is the too easy expression of excessive or obvious emotion; frigidity is when neither author nor characters seem to care sufficiently; see, for example, the way murders are typically presented in thrillers. In both cases the reader feels no incentive to experience an emotion. Why should readers care if someone else is feeling too much or too little? And if we manage to negotiate these two dragons then there is a third one to slay: cliché. So much has been written and sung about the emotions that many of our most common phrases—her heart leapt, his eyes filled with tears—can be used only with the utmost awareness and caution.

Writers have been aware of this dilemma for some time. Chekhov admonished his brother in a letter to use details and beware of commonplaces. "Best of all is to avoid depicting the hero's state of mind; you ought to make it clear from the hero's action." And in 1919 T. S. Eliot famously claimed that emotion could no longer be expressed directly: "The only way of expressing emotion in the form of art is by finding an 'objective correlative'; in other words, a set of objects, a situation, a chain of events which shall be the formula of that *particular* emotion; such that when the external facts, which must terminate in sensory experience, are given, the emotion is immediately evoked" ("Hamlet and His Problems").

So what is to be done? One strategy is to withhold depicting or commenting on obvious emotion, and again we see writers experimenting with this for well over a hundred years. Kleist, Lermontov, and Robbe-Grillet all resolutely avoid the statement, and sometimes even the depiction, of emotion. This can work wonderfully well but only, I think, if it is obvious that emotion is being withheld—as, for instance, in Hemingway's famous story "Hills Like White Elephants." If the reader doesn't intuit the buried emotion, this kind of withholding turns into frigidity.

Another strategy is to surprise the reader. Your heroine comes home to find an eviction notice on the door. Don't have her burst into tears or swear. Have her laugh or use the notice to line the bottom of her parrot's cage. Flannery O'Connor claimed that at the heart of a story lies some action or gesture quite unlike any other in the story. "This would have to be an action or gesture which was both totally right and totally unexpected," she said. "It would have to be one that was both in character and beyond character; it would have to suggest both the world and eternity."

A third strategy is to find a new way of describing familiar emotions, or to find an action that conveys how the character feels. As writers, our primary tool for creating emotion is language, which is to say that in writing we need to take account of both the connotation and the denotation of words and also to be aware of how the rhythm of our prose conveys meaning. Our secondary tools are action, dialogue, gestures, setting, narration, and exposition. Clearly how expression is conveyed in fiction depends on the voice of your story.

THE EXERCISE

Take a story or a chapter you've written and choose a scene that you hope depicts and conveys emotion. Try one or several of these strategies:

1. Go through it checking for the word *feel*. Wherever possible, replace the word with something stronger and more precise. Check for clichés and obvious emotions: women crying, men being tough. Again replace with something more precise and appropriate for these particular characters. Or something more surprising.
2. Try radically overwriting the scene. Don't be afraid of purple prose, outrageous metaphors, piling on details, excess of all kinds. Reread and see what you've written that might be useful.
3. Try withholding all obvious expression of emotion. Can you signal the missing emotions in other ways—through gestures, pauses, descriptions of setting, having a character say or do something that's the opposite of what she actually feels? Imagining your characters on a stage can be helpful.
4. Follow T. S. Eliot's advice and invent an objective correlative.

REVISION

ON REVISION

Words cluster like chromosomes, determining procedure.

—Marianne Moore

I see but one rule: to be clear.   —Stendhal

I've done as many as twenty or thirty drafts of a story. Never less than ten or twelve.   —Raymond Carver

HAVE A THEORY THAT MOST (IF NOT ALL) WRITERS LOVE washing dishes. I would also submit that they love mowing lawns, raking leaves, shoveling snow. And alphabetizing the books on their shelves. And changing the oil in their cars. And running errands, folding laundry, balancing checkbooks, bathing pets, even doing taxes. My reasoning here is that washing dishes and such are self-contained, finishable tasks. That is to say, unlike with writing, you know when you're done, know when the project is unambiguously completed.

The cliché is that books are never finished; they're abandoned.

As with most clichés, there's more than a little truth here. If writers had the time, they would continue tinkering and rewriting and polishing and restructuring and revising ad nauseam, attempting to perfect the imperfectable. (Practically speaking, many writers would attest that once something is published, it's done; however, the superb writer James Salter raised the stakes on that premise when he revised two of his early novels and republished them.) Such restlessness is true of all art forms. Think of the times when you go to a concert and the band "revises" your favorite song—the guitarist changes the solo, the singer throws in a different verse, the pianist improvises a riff no one expects. Think of the recent trend in moviemaking where DVDs come with alternate endings of films, or where the film is completely overhauled as the "director's cut." Remember that there are accounts of Michelangelo breaking into St. Peter's and chiseling away at the *Pietà* after it was "finished." Remember that Hemingway rewrote the last page of *A Farewell to Arms* thirty-nine times, and when George Plimpton asked him why, he said, "Getting the words right."

In many ways, getting the words right epitomizes the writer's essential hope and challenge. Rarely, though, does this translate to simply grooming the language; yet writers often approach revision with that very limited and limiting goal. Maybe this is related to the fact that so few writing workshops or books on writing afford much attention to the "final" stage of the writing process. Such books and workshops can prove invaluable in helping a writer jump-start her work or locate blind spots where the project isn't yet reaching its potential; however, those same books and workshops might offer nothing in the way of follow-up care, the equivalent of a physician's diagnosing an aggressive and potentially fatal illness and giving the patient not a prescription for treatment but a Get Well Soon card. We've been led to believe (or lead ourselves to believe) that revision should be easy and fast. We tinker with punctuation, polish the prose, change the font, add some italics, and generally trick ourselves into believing we're revising when really we're only procrastinating.

Another theory: if the blank page is the legendary white bull that intimidates writers into not beginning, then the worded page, the sheet of paper with black spots, is the killer Dalmatian that scares writers into not finishing. Or it confuses us with its spots—that is, with our own words—and the black markings on the page mesmerize the writer until their placement seems unavoidable, unchangeable. This sense of unchangeableness is even more mesmerizing and confusing because the writer's goal is to achieve exactly that kind of linguistic and narrative inevitability. That is, we want to finish a story or essay and feel assured that not one word is misplaced, not one sentence too dinky or lax, and so it makes sense that we'd be preoccupied with getting the words right as soon as possible. Yet addressing the language is often best reserved for the very end of the revision process. (No coincidence, of course, that this is the last section of exercises in the book.) Think of it this way: What if you spend two weeks writing and polishing a four-page scene—and, yes, many publishing writers will spend that long on four pages—and then you realize (or your editor realizes) that those four pages don't belong in the book at all? They're brilliantly written, but they have no place in this narrative. Or think of it this way: You wouldn't splurge on really expensive and gorgeous carpet before you were sure the leaky roof was repaired. And you certainly wouldn't start laying the really expensive and gorgeous carpet before the foundation was poured and dry and level. Would you?

But again, it's not always so clear. Clean and lyrical and vivid and original language was what first attracted every writer to writing; when we read work by authors we admire, we respond to how smoothly and effortlessly their sentences flow, so returning to our own flabby prose is all the more embarrassing and we feel compelled to spruce up the language. And we're compelled to spruce up the language—whether we know it or not—because that job seems manageable, like washing dishes, like almost anything other than writing. Revision is messy and nonlinear and time-consuming, a harrowing period of indeterminate length wherein the writer relegates her favorite passages and scenes to the wastebasket (Nabokov claimed to go through more erasers than pencils; Capote trusted his scissors more than his pen) and wherein beautifully rendered but superfluous characters are killed off, wherein the POV shifts from first-person to third-person then back to first again, wherein your original idea for the project is consumed and supplanted by the project itself. If beginning a story or novel or memoir takes courage, finishing it takes faith.

Writers tend to begin projects with terrific bursts of vigor and enthusiasm—read: hope. Hope that this will be the easy one, the good one, the One—and because that adrenaline and momentum of newness, of creation, is addictive, it's often difficult to slow down and settle into the more concentrated and measured rhythm of revising. The writers in this section offer up the tools you'll need to begin, sustain, and finish the rewriting process. They dispel the fear—an utterly unfounded fear, I assure you, but nonetheless real and omnipresent in all writers—that even tinkering with the prose, let alone undertaking a full-scale revision, will make an already bad piece worse. And just as important, through their examples and exercises, the authors assert that revision is not a sign of bad or hopeless writing. It's not punishment. The process may be punishing, but to commit to a rewrite is never a confirmation of a narrative's failings; rather, it's a testament to the project's merit and promise.

Don Lee

THE FIRST DRAFT OF ANYTHING

THE FIRST DRAFT OF ANYTHING, HEMINGWAY ONCE SAID, is always crap—or words to that effect. But sometimes it's difficult to convince students of this. Particularly after having their stories critiqued in a couple of workshops, writers can develop a certain self-consciousness, and they might begin to hesitate during the act of composition, especially when beginning a new story or chapter. They'll berate themselves if they're not able to lay down perfect, burnished lines from the get-go, and utter rigor mortis can set in. Of course, as we all know, writing is all about the process of revision. Almost invariably, everyone's first drafts are awful. The important thing is to get the story down, figure out what you're trying to convey, just finish a rough draft.

The trick, as you're doing this, is in allowing yourself to live momentarily with your bad prose and in believing that it will be possible—in fact, relatively *easy*—to fix it later. To demonstrate, I'll give my students several examples of truly wretched writing and ask them to take a quick pass at revising them. The following passage, for instance, presents a writer who is generally trying much too hard to impress:

Her eyelids were knifed by the demented morning sun, her body jolted awake as the train shot out of the tunnel. Her nerves were still sizzling from last night, but the miles were rumbling away from her, graciously rolling the past far away from her jangled consciousness, she inhaled deeply.

"You had a nice long sleep." the man seated in the next chair snapped her back to the present, butting into her subtle contemplation. "I can never sleep on trains. The same is true for airplanes. Are you going to Montreal for vacation or business?" he viewed her with lecherous appreciation of her appearance.

"I do not think it is any of your business." She replied to the man, not caring to talk to him, "Pardon me. I want to be alone," she stood up. she sat down in a chair at the other end of the train car.

The first paragraph combines hackneyed phrasing with a passive voice (and a comma splice). The second paragraph employs an unnecessary transition and a break in point of view (and a couple of capitalization errors). The third paragraph incorporates a superfluous dialogue tag, not to mention dialogue that lacks subtext (and a few punctuation gaffes). But a few minutes of editing can salvage it into something like this:

She awoke as the train came out of the tunnel, into the morning light. Her nerves were still frayed from the previous night, yet with each mile she traveled, she felt history receding, and she was beginning to relax. She stretched her arms, arching her back.

The man in the adjacent seat watched her appreciatively. "You slept soundly," he said. "I can never sleep on trains. Planes, either. You going to Montreal for business or pleasure?"

Next he would suggest a way to combine business with pleasure. "*Désolé, je ne parle pas l'anglais,*" she said. "*Pardonnez-moi.*" She gathered her things and moved down the car to another seat.

It's not brilliant, but it's certainly better than the original. Students are always surprised by how quickly and easily they can turn a passage of absolutely putrid writing—lines that seem, at first glance, beyond repair—into something that's serviceable. I'll preach, over and over, that this is what they need to trust: It's only a rough draft. Don't worry about it. You can make it pretty later. Just write!

Here are four more miserable, god-awful passages—that read like inept translations—for students to revise themselves:

The warm wind tickled my skin, cradling me with comfort of blissful relaxation after the sterile air-conditioned cold of the hotel room as I walked through the door on the patio outside toward the languid turquoise water and silky luxury of the sand crystals cushioning my feet on the beach.

I peeled the confining clothes from my constricted existence and welcomed the freedom of the Caribbean air to cleanse my soul and buoy my excited, hopeful spirit. I was in love with Brian. I called to the sun God to send my thoughts across the glittering ocean to his office. Naked, I waded into the soothing water.

Brian, feel my desire!

Childishly Lenny snatched the bag from the sales clerk. she looked surprised. "I will never shop here again," He declared with anger. "you should know to treat me with respect. I am an important client."

The face on Monique was plastered with boredom—She had seen many disgruntled people in her retail experience. She never stooped to engage in being nice just because someone thought they could push her around. What was the point of expending her energy when this was just a summer job for pitiful money? She was thinking in her mind. Monique watches as Lenny hurriedly signs the receipt for the credit card and plucks his card away from her fingers before she can even say anything and storms out of the store in fury. She will make an excuse to her boss that it was not her fault, she did not do anything wrong, but she does not care if he believes her and decides to fire her.

The car displays its usual uncooperative personality and re-fuses to start for me. I turn the key over and over and press on the accelerator and pound the steering wheel. I hate this car. I hate this city. I hate my life. Fuming, I extract my cell phone tiredly from my pocket of my pants and try to remember the telephone number for AAA. I never have the foresight to an-ticipate these situations and prepare for emergencies like this one. My mother says I have a borderline personality. But she does not know that I have resources beyond her control. I have collected a plan in advance on the Internet to kill her tonight with an improvised explosive device. But I need to remember the telephone number for AAA first if I am able to start my blasted, frustrated, infernal car in order to drive to her house and execute my plan which guarantees to leave no trace of my whereabouts.

Flying through the air, the ball rolls off the boy's fingertips and circles the rim and lips off. Once again he is thwarted in this game. His team is one point behind, and there are ten seconds left in the state championship. He doesn't understand his deficient luck today. Ordinarily he is a star, and the audience in the ' stands, with a scout from the NBA firmly among them, is mystified as well. He must not miss this chance. He worked so hard to get to this pinnacle point in his basketball career, and this is the most important day of his young life. His grades and SATs are fruitless, and the possibility of college is a dim chance.

He bangs into the other players to wedge into position for a rebound. Today he feels dwarfed on the court. Desperately he jabs his elbow into the other team's sweaty forward. "Hey, asshole!" The forward responds grudgingly.

"Don't asshole me!" He admonishes and successfully grabs the rebound and zips down the court at full speed as he begins a fast break. Timing was everything in basketball. He knew this all his life. His every fiber knew this as instinct. But he was so aware of the importance of this game, the scout in the stands watching his every move, that his usual prowess was absent and he huffed down the gleaming parquet floor and choked as he futilely flung the ball just a precious split second too late to reach his teammate. The crowd groaned in unison at yet another mistake from their star player, their savior who was their proud son from this town that had nothing else to trumpet for pride.

John Smolens

ON THE WHEEL:
REVISING THE PERSONAL ESSAY

PERIODICALLY, I REMIND MYSELF, AND MY STUDENTS, that the literary term *essay* was coined by Michel de Montaigne in the sixteenth century, and what's important about this is that he chose the French word *essai,* which means "trial." This is really what we do when we write nonfiction: conduct a test to see what we think and feel about a given subject—we put our ideas on trial, so to speak, to see if they stand up to the laws of logic and the rigor of language. Montaigne lived at a time when it was common for a learned person to have a medal struck with an inscription that encapsulated his life's work and endeavors, and in 1576, at the age of forty-three, he had a medal created that read *Que sais-je?*—What do I know? My guess is that all the essays since Montaigne that have been entitled "On Love," "On Ambiguity," "On Boxing," and the like are, consciously or not, an homage to the writer who invented the wheel—established the literary form known as the personal essay.

Yet despite Montaigne's trailblazing, all writers must invent their own wheel. You can read all the great essays, study their linguistic subtleties, their approaches to rhetorical argument, but the fact is that when you sit down to write it is (and it should be) as though you were writing the first essay ever written. You try out an idea, creating a rough draft, which, except for the most brilliant or most fortunate, turns out to be anything but perfect. It's at this point that I—and my students—often get stuck. You get something down on paper, but you know it's not close to being finished. It's formless, bloated, sloppy; it's such a mess that at this point you question whether you'll ever attempt to write anything again. In many cases the way forward, the way toward clarity, is reduction. Take what you've got and pare it down to its essentials; determine the worth of every word and excise anything that's unnecessary. In order to demonstrate this to my students (in both fiction and non-fiction writing workshops), I give them an assignment that I call "The 80 Percent Solution."

THE EXERCISE

Write a first draft of a personal essay that is no longer than five hundred and no shorter than four hundred words.

Then write the second draft without going any longer than 80 percent of the number of words used in the first draft. (For example, a five-page essay's first draft will run no longer than four pages in the second draft.) The intention here is to provide the reader with the same experience as in the first draft, only in a more concise fashion. (This exercise is one of the few times when I think the computer's ability to provide word counts is truly beneficial.)

Here are several approaches to accomplishing the 80 percent draft:

- Be ruthless with the usual suspects, adjectives and adverbs; retain only those that are truly necessary, those that so dramatically alter the noun or verb they are modifying that the sentence would be significantly different without them.

- Take one paragraph and distill it until you've said the same thing in one sentence.
- Combine sentences (in particular, by using subordination, which often allows connecting words and entire phrases to be dropped).
- Employ the active voice as much as possible.

This exercise demonstrates the power of concise, direct prose. It may not result in a final draft, but it should give you a clearer idea of what you've said thus far. From there your true "trial" may take shape.

SILENCES AND BLANK SPACES

WHEN I FIRST STARTED WRITING, THE SPARK WAS IN that first heady scribble of words on the blue lines of my pristine notebook. Those words were precious and hard-won, and I was reluctant to cross any of them out. Not surprisingly, this habit devastated any story I tried to write. Many of my students feel a similar attachment to their first drafts, and who can blame them? To write fiction takes a kind of courage and energy that can seem magical. But, in my experience, stories come to life only when the right pieces are cut away.

I try to teach my students to see revision as more than just editing or fixing flaws, to get excited about letting things go. Here they are, pages of sentences and paragraphs and scenes, and the task is to discover the secret of the story in that text, the story's best version of itself, even if that means cutting everything except one sentence or phrase. To get to this stage, a writer needs to be writing regularly, so that he can say to himself (even if he needs to cut several pages), "Oh, well, there's more where that came from." It's also a good idea to save all the cut passages in a separate folder somewhere. Those pieces might never be used again (though they might very well be used again), but saving them makes the moment of cutting easier.

To think of the power in the unsaid, in empty space, sometimes it's useful to look at other art forms with narratives. In movies, the camera often cuts from one scene in a bedroom, say, to another scene on a city street, without an explanation of what happens in between those two moments—there is energy in that juxtaposition, and the filmmaker trusts the viewer to make the right connections. Pop songs almost always have a story, even if it's a bare minimum—"You left me, and now I'm miserable"; "I saw an ex, and remembered our love affair." Part of what makes the song catchy is its allusiveness, rhythms or images that refer to a specific situation that listeners have to imagine for themselves. Paintings that depict famous stories (for instance, the various portraits of the Annunciation, when the angel Gabriel visits Mary to tell her she is pregnant with the child of God, or Heironymus Bosch's versions of the apocalypse) include some visual details from the original story but omit others. Studying how and why certain details are included reveals much about how much information a single image can suggest.

Of course, there's a difference between juxtapositions and confusion, allusiveness and vagueness, a telling image and static description. One has to determine those boundaries. But finding the shape of any work of art is largely deciding what to leave out. And, ultimately, what's absent from a story can be as powerful as what's included—a writer's silences become part of a writer's style.

In Virginia Woolf's novel *To the Lighthouse,* the middle section, titled "Time Passes," reveals major events about the central characters—a marriage, three deaths—only through very brief, bracketed sections. Lydia Davis's stories, which tend to be no more than a few pages long, gain their resonance from their compression. She often uses very little exposition or context, so that the focus is on the rhythms of the sentences and the tensions beading up in the language. Woolf and Davis may not be creating traditional narratives, but they remind us of how blank space in a piece of writing can be eloquent and devastating.

This exercise is designed to help students see what they might accomplish in their own work by leaving something out. It also works from the premise that often the nascent story exists in one's best writing, that it may be obscured by weaker parts where the writing feels labored or wordy.

THE EXERCISE

First, take a draft of at least ten pages. Read it over once as if it were written by someone else and just by chance came to you. As honestly as possible, ask yourself, "What's the most important question this story asks?" Keep your answer in mind, even if the answer surprises you, and read the story again. As you read, trust your intuition, and work through the questions below.

1. Are there any unnecessarily repeated words or phrases? Circle them.
2. Are there any scenes that seem to impart the same information or suggest the same idea? If so, choose the one you like best and circle the other ones, or choose the best parts of each scene and circle the rest of the scene.
3. Are there any characters who seem to be serving the same purpose in the story? Two villains? Two mentors? Two best friends? If so, choose the character you think is the more vivid and compelling and circle all references to the other one.
4. Are there any scenes that seem boring? Paragraphs that seem show-offy or pedantic? Circle them.

5. Is there any part of the story that doesn't address the story's central question, as you understand it? Circle it.
6. Circle either the first paragraph or the last paragraph.

Cut everything you've circled (but remember to save the cut pieces). Read the story again (this is easiest if you have typed the story into your computer). Are there ways in which the story is stronger? At the very least, you should have cut the weaker characters and weaker prose sections. Does this give the work more authority, more movement? Are there ways in which what's left unsaid makes the action or description or characterization that remains more effective? Did you end up cutting a scene you thought was central to understanding the story? Was it as necessary as you thought? You may be surprised at how well the story works in its newly shorn form. But the point of the exercise is not that it creates a finished draft, only that it may help lead you to one. There will probably be holes that need to be filled, passages that need to be returned to their places. But hopefully, you can see now how silences can be used to press up against the words; how cutting a paragraph can sometimes be more effective than writing one; and you can begin to see how a story takes shape within the silences surrounding it.

Jason Brown

RESEEING IN REVISION

T HE LONG ROAD FROM THE FIRST DRAFT TO THE FINAL draft is an epic journey through foreign lands with no Frodo to guide me. No, that's not right. I can't believe that line came out of my head. It did, though, and I just have to remember that more than 90 percent of what pops into my thoughts doesn't belong on paper. So I try again: Revision is a month-long backpacking trip with a group of people I met in line at the DMV. No, no. Revision—it's like driving cross-country in a Chevy Nova with my aunt and uncle and delinquent cousins from Buffalo. Everyone's whining and my aunt yells, "What is wrong with us?" Though I can't answer her (I'm a member of the same family and have no perspective), I wonder if this miserable car ride might just serve as a metaphor for revision. It would work if only you knew my relatives from Buffalo (though believe me, you don't want to). You can't choose your family, but you can choose your words. So I need to revise again.

Revision is the process of taking what first comes out of my head and making it better, finding the right comparison, the right description, or the right language, and not just for me, but also for you, the reader I have never met and probably never will. I want you to share my vision and feel compassion, outrage, and fear for my characters.

Revision is the process of seeing what doesn't belong in your writing—passive voice, inaccurate language, cliché, awkward shifts in point of view, and so on. Revision is also the process of envisioning how your work can be clearer and more powerful with fully distinct characters and language that sings. Prose that is closer to your ideal. To resee your work, you have to look through the eyes of a better reader. It can help, of course, to show your work to smart readers and listen to what they think, but in the end only you can revise your own work. The only solution is to become your ideal reader. For instance, my ideal reader is not dyslexic and burdened with a caffeine-enhanced, MTV-warped attention span. I used to think that my ideal reader would smoke cigars, but cigars make me gag, so I gave that up. My ideal reader often doesn't shower for days and eats and drinks nothing but pizza and Diet Coke, but the people who care about me keep me from that ideal. For a short time when I was younger, my ideal reader was drunk all the time, but then my ideal reader went to rehab, so now my ideal reader does yoga, eats organic muesli, and dreams of traveling the world. It can be difficult, though, to become your ideal reader, especially on my budget. I find it helps to check books out of the library and read widely and deeply. It helps to put the manuscript in a drawer for six months and come back to it when I am more ideal. At this rate, though, revision would take years (and often it does). The few exercises listed below may help shorten and sharpen the process.

THE EXERCISES

1. When you reread your manuscript, start somewhere in the middle or near the end. Reread the story or chapter twice a

day for six straight days, starting at a different point in the narrative each time. We all know the first paragraph and first page have to be great. Bring fresh scrutiny to all the subsequent paragraphs and pages.

2. Read your manuscript sentence by sentence from back to front. We have a tendency to let the success of a great beginning sentence carry us through a series of duds. Make every sentence and word earn its place in the narrative and stand up to your ideal reader's discriminating tastes.

3. Read your manuscript out loud to someone whose opinion you value. Ideally, you can trap two or more into listening. Read with a pen in hand and make notations when you stumble, when your stomach contracts, or when you sense you are losing your audience.

4. Read your manuscript into a recording device and play it back with a notepad in hand. Where does your attention wander as you listen? Where does your voice stumble? Pretend you are listening to a story someone else wrote. Ideally, you can convince someone else to read the story into a recording device, so that when you play it, you hear another voice.

5. Choose short selections from at least three of your favorite writers to read before you sit down to revise. How can your own prose measure up to your ideal?

6. Identify a list of common problems in fiction: cliché, inappropriate diction, abrupt point-of-view switches, passive voice, needless detail, scenes that only convey information and could be put into narration, narration that relates dramatic material and should be put into scene, and so on. Read your manuscript once all the way through for every problem on your list.

7. Make a list of ideals for your manuscript. For instance: You

want your main character to be complex, funny, morally ambiguous, and fascinating. You want your description to be worthy of Hardy. Read through your manuscript once for every specific ideal and find places where you can change your story in order to come closer to your ideal.

REVISE, REENVISION, REINVENT

I COME TO FICTION WRITING AS A FAILED ACTOR, PERFOR-mance artist/waiter, boot painter, hummus maker, and vet's assistant, so the act of reinventing a story as one reinvents a job and a life is my favorite part of the writing process. For me, the act of revising a story isn't all that different from the process of exploring, rehearsing, and tearing apart a stage play someone else wrote a month or a few centuries ago. I always start by going through the text and creating a series of ten-minute writing exercises based on what I feel are the weak spots. I do this in an effort to see what I can learn and to discover what I may have missed in the first go-round.

Before I attempt to work directly on the story, I spend a long time doing these exercises in a cheap notebook; then I set them aside. Many times, I will use nothing that I've written, but they deepen my understanding of the worlds I am working within, and they let the characters be the writers of the story. As the author, I always feel it is my job to completely disappear.

THE EXERCISES

- Relax. In an attempt to quiet an overactive editing mind, I always begin the work session with a body relaxation, just as an actor does before a rehearsal or a show. I do the body relaxation in the hopes that I will be able to more adequately write what needs to be written. I want to get out of my own way and listen to my characters in their bodies as well as in their minds and imaginations. I concentrate on relaxing places in my body that hold both good and bad memories, or aspects of the human body that I don't understand. I try to relax my endocrine system, for example, even though I'm not absolutely sure what an endocrine system is. Lots of times in workshop I advise students to relax "the small place where the proctologist goes" because a theater director I admired said that to me once after a very difficult performance and it made me laugh.

- Choose a character that is the least developed right now and fashion a series of ten-minute exploratory exercises for him both inside and outside the story frame. For example, write a pivotal childhood memory for the character that could have ramifications within the context of the story currently being written.

- Write a dream or nightmare the character had the day before or the day after this story takes place.

- Write in the voice of the character thirty years later, describing the events of the story that is being told in the present. How does the character feel about these events now? How important was this day in the context of his life?

- With your story in mind, locate a copy of the Twelve Steps of Alcoholics Anonymous and do a (Step 4) "searching and fearless" moral inventory in the voice of one of your characters. For what and to whom does this character need to make amends?

- Are there behaviors or substances or habits that have become addictive and affect the story or its outcome? What are your characters powerless over? What do they need to surrender right now and can't?

- Write a list of everything your character resents or is ashamed of in the entire world.
- What is the most hideous thing that ever happened to his character? Does it occur within the context of the story or inform it somehow?
- What did your character used to daydream about in his childhood? What does he daydream about now? Are his daydreams different once the story is over?
- Locate the pivotal scene in your story. Rewrite the scene in the voice of an animate or inanimate something that resides in the scene, such as a painting on the wall or a housefly. What do you learn about the story?
- With your characters in mind, take out your Twelve Steps of Alcoholics Anonymous again. Rewrite the story now very quickly in the POV of God or a Higher Power. A totally omniscient voice. What do you learn?
- Read passages from *Waterland* by Graham Swift and/or *Purple America* by Rick Moody and study how these authors use voice to tell the story and elevate the emotional effect of the events at hand. Try rewriting at least the first page of your story with the aim of boosting the musicality of the language itself.
- Study the setting of your story, then describe something that happened in that same setting three years ago that has a strong effect on what is happening to your characters right now in this very same place. If it has nothing to do with your characters at all, that's fine too.
- Write down everything your characters need to know in order to survive the story you are telling. This can be a list.

- In the most corny, New Age voice you can find, write the story in the POV of a character's inner child.
- Locate a scene in your story where the vocal exchanges are something you'd like to work on. Rewrite the scene now as a silent movie. Physical, nonverbal action only. What do you discover that might inform the story you are writing?
- Select a scene with no dialogue from a story by an author you really admire and write dialogue for that scene. I often select scenes from "Goodbye, My Brother" by John Cheever or "A Romantic Weekend" by Mary Gaitskill, two of my favorite stories ever.
- To explore underwritten scenes, rewrite them as scenes in which your characters say every single thing they are actually thinking but not saying. Rewrite them as scenes in which your characters talk about everything else but the matter at hand.

Marlin Barton

HIDING THE *I* IN FICTION
AND NONFICTION

A GOOD NUMBER OF YEARS AGO NOW, I GAVE A DRAFT OF A short story written in the first-person point of view to Dale Ray Phillips, who is, in my estimation, a master of the first-person voice (see his collection *My People's Waltz*). He read the story, called "Longer Than Summer," said some nice things about it, offered suggestions, and then made the offhand comment, "And you need to go through it and hide the 'I.' " When I asked him what he meant, he said that I'd overused that particular personal pronoun. Too many of my sentences began with "I saw," "I thought," "I couldn't believe," and the repetition made for awkward prose. After reading back through the first few paragraphs, I realized his point was obvious. I tried my hand at rewriting a few lines and found it difficult. Then Dale Ray sat down, and in just a few minutes he'd hidden about fifteen *I*'s in the first three pages—and the difference was clear. The prose was much smoother, the story stronger.

Other than creating awkward and repetitive prose, overuse of the first-person pronoun can suggest to a reader that your character or narrator is self-centered and narcissistic, and if that's not the case your prose style is working against your story. If your character is self-centered and narcissistic, the constant use of *I* isn't the best way to demonstrate, or *show,* those qualities. The repetition will simply become obnoxious and irritating to your reader. Sometimes the small details can make or break a piece of fiction. So a little time spent practicing hiding the *I* can serve your writing well.

THE EXERCISES

EXERCISE 1: Below is a passage from the rough draft of the story I mentioned above. Read through it and look for simple phrases that can be cut or reworded and independent clauses that might be made dependent. Also, try shifting the focus from what the narrator sees the other character do to describing in a more direct manner what that other character's actions are. Then try your hand at a rewrite and see how many of the thirteen *I*'s you can hide.

> I picked Jimmy Neal like he was some kind of prize off the shelf at a carnival, like he was a stuffed bear or a box of candy. I picked him as sure as these summer nights are hot as oven heat. I didn't know I was going to choose anybody until I saw him at the Bait Shop. Then I knew, all of a sudden, that I had to pick someone. Someone for my summer. I had to pick him. And that's what I did.
>
> Maybe it was because of his sweet red mouth or his pale blue eyes, eyes the lightness of the watercolors I used to paint with when I was little. Jimmy Neal had such pale blond hair

too, I thought, like a little boy's before it darkens. He looked too sweet almost. I knew he wasn't my usual type.

EXERCISE 2: Take a look at one of your own first-person stories or narrative essays, count the number of *I*'s in the first five pages, and see if you can remove a fourth of them. Then work your way to the end of the story.

SHOPPING FOR CONFLICT IN
THE SECOND DRAFT

HERE'S A LACKLUSTER NARRATIVE FOR YOU: I WENT OUT to buy a birthday gift for my friend Kristen. We've known each other forever and we never fight. We like the same cute iron-on T-shirts, the same books, and, more often than not, the same music; assembling a care package for her is a breeze. I wrapped up a T-shirt, a book, and a CD, and upon receiving it, she called to say thanks. Six weeks later, when Kristen picked me up at the airport for a visit, we were both sporting tees we'd sent each other over the years. We giggled!

Tee-hee-hee indeed.

This is a nonstory. This is easy shopping and boring telling. There is no conflict, which, of course, means there's really no *story* at all.

But take, by contrast, this recent episode of gift-giving torment, wherein I spent a glorious spring day anxiously trolling the boutiques of Brooklyn, racked with indecision over what to get my friend Frank. Frank and I have been friends for a long time—with a pretty regrettable drunken episode not far enough in the past. Surely, I thought, somewhere between the sweater and the six-pack, there had to be the perfect gift to accurately encapsulate where we stood. *Does this seem too romantic? Too glib? Does this? Or this?*

If a gift marks the locus where two people intersect, gift giving is easy when this point of connection is clear. But when the point of connection has morphed and muddied, the gift—like any antagonist introduced into a narrative—has the capacity to prod and agitate the sludge of conflict lurking beneath the surface of a relationship.

In such fraught gifting circumstances, I worry and second-guess options, fearing I'll offend with too much exuberance or not enough. I'll spend the first beach day of the year pounding pavement and gnawing on my neuroses, selecting an object for purchase and putting it back until I'm so ambivalent about what I wish to express that, for example, I won't show up at Frank's birthday party at all. I find myself asking the following questions: *Why is this such a big deal? What is the conflict here? What do I want from this person? What does he want from me? What do I hope for this gesture to accomplish? What do I fear? And what, really, is at stake after all?*

Sound familiar?

These questions address the same sort of subterranean conflict that is the very stuff of fiction, that spring-loads tension into narrative. They are, in fact, almost exactly the questions I ask myself when writing, particularly when I'm staring down a finished first draft. *What the hell is this thing about? What do these people want from one another? What is the conflict? What is at stake?*

It's no surprise then to find that gifting in fiction, as in life, can help in sifting through the first-draft murk to discover—and to dramatize—with startling clarity what is truly at stake between people.

When I have an early draft—when it's clear I have a story but unclear what it's really *about;* when my characters are in place, but sort of blandly bumbling about the page; when the situations, if not the conflicts, have taken on a ghostly outline—I've found that the gift (or even the planning of a gift) can be a tremendous help in further discovering the story and in shaping its arc. Introducing a gift into a narrative can stir underlying conflicts to the surface, tether desire and disappointment to a seemingly simple action, and, ultimately, serve as a vehicle for transforming latent tension into vibrant scene.

Further, the act of gift giving is inherently friendly to narrative structure—containing, unto itself, a beginning, middle, and end:

The selection of a gift (or the anticipation of receiving it) creates an expectation.

The receipt of the gift delivers the fulfillment or failure of that expectation.

And, finally, the success or failure of the gesture is reconciled—for better or worse—into the relationship, offering a resolution of some sort.

THE EXERCISE

Incorporate a gift (or a plan for a future gift) into the second draft of a story lacking adequate conflict.

Try arming your point-of-view character with a gift. What is this gift? Who is it for? What kind of intersection does it assert between the two characters? Does it seem perfect—or half-assed, or somehow inadequate, or, for some reason, absolutely urgent to give? (You might consider trying out each of these possibilities in subsequent revisions of the story, mining the material and each draft until you strike gold.) What response is the POV character hoping for?

What actually occurs?

How does this inform the future of the relationship?

Try weaving the gift throughout the narrative, considering the planning, the giving, and the reaction as structural support to the beginning, middle, and end of your story or scene.

Stephen D. Marlowe

THE RIGHT WORD IN TAILS

MAKING ART — IN OUR CASE, OF SYMBOLS ON A PAGE — IS hard. How do good writers choose between right words when several may pass muster? More important, how can we make that choice a part of our revision process?

Let's look at a few techniques—a nonexclusive list, for sure— for going the extra step in revision, moving past the craft of choosing a right word and into the art of making the right word unforgettable, thereby imbuing stalled prose with verve.

Think about these techniques, in a baseball metaphor, as relief pitchers. When your starters seem to have tired, consider sending these, among others, to warm up. You never know. They might put you on the way to a save.

1. KISS, SLAP, KISS.

A word chosen judiciously that might otherwise seem out of place can starch the prose and slap the reader to attention, when that's needed. In Stephen King's *Rage,* the author invites us to the story with this gem:

The lawn of Placerville High School is a very good one. It does not fuck around. It comes right up to the building and says howdy.

This example uses a word that is usually *never* right—in this case the loathed and dreaded F-bomb. Yet here it works. It's dressed down—or leathered up—and is busy making good mischief. Also, King's framing *fuck* with *a very good one* and *howdy* softens the curse, which can seem ugly when it unexpectedly appears in print.

2. HAVEN'T SEEN *YOU* IN A WHILE.

For our purposes, the mischief-making revision needn't necessarily be profane; imagine it, if you will, as the uninvited, underdressed, party crasher who, nevertheless, makes the event memorable. Sometimes a word on its own, by virtue of being archaic, or because it is spoken more than written and thus rare on the page, can do wonders. In his essay "Big Boy," David Sedaris opts for *turd* instead of *piece of shit* or *load of crap:*

Everyone had taken their places, when I excused myself to visit the bathroom, and there, in the toilet, was the absolute biggest turd I have ever seen in my life—no toilet paper or anything, just this long and coiled specimen, as thick as a burrito.

It's as great as it is uncommon to see *turd* in print; Sedaris's choice seizes both attention and envy.

3. CAN SHE SAY THAT?

Likewise, lower-level definitions of words can be gold mines, and we ought to dig them. For instance, a writer might use *queer* to good effect in describing something as out of place, because other associations have rendered that word almost taboo and left a sense of awe around it. For many, the word *fetish* carries sinister (and perhaps titillating) overtones; yet it means only that a thing is the object of obsessive or religious focus. A person can fetishize something without the obsession's being sexual, and a revision using a known but often-neglected definition can edify your prose.

4. THE RIGHT WORD IN TAILS.

Occasionally, the right word may need to put on a little swank. In *The Enemies List,* P. J. O'Rourke clothes his lovelies in white-tie formal in defense of the 1950s:

> Indeed, we are experiencing anew many of the pleasures and benefits of that excellent decade: a salubrious prudery, a sensible avariciousness, a healthy dose of social conformity, a much-needed narrowing of minds, and a return to common-sense American political troglodytism.

Excellent, salubrious, troglodytism. But finery was needed, no? O'Rourke slaps tails and a top hat on concepts we might otherwise reject—and good for him: readers go crazy 'bout a sharp-dressed word! We would be less likely to take his point, and far less likely to smile, or laugh, as we often do when holding O'Rourke's books, if he had described his list of pleasures and benefits as the following, instead:

> . . . fear of sex, greed, groupthink, a dumbed-down populace, and reactionary politics.

THE EXERCISE

Craft alone rarely does the trick; the artist, by making conscious choices about where to insert grace notes, returns humanity to a finely honed text. So let's do it: Go get your manuscript—or that otherwise unfinished piece of writing you have stowed away in your writer's trunk. You know the one. The one with the competent, flaccid prose. The one your readers sort of shrugged at and said, "It's technically flawless, but . . ."

Arm yourself with a Web browser and the URLs of good online writing resources, dictionaries, and so on, or surround yourself with good print references: dictionaries, thesauri, compendiums of synonyms and antonyms. Take a highlighter—I prefer pink, for whatever reason—and concentrate on one troubling passage. At first. Identify necessary, adequate words that nevertheless aren't pulling their weight.

Within the purview of the "right word," allow yourself to play with word choice—move out, up, down, complicate, simplify, transgress, declutter, mix, return to go, curse, flail, mitigate the curses, rescue abandoned words, dress them up in tails. Watch how the changes you make affect the sentence- and paragraph-level impacts of the idea you're trying to convey. Squeeze the words. Work them. Make them sing. Take your time, choose wisely, and mind the reader. Go where the change takes you. Expect magic.

DAILY
WARM-UPS

A NOTE ABOUT DAILY WARM-UPS

THIS SECTION OF THE BOOK WAS INSPIRED BY THE WONderful artist Don Bachardy. I had the good fortune to meet him in Santa Monica, and he had the misfortune of painting my portrait because I'd received a Christopher Isherwood fellowship from the Isherwood Foundation. (Why they make him do this, I have no idea.) When I entered his airy and bright studio, I found the artist completing his morning ritual of painting random colors on a rectangular sheet of canvas paper. There were palettes of completed sheets beside a worktable, stacks of wavy dried color; they looked tie-dyed. Each sheet had a circle of color in the middle; then he'd rippled different shades and hues out and out and out until the canvas was covered; then he'd set it to dry. He's been doing one a day for decades; they usually take only a few minutes. He uses them to see what colors interest him before starting his "real" work, to see how his mind and vision and heart have changed since he closed up shop the day before.

This ritual made immediate sense to me, the emotional and physical engaging of the senses as a way of clearing out and focusing the mind, and ever since that Santa Monica morning, I've been using such prompts in my own daily routine and my teaching. (I've been heartened to learn how many writers, as well as visual artists, musicians, athletes, and actors, also subscribe to the same kind of daily regimen.) I employ these warm-ups the way musicians practice scales, the way boxers work a speed bag, to heighten concentration and to awaken creativity. The narrative calisthenics have essentially no bearing on the major project at hand, but for all of their whimsy, they serve that deep and abiding purpose: they purge everything from the writer's mind except a concerted attention to language. They make it easier to get your butt in the chair, and to keep it there. (For this reason, they're also a terrific antidote for writer's block. They bring your fingers to the keys, or your pen to the paper, without bias or expectation.) Because each of us has so many pressures and responsibilities outside of our writing rooms—studying for biology tests, walking the dog, paying the mortgage, finding a soul mate—and because so many distractions and indulgences conspire to lure us away from our art—exotic vacations, the aforementioned soul mates, sitcom reruns, a long-overdue root canal without anesthesia—devising strategies to capitalize on whatever time we can afford our writing is tantamount to success. My experience, and the experience of my students, has been that these warm-ups address this need ideally. I mean nothing less: if you devote the first few minutes of your writing day to completing one of these prompts, your work, and likewise your chances of getting published, will exponentially improve.

Jacob M. Appel, Tom Bligh, Sarah Shun-lien Bynum, Josh Emmons, Amy Hassinger, Vanessa Furse Jackson, Adam Johnson, Bret Anthony Johnston, Michael Knight, Paul Lisicky, Thisbe Nissen, Colette Sartor & Michelle Wildgen

DAILY WARM-UPS

Spend five minutes describing:
- An eighth dwarf to go along with Snow White's seven.
- A crime you wish you'd committed but lacked the courage for.
- The childhood of the oldest person you know.
- A homemade invention.
- An unusual pet.

Spend fifteen minutes finishing a paragraph that begins:
- "George never would have guessed a coffin could hold so many marbles."
- "My mother broke every dish in the house that day."
- "As Bettina pushed him down the stairs, Jack was certain he saw her smile."
- "No one could blame her for trying. The ring was just sitting on the counter, begging to be stolen."
- "The freezer door wasn't supposed to lock behind him. That wasn't part of the plan."

Spend five minutes listing:
- Fifty phrases that would make good titles for a short story.
- Fifty interesting settings for stories.
- Fifty things a potential character of yours might long for.
- Stories you would write if the most important person in your life (parent, spouse, boss, etc.) were guaranteed never to read them.
- All the things you'd be doing right now if you weren't making yourself write.

Spend five minutes describing:
- A strange experience in a car.
- A strange experience in a restaurant.
- An unmerited award.
- A good deed that backfires.
- A famous painting; add something original to the image.

Spend twenty minutes writing a scene that involves:
- An airport baggage claim.
- A department store that's going out of business.
- A character who steals a pair of fingernail clippers.
- An e-mail sent to the wrong person.
- An encounter with a television weatherman.

Spend ten minutes describing:
- Your boss's shoes.
- Your boss's hairstyle.
- The interior of your boss's car.
- Why you should move someplace else.
- Why you're living exactly where you should be living.

Spend five minutes listing:
- Verbs that have to do with the ocean.
- Nouns that have to do with the plains.
- Verbs that have to do with the city.
- Nouns and verbs that have to do with your home landscape.
- Fifty phrases that would make good titles for a novel.

Spend five minutes describing:
- A new national holiday and how it should be celebrated.
- How the color blue would taste, smell, sound.
- An amusement park with an odd theme; focus on one of the rides.
- A strange tourist attraction.
- An unusual contest, including the winning prize.

Spend five minutes describing:
- The oddest coincidence you've ever encountered.
- A family legend.
- An unusual piece of furniture.
- A recipe to cure writer's block.
- A recipe to stop the rain.

Spend twenty minutes writing a scene that involves:
- An adult child trying to convince his or her fifty-something mother not to adopt a baby.
- A swap meet.
- A mirror.
- A page missing from a phone book.
- A doughnut for dinner.

Spend ten minutes describing:
- An item you've stolen and never told anyone about.
- A time when you felt elated, without using the word *happy*.
- A time when you felt miserable, without using the word *sad*.
- A time when you felt pissed off, without using the word *angry*.
- A time when you felt at peace, without using the word *content*.

Spend fifteen minutes finishing a paragraph that begins:
- "This morning I couldn't find . . ."
- "What I see in the sky is . . ."
- "Walking along a path at dawn, I . . ."
- "Coming up against bureaucratic rules, I . . ."
- "A wonderful excuse for failing to turn up for work would be . . ."

Spend five minutes describing:
- A recipe to cure depression.
- A recipe that would bring back a vivid memory.
- A remedy to soothe anger.
- A car wreck.
- A eulogy at a funeral (serious or unintentionally funny).

Spend twenty minutes writing a scene that involves:
- The dining car of a train.
- Two lovers arguing about whether or not to terminate a pregnancy.
- A dialogue with the same premise as above, but switch the characters' desires: the person who wanted to terminate the pregnancy is now the one who wants to keep it.
- A mother and daughter arguing over whether the unmarried daughter should bear a child.

- A father and son arguing over whether the unmarried son should become a father.

Spend five minutes describing:
- A chair in terms of a lover. ("I draped myself over his arm . . .")
- A house fire in terms of a lion.
- An argument in terms of a storm.
- A person's physical characteristics in terms of food.
- A pet animal in terms of a human being.

Spend five minutes listing:
- Everything that comes to mind when you think of stained glass.
- Everything that comes to mind when you think of air travel.
- Everything that comes to mind when you think of a rock concert.
- Everything that comes to mind when you think of a doll-house.
- Nouns that have to do with the woods.

Spend five minutes describing:
- A memory in terms of a movie.
- The contents of someone's glove compartment.
- The contents of your sixth-grade teacher's desk.
- Your sister or brother's backpack.
- Your father's briefcase.

Spend five minutes listing:
- What used to be true that is no longer (e.g., Pluto was once a planet but now is not).
- All the names you'd like to give your characters.
- All the names you'd never give your characters.

- Everything that comes to mind when you think of light-bulbs.
- Everything that comes to mind when you think of a park bench.

Spend twenty minutes writing a scene that involves:
- A hair salon or barbershop.
- A greenhouse.
- A clothing boutique.
- A public restroom.
- A city council meeting.

Spend five minutes describing:
- Your grandmother's jewelry box.
- The contents of a character's medicine cabinet.
- An unwelcome surprise.
- An account of your birth from your father's perspective. (Other possibilities: mother, sibling, aunt, uncle, grandparent.)
- A competitive colleague.

Spend twenty minutes writing a scene that involves:
- A bowling alley.
- A hospital psychiatric ward.
- A submarine.
- A rooftop.
- A bookstore.

Spend five minutes describing:
- An unusual hobby.
- A shopping mall through the eyes of a person walking through it. Invent the stores that person sees.
- Two people who pretend to get along but secretly despise each other.

- Overhearing your students (or friends or family) discussing your work at a party.
- One of your characters manages to write you a postcard. What does it say?

Spend five minutes listing:
- Things you've bought and never used.
- What made you happiest as a child. Or as an adolescent. Or as an adult.
- All the medical conditions you or people in your family have had.
- The most interesting names of people you know directly.
- Products that have prominent warning signs on them.

Spend ten minutes describing:
- How you got your biggest scar.
- Your craziest friend.
- Something strange that you've learned about your neighbor.
- The lost object you wish you still had.
- The object you wish you could lose.

Spend five minutes describing:
- A brief scene in which a character does something impossible.
- Your discovery of convincing evidence that your parents are both robots. What do you do next?
- Your arrival at a party where every guest is naked except you. What do you do?
- A safe space.
- A rude encounter over the phone.

Spend twenty minutes writing a scene that involves:
- A computer disk.
- A bonfire.

- An antique vase.
- A church pew.
- An elevator.

Spend ten minutes describing:
- The last creature (probably a bug) you've killed.
- Someone for whom you feel great sympathy.
- The most recent news item that made you angry.
- Why God does or does not exist.
- The person or thing or image that most frightened you as a child.

Spend five minutes listing:
- Animals that are sinister and horrible.
- Places you've been to which you never want to return.
- The most overrated songs, books, or movies in the world.
- Synonyms for your favorite color.
- The various nicknames (including terms of endearment) you've had in your life.

Spend five minutes describing:
- The strangest diet you can imagine.
- A doomed wedding.
- The physical appearance of your idealized self.
- The physical appearance of your grotesque self.
- What you'd like to dream about tonight.

Spend five minutes describing:
- A bird perched on a wire, looking for its morning meal. Write from the bird's perspective, without mentioning that you're a bird. Next, describe the same bird looking for its morning meal, only from the perspective of a person watch-

ing the bird. Finally, write from the perspective of the morning meal, but don't mention the bird.
- Being trapped underneath a saggy mattress by a dead body.
- Piloting a runaway hot-air balloon.
- Riding a roller coaster with a broken safety bar.
- Speeding along the freeway in the trunk of a car.

Spend twenty minutes writing a scene that involves:
- A parachute.
- A magnifying glass.
- A centipede.
- A tambourine.
- A celebrity.

Spend ten minutes describing:
- The funniest joke you've ever heard.
- The most ridiculous outfit you've seen lately.
- Your most secret fantasy.
- Your most amazing trick or physical ability.
- The most interesting house in your neighborhood.

Spend five minutes listing:
- The most popular students from your high school class.
- Your favorite songs from your teenage years.
- What makes you angry about the person closest to you.
- Things at work or school that you would change if given Aladdin's magic lamp.
- Things you find most tempting.

Spend twenty minutes writing a scene that involves:
- Someone taking the law into his or her own hands.
- A conflict over an umbrella.

- A mishap with a musical instrument.
- An encounter with the supernatural.
- A ladder.

Spend five minutes listing:
- Values you truly believe in.
- Things a pet would love.
- What gifts your partner should buy you.
- Every word you can think of that starts with the letter *A*. (For the next twenty-five days, do the same for another letter in the alphabet.)
- Street names you remember from your childhood neighborhood.

Spend ten minutes describing:
- Your best feature.
- Your worst feature.
- The last time you successfully resisted temptation.
- The last time you gave in to temptation entirely.
- An urban legend you once believed.

Spend twenty minutes writing a scene that involves:
- An odd neighbor.
- A disagreement between two strangers.
- An occurrence underground.
- An incident underwater.
- A zoo.

Spend twenty minutes writing a scene that involves:
- A man in a tuxedo walking barefoot on the side of the road.
- Being lost somewhere geographically.
- Sitting on a porch at night.

- Getting caught in a storm.
- A leaky faucet.

Spend five minutes listing:
- The kinds of food in the grocery store that you never buy.
- As many clichés as you can remember.
- Metaphors that best describe you.
- Verbs that best describe you.
- Highlights in your life.

Spend ten minutes describing:
- The last activity after which you collapsed into a chair or bed, too exhausted to move. Don't use the words *exhausted* or *tired.*
- The last time you said something you instantly regretted.
- Your most recent brush with danger.
- Your enemy's best qualities.
- How your boss or teacher abuses his or her power.

Spend five minutes listing:
- What turns you on.
- The types of junk mail and spam you most often receive.
- The kinds of clothes you least like to wear.
- What vacations you dream of taking.
- The types of people you dread having to talk to.

Spend five minutes listing:
- Things that terrify you the most.
- Memories that recur to you most often.
- What best defines you as a person.
- What you feel like as you're writing.
- What you hate about getting up in the morning.

Spend ten minutes describing:
- An occasion on which your opposite-gender parent took you shopping for clothes.
- A time when you wore an outfit that turned out to be inappropriate for the occasion.
- When a student from your elementary school or high school was ostracized by other students.
- A time when one of your parents surprised you.
- A time you surprised yourself by acting like one of your parents.

Spend ten minutes describing:
- A conversation between a doctor and a patient.
- A homeless person; strive for unusual yet believable details and avoid clichés.
- Your first bicycle or bicycle ride. Invent the details you can't remember.
- The last incident that made you cry with sadness.
- The last incident that made you cry with laughter.

Spend twenty minutes writing a scene that involves:
- A lost dog.
- A number (and ways in which people have used it).
- The color orange (and images you associate with it).
- A city street at night.
- Clouds.

Spend five minutes listing:
- Every homonym you know.
- Things you dream of possessing.
- Things you've lost that you most regret.

- Things you keep in your purse or pocket.
- Things that best define home for you.

Spend ten minutes describing:
- Your best friend's backyard. (Other possibilities: living room, bedroom.)
- One of your birthday parties.
- Attending a religious service in a tradition in which you weren't raised.
- A gift you were given that struck you as inappropriate to your character.
- A time when you bought a gift that turned out to be a mistake.

Spend twenty minutes writing a scene that involves:
- Rain.
- Snow.
- Heat.
- Wind.
- Bad hair.

Spend ten minutes describing:
- An early experience of otherness.
- Your first crush.
- An experience in which you conceded that you weren't going to get something you wanted.
- Taking care of a child, pet, or person you didn't really like.
- Staying with a couple or family you didn't really know.

Spend five minutes listing:
- The opening line of every literary work you can quote from memory.

- As many bird species found in your hometown as you can name.
- The many different types of shops you might find in a small town.
- All the fictional dogs you can think of.
- All the different parts of a car you can name.

Spend ten minutes describing:
- A bad habit.
- Leaving for college.
- First communion, bar mitzvah, or other coming-of-age ritual.
- Trying a new and bizarre food.
- The face of someone you saw yesterday.

Spend twenty minutes writing a scene that involves:
- Checkout lines.
- Bird droppings.
- Throwing up.
- A story set in your kitchen.
- A novel entitled *Disappearance at the Circus.*

Spend ten minutes describing:
- The art of shopping.
- A room you'll never visit again.
- A terrible party.
- A time when you got in trouble at school.
- Shopping for something you don't want to buy.

Spend twenty minutes writing a scene that involves:
- Being unfairly dismissed from a job.
- A science fiction story set in the White House.

Spend ten minutes describing:
- A time you decided to take the day off.
- An apology that is long overdue.
- The most beautiful aroma you've ever encountered.
- Someone you never want to meet again.
- A nursery rhyme or fairy tale, only in a different setting.

Spend twenty minutes writing a scene that involves:
- A parking garage.
- A riverboat casino.
- A lighthouse.
- A furniture showroom.
- A place you've visited in the last week.

Spend ten minutes describing:
- A childhood memory you wish you could forget.
- A time you had to undress in a public place.
- The most frightening experience you've had.
- The strangest wedding you've ever attended.
- An unjust punishment.

Spend twenty minutes writing a scene that involves:
- A place you've never visited.
- A police station.
- An abandoned warehouse.
- A flustered coworker.
- An annoying relative.

Spend twenty minutes writing a scene that involves:
- A discussion between a young couple standing beside a U-Haul in front of an old-age home.
- A trip on a subway or train. Who are the other passengers? What are they doing?

- A children's fable about a cow and an elephant.
- A dumpster behind a library.
- A FedEx package.

Spend ten minutes describing:
- The worst gift you've ever received.
- The first person you remember hating as a child.
- Why you always lock the doors at night.
- Going to a restaurant you can't afford.
- Church smells.

Spend twenty minutes writing a scene that involves:
- A pair of broken spectacles.
- A snow shovel.
- A lottery ticket.
- A pothole.
- A tree house.

Spend ten minutes describing:
- The worst idea you've ever had.
- What you dreamed of becoming as a child.
- The very first thing you remember from your childhood.
- The last time you were lied to. Write a descriptive scene showing the conversation that reveals the telltale signs of a lie.
- A secret from your childhood.

Spend twenty minutes writing a scene that involves:
- A seesaw.
- A hammock.
- A desk globe.
- A man cutting off his beard.
- A bakery.

- Two old friends unexpectedly meeting in a store. Have them each shopping for an item that reveals something about their present situations.
- A man and woman who want to go to different movies.
- A skateboard.

Spend twenty minutes writing a scene that involves:
- A stained rug.
- A missing photograph.
- A Tiffany lamp.
- A walking cane.
- A cassette tape.

Spend twenty minutes writing a scene that involves:
- A flat tire.
- An artist's easel.
- A dog leash.
- A motel key.
- A broken window.

Spend twenty minutes writing a scene that involves:
- A stringless guitar.
- A pizza cutter.
- A duffel bag.
- A Bible.
- A bonsai tree.

Spend twenty minutes writing a scene that involves:
- An autographed football.
- A Civil War artifact.
- A mechanic.
- An aquarium.
- A nurse.

Spend twenty minutes writing a scene that involves:

- A Cadillac.
- A snake.
- A television antenna.
- A tandem bicycle.
- A lobster.

ACKNOWLEDGMENTS

For encouragement along the way, I'm deeply indebted to these good, good souls: Ethan Canin. Marilynne Robinson. Samantha Chang. Connie Brothers. Jim McPherson. Jorie Graham. Peter Sacks. Jim Engell. Sven Birkerts. Peter Richards. Ellen "the Constant Gardner" Silva. Deb West. Jan Z. Patrick Cotter. Harriet and Liadain O'Donovan. Hansjorg Schertenleib. Leslie Shipman, Harold Augenbraum, Adah Nuchi, and every last person at the National Book Foundation. Chris Offutt. Adam Haslett. Ron Chen. B. H. Fairchild. Steven Bauer and the fine folks at Miami University. Katherine Vaz. Michael Collier, Jennifer Grotz, Noreen Cargill, and everyone at the Bread Loaf Writers' Conference. Mike Vause, Carl Porter, and the National Undergraduate Literature Conference. Mike Anzaldua. Cheryl Pfoff. Liz Flores. Amy Margolis. Jim Gilbert. Sonny Brewer. Whitney Scharer, Sonia Larson, and all things Grub Street. Elfrieda Abbe. Serenity Gerbman. Katie McManners. Clay Smith. Anne Greene and the Wesleyan Writers Conference. Marc Smirnoff and Carol Ann Fitzgerald and Paul "Panama" Reyes and the whole OA crew. Joe Wilson. Jan Williams, and Susan and Dee and Jed, and the Corpus Christi Literary Reading Series, which pretty much started it all. Ron, Velda, and Chris Schalk. Shannon Ravenel. Kathy Pories, whose idea this kind of was in the first place. And my students, who make me want to read, who make me want to write. For generous support, without which this book wouldn't exist, I'm grateful to the James A. Michener/Copernicus Society of America. The National Endowment for the Arts. The Isherwood Foundation. The Arthur and Margaret Glasgow Endowment. For all things family: Bill, Michelle, and Camryn Kuykendall. Joseph "the Jackrabbit" Martinez. Brad, Brie, Nathan, and Austen. Ivan, Betty, Anthony, and Americus Pena. Gary, Lizz, Chloe, Samantha, Natalie, and Katie. And, of course, my parents, who always read, and to whom I owe more than I can write. At Random House, I'm so, so thankful for the incandescent and brilliant and fire-streaming-from-her-eyes-in-a-good-way and always map-carrying and compassionate and exuberant Judy Sternlight. (With a special nod to Daisy!) And thanks, too, to Becca Shapiro, Stephanie Higgs, Karen Fink, and Dennis Ambrose. And to Daniel Menaker, whose light is so pure and strong and inspiring, and who looks like a young Burt Reynolds and not at all like Alex Trebek. The utterly amazing and cool and radiant and way stylish and way, way smart Nina Collins, of Collins Literary, deserves a shopping spree in that store on Newbury Street (with the pink bags) for all her passion for this project. Matt Elbonk deserves a lottery ticket with the numbers 4, 8, 15, 16, 23, and 42 on it. This book is for all of you, and it's for Jennifer, my name and my world.

NOTES ON CONTRIBUTORS

DOROTHY ALLISON's first novel, *Bastard Out of Carolina,* was a finalist for the National Book Award and was made into a film produced by Anjelica Huston. Her novel *Cavedweller* was a national bestseller. Her short stories have appeared in *The Best American Short Stories* and *New Stories from the South: The Year's Best.*

STEVE ALMOND is the author of two story collections, *My Life in Heavy Metal* and *The Evil B. B. Chow,* and a nonfiction book, *Candyfreak.* He lives in Somerville, Massachusetts. To find out what kind of music he listens to, check out www.bbchow.com.

JACOB M. APPEL's short fiction, which has appeared in *Agni, The Southwest Review, StoryQuarterly,* and elsewhere, has been short-listed for the O. Henry Award and the Pushcart Prize. He is a graduate of the MFA program in fiction at New York University and teaches at Brown University in Providence, Rhode Island, and the Gotham Writers' Workshop in New York City. Jacob can be reached via e-mail at jma38@columbia.edu; his Internet presence is located at www.jacobmappel.com.

NICK ARVIN is the author of a collection of stories, *In the Electric Eden,* and a novel, *Articles of War.* His short fiction has appeared in *The New Yorker,* and his work has been recognized with the James A. Michener/Copernicus Society of America fellowship, the Rosenthal Foundation Award from the American Academy of Arts and Letters, and the W. Y. Boyd Award from the American Library Association. He teaches occasional classes for the Lighthouse Writers Workshop in Denver.

TOM BARBASH is the author of the novel *The Last Good Chance,* which won the California Book Award and was a *Publishers Weekly* Best Book of the Year, and the *New York Times* nonfiction bestseller *On Top of the World: Cantor Fitzgerald, Howard Lutnick and 9/11.* He is an assistant professor in the graduate MFA program at California College of the Arts.

MARLIN BARTON is from the Black Belt region of Alabama. He has published two collections of short stories, *The Dry Well* and *Dancing by the River,* and a novel, *A Broken Thing.* His stories have appeared in such journals and anthologies as *The Sewanee Review* and the annual *O. Henry Prize Stories* collection. He teaches creative writing to juvenile offenders in a program called Writing Our Stories.

RICHARD BAUSCH is the author of nine novels and five collections of short stories, including *Take Me Back,* which was nominated for the PEN/Faulkner Award; *The Last Good Time; Mr. Field's Daughter; Violence; The Selected Stories of Richard Bausch; In the Night Season;* and *Hello to the Cannibals.* His short stories have appeared in numerous prize-winning anthologies, including *The Best American Short Stories, The O. Henry Prize Stories,* and *The Pushcart Prize.* He has received several awards, including a National Endowment for the Arts fellowship, a Guggenheim fellowship, the Lila Wallace–Reader's Digest Writer's Award, and the Award in Literature from the Academy of Arts and Letters. Previously a professor of English and the Heritage Chair of Creative Writing at George Mason

University, Bausch now holds the Lillian and Morrie A. Moss Chair of Excellence at the University of Memphis.

TOM BLIGH's fiction has appeared in *The Southern Review, Black Warrior Review,* and *The Cincinnati Review* and his nonfiction in *The Believer, Oxford American,* and *Five Points.* He is a doctoral candidate in the creative-writing program at Florida State University.

ROBERT BOSWELL is the author of *Century's Son, American Owned Love, Living to Be 100, Mystery Ride, The Geography of Desire, Dancing in the Movies,* and *Crooked Hearts.* He has received two NEA fellowships, a Guggenheim fellowship, and numerous prizes for his fiction. His stories have appeared in *Esquire, The New Yorker, The Best American Short Stories, The O. Henry Prize Stories, The Pushcart Prize* volumes, and in many literary magazines. He teaches at New Mexico State University, the University of Houston, and in the Warren Wilson MFA Program. He lives with his wife, Antonya Nelson, and their two children in Texas, New Mexico, and Colorado.

JAMES BROWN teaches at the California State University at San Bernardino. He is also the author of *The Los Angeles Diaries: A Memoir.*

JASON BROWN grew up in Maine. His first book was *Driving the Heart and Other Stories;* his second, a collection of linked stories, is *Why the Devil Chose New England for His Work.* His stories have appeared in *The Best American Short Stories, Harper's, The Atlantic,* and elsewhere and have been read on NPR's *Selected Shorts.*

SARAH SHUN-LIEN BYNUM's short fiction has appeared in *Tin House, TriQuarterly, The Georgia Review,* and *The Best American Short Stories.* Her first novel, *Madeleine Is Sleeping,* was a finalist for the National Book Award. A recipient of a Whiting Writers' Award and an NEA fellowship, she lives with her family in Los Angeles and teaches at the University of California at San Diego.

Norma E. Cantú, born and raised along the U.S.-Mexico borderlands, writes and teaches about that region. Her award-winning novel *Canícula: Snapshots of a Girlhood en la Frontera* is part of a border trilogy that includes the unpublished works "Papeles de Mujer" and "Cabañuelas: A Love Story." Among her current projects are a coedited anthology on dance, *Dancing Across Borders: Danzas y Bailes Mexicanos,* and a novel, *Champú, or Hair Matters.* Her work has appeared in numerous journals and collections. She currently serves as professor of English and U.S. Latina/o literature at the University of Texas at San Antonio.

Christopher Castellani has an MA in creative writing from Boston University and is ABD in English literature at Tufts. His most recent novel, *The Saint of Lost Things,* was published in 2005. He is also the author of the novel *A Kiss from Maddalena,* which won the Massachusetts Book Award. Christopher works as artistic director of Grub Street, Inc., a Boston-based nonprofit writing center, and teaches at Swarthmore College. He lives in Arlington, Massachusetts. For more information, visit www.christopher castellani.com.

Dan Chaon is the author of several books, including the short-story collection *Among the Missing,* which was a finalist for the National Book Award. He teaches at Oberlin College.

Alan Cheuse is a novelist, story writer, and journalist, the author, among other books, of *The Fires, The Grandmothers' Club, The Light Possessed,* and *Lost and Old Rivers* and the memoir *Fall Out of Heaven.* He serves as book commentator for NPR's evening newsmagazine *All Things Considered* and teaches in the writing program at George Mason University. His short fiction has recently appeared in *Ploughshares, The Antioch Review, Prairie*

Schooner, New Letters, and *The Southern Review.* He is the coeditor of *Writers Workshop in a Book: The Squaw Valley Community of Writers on the Art of Fiction* and the editor of *Seeing Ourselves: Great American Short Fiction.*

RACHEL CLINE's first novel, *What to Keep,* was published in 2004. Her second novel, *My Liar,* will appear in 2008. Cline spent nine years in Los Angeles, where she wrote unproduced screenplays, teleplays for *Knots Landing,* and profanity-free dialogue for the movie *Glengarry Glen Ross.* She has taught at Sarah Lawrence, New York University, and the University of Southern California.

C. MICHAEL CURTIS is the John C. Cobb Professor of Humanities at Wofford College. He also edits fiction for *The Atlantic Monthly,* for whom he has worked since 1963. He is the editor of six anthologies of short fiction— *American Stories: Fiction from* The Atlantic Monthly (volumes 1 and 2), *Contemporary New England Stories, Contemporary West Coast Stories, God: Stories,* and *Faith: Stories*—and has published poetry, essays, reporting, and reviews in *The Atlantic Monthly, The New Republic, The National Review,* and many other periodicals. He has taught creative writing and composition at Harvard, Cornell, MIT, Tufts, Boston University, Simmons College, Bennington College, Northeastern University, and elsewhere. He lives in Spartanburg, South Carolina, with his wife, the novelist Elizabeth Cox, with whom he shares the Cobb Chair.

JOHN DUFRESNE teaches creative writing at Florida International University, in Miami, and is the author of, most recently, *Johnny Too Bad.*

JOSH EMMONS is the author of *The Loss of Leon Meed,* which won a James A. Michener/Copernicus Society of America award. He lives and writes in Portland, Oregon.

MERRILL FEITELL's first book, *Here Beneath Low-Flying Planes,* won the Iowa Award for Short Fiction. Her stories have appeared in many publications and have been short-listed in *The Best American Short Stories* and the *The O. Henry Prize Stories.* She is now part of the creative writing faculty at the University of Maryland and lives in Baltimore.

JULIA FIERRO, a graduate of the Iowa Writers' Workshop, has taught creative writing at Hofstra University and the University of Iowa. She founded the Sackett Street Writers' Workshop in 2002 and is at work on a novel.

ERIC GOODMAN is the author of four novels, most recently *Child of My Right Hand* and *In Days of Awe.* His short stories and essays appear in a wide range of publications. He's won Individual Artist Fellowships from the Ohio Arts Council and has enjoyed residencies at the MacDowell Colony, the Ragdale Foundation, and the Headlands Center for the Arts. He directs the creative writing program at Miami University, in Oxford, Ohio.

TOM GRIMES is the author of the novels *A Stone of the Heart, Season's End,* and *City of God.* His fiction has twice been among the finalists for the PEN/Nelson Algren Award. His work has also been a *New York Times* Notable Book of the Year, an Editors' Choice, and a New & Noteworthy Paperback. In 1992 he was awarded a James A. Michener/Copernicus Society of America fellowship. He is the author of three plays, *Spec* (for which he won three Los Angeles *Dramalogue* Awards), *New World,* and *Rehearsal.* He raised $2 million to preserve the childhood home of Katherine Anne Porter, which now serves as a literary center for visiting writers and for teaching creative writing to high school children; his essay about the project appeared in *Tin House* magazine. He is at work on a cycle of linked stories, two of which have appeared, "The Bridge" in *The*

Southeast Review, and "Superbad, 1979" in *Narrativemagazine.com.* He directs the MFA Program in Creative Writing at Texas State University.

KATE MYERS HANSON received her MFA from the University of Iowa's Iowa Writers' Workshop and is currently on the writing faculty at Northern Michigan University, where she is editor in chief of *Passages North.* Her fiction has appeared in several reviews, including *The North American Review, Prairie Schooner,* and *Shenandoah;* she has also published a collection of short stories, *Narrow Beams.*

AMY HASSINGER graduated from Barnard College and the Iowa Writers' Workshop, where she received her MFA in fiction writing. She is the author of *Nina: Adolescence* and *The Priest's Madonna.* Her novels have been translated into Dutch, Spanish, Indonesian, Russian, and Portuguese. She received a 2006 Finalist Award in prose from the Illinois Arts Council and was named a semifinalist for the 2005 Julia Peterkin Award. Her stories have appeared in many journals, including *Hunger Mountain, Arts and Letters, Salt Hill,* and *Natural Bridge,* and have been anthologized in *Best Lesbian Love Stories.* She is also the author of *Finding Katahdin: An Exploration of Maine's Past.* She's taught English to middle school students, writing and literature to undergraduates, and is currently on the faculty of the University of Nebraska's MFA in Writing program. She lives in Illinois with her family.

DEWITT HENRY's *The Marriage of Anna Maye Potts* won the Peter Taylor Award for the Novel. The founding editor of *Ploughshares,* he has also edited *Breaking into Print* and *Sorrow's Company,* among other anthologies. He teaches at Emerson College.

VANESSA FURSE JACKSON is the author of a critical study, *Henry Newbolt: Patriotism Is Not Enough,* and of a collection of short stories, *What I Cannot*

Say to You. She's originally from England but writes and teaches at Texas A&M University in Corpus Christi, on the hot and bird-rich Gulf of Mexico.

MICHAEL JAIME-BECERRA is the author of *Every Night Is Ladies' Night: Stories.* He teaches at the University of California at Riverside.

REBECCA JOHNS is the author of *Icebergs: A Novel,* as well as numerous magazine and newspaper articles. She teaches in the UCLA Extension Writers' Program.

ADAM JOHNSON is the Draper Fellow at Stanford University, where he teaches creative writing. He is the author of *Parasites Like Us,* a novel, and the short-story collection *Emporium.* His work has appeared in *Harper's, Esquire,* and *The Paris Review.* He lives in San Francisco with his wife and three children.

MICHAEL KNIGHT is the author of a novel, *Divining Rod,* and two collections of short fiction, *Dogfight & Other Stories* and *Goodnight, Nobody.* His stories have appeared in such journals as *The New Yorker* and *The Paris Review* and have been anthologized in *The Best American Mystery Stories* and *New Stories from the South.* He directs the creative-writing program at the University of Tennessee.

DON LEE is the author of the novel *Country of Origin,* which won an American Book Award, and the story collection *Yellow,* which won the Sue Kaufman Prize for First Fiction. A new novel, *Wrack and Ruin,* is due out in 2008. Formerly the editor of the literary journal *Ploughshares,* he now teaches creative writing at Macalester College.

JONATHAN LIEBSON teaches writing at Eugene Lang College of the New School and has taught at New York University, the Gotham Writers

Workshop, and the College of Charleston. His work has appeared in *Chelsea, South Dakota Review, The Georgia Review,* and *Meridian,* and he has finished his first novel, *A Body at Rest.*

PAUL LISICKY is the author of *Lawnboy* and *Famous Builder.* His work has appeared in *Ploughshares, Short Takes, Open House, Boulevard, Flash Fiction,* and many other anthologies and magazines. A graduate of the Iowa Writers' Workshop, he's the recipient of awards from the National Endowment for the Arts, the James A. Michener/Copernicus Society of America, the Henfield Foundation, the New Jersey State Council on the Arts, and the Fine Arts Work Center in Provincetown, where he was twice a fellow. He lives in New York City and teaches in the graduate and undergraduate writing programs at Sarah Lawrence College. He recently completed a new novel, *Lumina Harbor.*

MARGOT LIVESEY is the author of a collection of stories and five novels, including *The Missing World, Criminals, Eva Moves the Furniture,* and, most recently, *Banishing Verona.* She has taught in numerous writing programs, including those at the Iowa Writers' Workshop, Boston University, and the University of California at Irvine, and is currently writer in residence at Emerson College in Boston.

STEPHEN D. MARLOWE teaches English at Edison State Community College, writes fiction, blogs intermittently, and practices law when the mood strikes him. He lives in Tipp City, Ohio.

LEE MARTIN is the author of the novel *The Bright Forever,* a finalist for the 2006 Pulitzer Prize in Fiction; the novel *Quakertown;* the story collection *The Least You Need to Know;* and the memoirs *From Our House* and *Turning Bones.* He directs the MFA in Creative Writing Program at Ohio State University.

ELIZABETH MCCRACKEN is the author of two novels, *The Giant's House* and *Niagara Falls All Over Again,* and a collection of stories, *Here's Your Hat, What's Your Hurry.* She has received grants from the Guggenheim Foundation, the James A. Michener/Copernicus Society of America, the Fine Arts Work Center in Provincetown, and the National Endowment for the Arts.

KATHERINE MIN is the author of the novel *Secondhand World.* Her stories have appeared in numerous publications and anthologies, including *TriQuarterly, Ploughshares, The Threepenny Review, Prairie Schooner,* and *The Pushcart Book of Short Stories.* In addition, Min had a story listed in *The Best American Short Stories 1998* and another read on National Public Radio's *Selected Shorts.* She received a National Endowment for the Arts grant in 1992 and New Hampshire Arts Council fellowships in 1995 and 2004. She has been a Tennessee Williams scholar at the Sewanee Writers Conference and a fellow at Ledig House, Millay Colony for the Arts, and the MacDowell Colony. She currently teaches at Plymouth State University, in Plymouth, New Hampshire, and at the Iowa Summer Writing Festival, in Iowa City, Iowa.

KYOKO MORI is the author of three novels (*Shizuko's Daughter; One Bird; Stone Field, True Arrow*) and two nonfiction books (*The Dream of Water; Polite Lies*). She lives in Washington, D.C., and teaches creative writing at George Mason University.

THISBE NISSEN is the author of two novels, *Osprey Island* and *The Good People of New York,* and a story collection, *Out of the Girls' Room and into the Night.* She is also the coauthor (with Erin Ergenbright) of *The Ex-Boyfriend Cookbook.* She spends a lot of time amassing junk and figuring out what to do with it.

JOYCE CAROL OATES is the author of numerous novels, including the national bestsellers *We Were the Mulvaneys* and *The Falls.* She is a recipient of the National Book Award, the PEN/Malamud Award for Excellence in Short Fiction, the Commonwealth Award for Distinguished Service in Literature, and the Kenyon Review Award for Literary Achievement. She is the Roger S. Berlind Distinguished Professor of the Humanities at Princeton University.

VARLEY O'CONNOR's newest novel is *The Cure,* loosely based on her father's polio as a child in the 1930s and '40s. She is also the author of *A Company of Three,* a novel about the world of theater and acting, and *Like China.* Her prose has appeared and is forthcoming in *The Sun* magazine and the AWP *Writers' Chronicle.* An MFA graduate of the Programs in Writing at the University of California at Irvine, O'Connor is on the faculty of Kent State University and teaches fiction and creative nonfiction writing in the Northeast Ohio Universities Consortium MFA program.

ANN PACKER is the author of the novel *The Dive from Clausen's Pier* and the short-story collection *Mendocino and Other Stories.* She is a past recipient of a James A. Michener/Copernicus Society of America award and a National Endowment for the Arts fellowship. Her work has appeared in *The New Yorker, Ploughshares,* and other magazines, as well as in *Prize Stories 1992: The O. Henry Awards.* She lives in northern California with her husband and their two children.

AIMEE PHAN's first book of fiction, *We Should Never Meet,* won the 2004 Association for Asian American Studies Book Award in Prose. It was also a finalist for the Asian American Literary Awards and a Kiriyama Prize Notable Book of 2005. Her fiction has appeared in *Virginia Quarterly Review, Michigan Quarterly Review,* and *Chelsea,* among other journals. She is an assistant professor of creative writing at California College of the Arts.

DAN POPE is the author of the novel *In the Cherry Tree.* His short stories have been published in *Crazyhorse, Post Road, The Iowa Review,*

McSweeney's, Shenandoah, The Gettysburg Review, Night Train, Witness, and other magazines. Dan is a graduate of the Iowa Writers' Workshop, which he attended on a Truman Capote Fellowship. He is a winner of the Glenn Schaeffer Award from the International Institute of Modern Letters.

PAULA PRIAMOS's work has been featured in the *Los Angeles Times Magazine, West Magazine,* and *The New York Times Magazine.* She received her MFA in fiction writing from California State University at Long Beach, and teaches English and creative writing at California State University at San Bernardino.

MELISSA PRITCHARD is the nationally acclaimed author of three short-story collections, *Spirit Seizures, The Instinct for Bliss,* and *Disappearing Ingenue,* and three novels, *Phoenix, Selene of the Spirits,* and *Late Bloomer.* A recipient of numerous awards, including the Flannery O'Connor Award, the Carl Sandburg Award, and the James Phelan Award, and of fellowships from the National Endowment for the Arts, Pritchard has published fiction widely, in such literary journals as *The Southern Review, Boulevard, Open City, The Gettysburg Review, Conjunctions,* and *The Paris Review.* She is currently a professor of English and women's studies at Arizona State University.

HOLIDAY REINHORN is the author of *Big Cats: Stories.* Her work has appeared in numerous literary magazines, including, *Zoetrope, Tin House, Ploughshares,* and the anthology *This Is Not Chick Lit.* She lives and teaches in Los Angeles, where she is at work on her first novel.

JEWELL PARKER RHODES is the artistic director and the Piper Endowed Chair of the Virginia G. Piper Center for Creative Writing at Arizona State University. She is the author of four novels, *Voodoo Dreams, Magic City, Douglass' Women,* and *Voodoo Season,* and the memoir *Porch Stories: A Grandmother's Guide to Happiness.* She has published two writing guides:

Free Within Ourselves: Fiction Lessons for Black Authors and *The African American Guide to Writing and Publishing Nonfiction.* Her literary awards include a Yaddo Creative Writing fellowship, the American Book Award, the National Endowment of the Arts Award in Fiction, the Black Caucus of the American Library Award for Literary Excellence, and the PEN Oakland/Josephine Miles Award for Outstanding Writing.

TOM ROBBINS has eight novels and one collection currently in print, and while his books are decidedly offbeat, they have consistently been international bestsellers.

THANE ROSENBAUM is the author of the novels *The Golems of Gotham* (2002) (*San Francisco Chronicle* Top 100 Book), *Second Hand Smoke,* which was a finalist for the National Jewish Book Award in 1999, and the novel-in-stories *Elijah Visible,* which received the Edward Lewis Wallant Award in 1996 for the best book of Jewish-American fiction. He is the editor of the anthology *Law Lit, from Atticus Finch to* the Practice: *A Collection of Great Writing About the Law* (2007).

ROBERT ROSENBERG is the author of the novel *This Is Not Civilization.* He served as a Peace Corps volunteer in Kyrgyzstan and has taught on the White Mountain Apache Reservation in Arizona and in Istanbul, Turkey. He now teaches creative writing at Bucknell University.

COLETTE SARTOR is a graduate of Yale University, Harvard Law School, and the Iowa Writers' Workshop, where she held the Truman Capote fellowship. She has taught creative writing at the University of Iowa and currently teaches writing at the University of Southern California Gould School of Law. She has edited numerous fiction and nonfiction projects, including a creative-writing textbook. She also served as senior fiction editor for the award-winning online journal *Pif Magazine.* Her stories have appeared in various journals, such as the *Harvard Review.* She lives with her husband and son in Los Angeles, where she is working on a novel and a short-story collection.

José Skinner worked as an English-Spanish translator and interpreter before earning his MFA at the Iowa Writers' Workshop. His collection *Flight and Other Stories* was a finalist for the Western States Book Award for Fiction and a Barnes & Noble Discover selection. He currently teaches creative writing at the University of Texas–Pan American.

R. T. Smith's stories have appeared in *The Best American Short Stories, The Best American Mystery Stories,* the Pushcart Prize anthology, *New Stories from the South,* and his collection *Uke Rivers Delivers.* He lives in Rockbridge County, Virginia, and edits *Shenandoah* for Washington and Lee University.

John Smolens has published five novels and a collection of short stories, including *Cold, The Invisible World,* and *Fire Point.* His new novel is entitled *'01.* In 2006 he was the recipient of a Distinguished Faculty Award from Northern Michigan University, where he is a professor of English.

Debra Spark is the author of the novels *Coconuts for the Saint* and *The Ghost of Bridgetown* and the editor of the anthology *Twenty Under Thirty: Best Stories by America's New Young Writers.* Her most recent book is *Curious Attractions: Essays on Fiction Writing.* Spark has also written for *Esquire, Ploughshares, The New York Times* (the travel section and the book review), *Food and Wine, Yankee, The Washington Post,* and the *San Francisco Chronicle,* among other publications. She has been the recipient of several awards, including an NEA fellowship, a Bunting Institute fellowship from Radcliffe College, and the John Zacharis/*Ploughshares* award for best first book. She teaches at Colby College and in the MFA Program for Writers at Warren Wilson College. She lives with her husband and son in North Yarmouth, Maine.

RENÉ STEINKE is the author of the novel *Holy Skirts,* which was a finalist for the National Book Award and was included among the Best Books of 2005 by the *Chicago Tribune* and *The Washington Post.* She is also the author of *The Fires.* Her writing has appeared in anthologies and in *The New York Times, Vogue, Bookforum,* and *TriQuarterly.* She is editor at large for *The Literary Review* and teaches in the graduate and undergraduate writing programs at Fairleigh Dickinson University. She lives in Brooklyn.

SUSAN STRAIGHT is the author of the novel *Highwire Moon,* which was a finalist for the National Book Award. Her other novels include *Aquaboogie, The Getting Place, Blacker Than a Thousand Midnights,* and, most recently, *A Million Nightingales.* She has received a Lannan Foundation Award and a Guggenheim fellowship, and is the chair of the graduate writing program at the University of California at Riverside.

ELIZABETH STROUT's first novel, *Amy and Isabelle,* won the *Los Angeles Times* Art Seidenbaum Award for First Fiction and the *Chicago Tribune* Heartland Prize and was a finalist for the PEN/Faulkner Award, as well as the Orange Prize in England. Her short stories have been published in a number of magazines, including *The New Yorker.* Her second novel, *Abide With Me,* received much critical acclaim. Currently she is on the faculty of the low-residency MFA program at Queens University in Charlotte, North Carolina. She lives in New York City.

ROBERT TORRES is an illustrator and interactive-design director living and working in the San Francisco Bay Area. Originally from Texas, Robert has spent the last ten years of his career in the newspaper industry, building award-winning Web sites and multimedia presentations. Now in his mid-thirties, he can still be found on his skateboard most weekends. A current portfolio of work can be found at his Web site, www.rctorres.com.

Vu Tran was born in Saigon in 1975 and grew up in Tulsa, Oklahoma. He is a graduate of the Iowa Writers' Workshop and was a Glenn Schaeffer fellow at the University of Nevada at Las Vegas, where he currently teaches. His fiction has appeared in such publications as *The O. Henry Prize Stories 2007, The Southern Review, Glimmer Train Stories, Fence,* and the *Harvard Review.*

Danielle Trussoni has written for *The New York Times Book Review, Tin House,* and *The New York Times Magazine,* among other publications. Her first book, *Falling Through the Earth: A Memoir,* was awarded the 2006 James A. Michener/Copernicus Society of America award and was chosen by *The New York Times* as one of the ten best books of 2006.

Daniel Wallace is the author of three novels: *Big Fish, Ray in Reverse,* and *The Watermelon King.* To learn more about him and his work, go to www.danielwallace.org.

Michelle Wildgen is the author of a novel, *You're Not You,* and the editor of an anthology, *Food & Booze: A Tin House Literary Feast.* Her work has appeared in the anthologies *Death by Pad Thai, Best New American Voices 2004,* and *Best Food Writing 2004* and in journals including *Tin House, StoryQuarterly, TriQuarterly, Prairie Schooner,* and *Gulf Coast.* She is a senior editor at *Tin House* magazine and an editor at Tin House Books.

Mark Winegardner is the author of *The Godfather Returns,* which reached number five on the *New York Times* bestseller list. He has also written two other novels, *Crooked River Burning* and *The Veracruz Boys,* and the story collection *That's True of Everybody.* He is the director of the graduate writing program at Florida State University.

ABOUT THE EDITOR

BRET ANTHONY JOHNSTON is the internationally acclaimed author of *Corpus Christi: Stories.* His many awards include the James A. Michener/Copernicus Society of America Fellowship, the Glasgow Prize, an NEA Fellowship, and a National Book Award honor for writers under thirty-five. An occasional commentator for NPR's *All Things Considered,* he is a graduate of the Iowa Writers' Workshop. Currently, he is the director of the creative writing program at Harvard University. For more information, please visit: www.bretanthonyjohnston.com.

ABOUT THE TYPE

This book was set in Granjon, a modern recutting of a typeface produced under the direction of George W. Jones, who based Granjon's design upon the letter forms of Claude Garamond (1480–1561). The name was given to the typeface as a tribute to the typographic designer Robert Granjon.